AF540572

World Conference on Higher Education

Editor

Dr. Digumarti Bhaskara Rao
M.Sc., M.A., M.A., M.Ed., Ph.D.
R.V.R. College of Education
Guntur–522006
Andhra Pradesh
INDIA

DISCOVERY PUBLISHING HOUSE
New Delhi

First Published–2001
Reprinted: 2013
ISBN 81-7141-610-1

Published by :
DISCOVERY PUBLISHING HOUSE
4831/24, Ansari Road, Prahlad Street,
Darya Ganj, New Delhi-110002 (INDIA)
☎ : 3279245 • Fax : 91-11-3253475
E-mail : dphtemp@indiatimes.com

Printed at: Dynamic printers, Delhi

CONTENTS

Preface

Foreword

Introduction

1. **Oral Report by Ms Suzy Halimi, Rapporteur-General of the World Conference on Higher Education** 1

2. **World Declaration on Higher Education for the Twenty-first Century: Vision and Action** 14

3. **Framework for Priority Action for Change and Development in Higher Education** 33

ANNEXES:
Regional Declarations and Action Plans 43

Africa

Arab States

Asia and the Pacific

Europe

Latin America and the Caribbean

Bureau of the Conference *136*

Advisory Group on Higher Education *138*

List of Participants *140*

Index

FOREWORD

For the world of education, science and culture, the dates from 5 to 9 October 1998 will go down in history as the period of the first-ever World Conference on Higher Education. Representatives of 182 States responsible for education and higher education, teachers, researchers, students members of parliament, representatives of intergovernmental and non-governmental organisations from various sectors of society, the world of work and business, financial organisations, publishing houses, etc.- in all more than 4,000 participants - have come to Paris to discuss matters of higher education to agree on the higher education we need for the next century: for whom, with whom, and why, for what kind of society and what kind of world.

No conference convened until now by UNESCO has brought together such a large number of participants nor - I believe I can safely say- has represented society as fully as this World Conference on Higher Education. These past five days have seen the largest international gathering on higher education held this century.

The interest shown by such widely different circles from across the world in the work of the Conference is the expression of a clear realisation of the growing importance of education, and in particular of higher education, for the destiny of humankind and society itself. In a world in which inequalities between nations and countries are growing more acute, where economic considerations dominate and the absolute power of money and the pursuit of profit at all costs brush aside ethical values and all sense of human solidarity, and where violence, far from retreating, proliferates in various and often hitherto unknown forms, and thus constitutes a real threat to civil and international peace, all education systems, and higher education in particular, are directly challenged.

It is no longer necessary to demonstrate the importance of education and higher education for sustainable, endogenous development, for democracy and peace, for a strengthening of the defence of peace as a human value, and for the respect and protection of all human rights and fundamental freedoms. The far-reaching changes now taking place in the world, and the entry of human values into a society based on knowledge and information, reveal how overwhelmingly important education and higher education are. It is appropriate to note, as the head of the one of the delegations to the Conference has said, that "science and education are what will determine the future well-being of individuals and of nations." And it is above all within the framework of higher education that science and education meet, unite and stimulate one another, by advancing and disseminating knowledge. Because one of the tasks of higher education is to educate the educators, to further research into education and to make recommendations about the content, methods and organiszation of education at each of its different levels and in its various forms, higher education has a decisive contribution to make to the progress of the educational task within society towards lifelong education for all.

When I opened this Conference, I expressed the wish that we might make the completion of the long process of preparation for it a new beginning, that we might gather its harvest in order the better to use it, like food and seed, and that our Conference might plant the seeds of better education for the twenty-first century.

And that is what the Conference has done. It has answered the questions that were asked of it. It has set the direction needed to prepare higher education for the tasks that await it in the twenty-first century, and to help humankind, society and the community of nations to stride out towards a better future, towards a world more just, more humane, more caring and more peaceful. The Conference has established the principles and determined the ways of achieving this in the texts of the World Declaration and the Framework for Priority Action adopted at the close of its deliberations.

Several factors have come together to enable the Conference, despite different national and regional situations, to adopt texts of particular importance, which concern all participants. It is the result of the work of five regional conferences, which took place in Havana, Dakar, Tokyo, Palermo and Beirut between 1996 and 1998. It is the result of the reflections and the commitment of vice-chancellors and presidents, and of the teachers, staff and students of universities and other institutions of higher education. It is also, and above all, the result of active and constructive enrolment by a number of States in various regions and by many intergovernmental and non-governmental organiszations in the process of the development of draft declarations and action plans in particular within the framework of the two stages of consultation which preceded the Conference. It is largely the result of participants' commitment to opening up ways of renewing and transforming higher education in the direction that the history and development of the world require. It is largely the result of the will and the remarkable spirit of cooperation that everyone has shown throughout this Conference. Lastly, it is the result of the objective fact that, in the field of higher education, there is greater convergence and a greater community of problems, trends, challenges and concerns than national and regional differences and specificities would suggest, although the problems confronting many developing countries are more serious and more urgent than those experienced by the industrialised countries.

In their scope, in their global vision of the problems of higher education and in their constructive approach, the texts adopted by this first World Conference are probably without precedent.

This Conference has provided a forum for a wealth of debates and exchanges of views, and I should like to raise here some of the main ideas which have emerged from them.

The Conference was unanimous in considering that a **renewal** of higher education is essential for the whole of society to be able to face up to the challenges of the twenty-first century, to ensure its intellectual independence, to create and advance knowledge, and to educate and train responsible, enlightened citizens and qualified specialists, without whom no nation can progress economically, socially, culturally or politically.

As the Declaration of the World Conference emphasizes, since society is "increasingly **knowledge-based** (...), higher education and research now act as essential components of cultural, socio-economic and environmentally sustainable development of individuals, communities and nations." The development of higher education must therefore feature among the highest national priorities.

It is now clear that, to fulfil its mission, **higher education must change** radically, by becoming organically flexible, and at the same time more diverse in its institutions, its structures, its curricula, and the nature and forms of its programmes and delivery systems, and by mastering the information technologies which can help it achieve its purpose. Higher education must anticipate the developing needs of society and individuals, and it must be opened to the needs of adults for continuing education and the updating of their knowledge and skills, whether in the pursuit of retraining, redeployment or cultural improvement in general. In short, **higher education in the twenty-first century must be seen to be part of the global project of continuing education for all,** it must become the motivating force of that project, the place where it all happens, and it must help to integrate into that project all other levels and forms of education by strengthening its links with them.

One central question which was present throughout the debates, and which is closely related to the preceding one, is that of access to higher education. This principle has been clearly defined by the World Declaration, which was itself inspired by the great prescriptive texts of the United Nations and above all by Article 26 of the Universal Declaration of Human Rights.[1] "Admission to higher education," the Declaration of the World Conference stipulates, "should be founded on the merit, capacity, efforts, perseverance and devotion showed by those seeking access to it, and can take place in a lifelong scheme, at any time, with due recognition of previously acquired skills." **The concern for equity** in this respect, strongly emphasized in the Universal Declaration of Human Rights, the UNESCO Convention against Discrimination in Education (1960) and the International Covenant on Economic, Social and Cultural Rights (1966), **as the first principle** governing access to higher education, is vigorously reaffirmed by the World Conference in its Declaration. It is the duty of all States, and of all those who have taken part in the Conference, to work, with the support of UNESCO, to promote the relevant provisions of the Declaration through legislative and national regulatory channels and through actual educational practice.

All citizens must be aware that, as stated in the Universal Declaration of Human Rights, it is the merit and effort of the individual which should determine access to higher education. Anyone who possesses the "merit" and the means may be admitted to higher education, and is expected to contribute financially to the institution providing it; anyone who possesses the "merit" but not the means may be admitted to higher education, but society provides for its financing;

lastly, anyone who possesses the means but not the "merit" must endeavour to acquire the "merit" and to have it recognised in order to enter higher education, which thus becomes a permanent space for higher learning. From élite-based to merit-based: these words accurately express, in my opinion, the new face of higher education.

Beyond these general principles governing access, the debates revealed particular emphasis on certain points. Above all, the importance of continuing and intensifying our efforts to extend and improve access for women to all areas of higher education, especially to scientific and technological studies, to teaching positions in higher education and to management responsibilities.

Another point concerning equity and social justice emerges from the discussions of the Conference. Economic, social and educational measures are needed throughout the educational careers of children and young people from underprivileged backgrounds and modest circumstances to enable them to acquire the necessary preparations for access to and success in higher education.

Lastly, conference participants were clearly inspired by this same concern when they recommended appropriate measures to eliminate discrimination and to overcome the inequalities concerning access to higher education suffered by the disabled, minorities, refugees and peoples displaced following natural disasters or conflicts.

The question of access takes on a new dimension as we approach the twenty-first century, which will necessarily transform higher education and see the implementation of lifelong learning **for all.** The popularization of higher education, frequently mentioned during the debates, is only one manifestation of a marked trend, already well-established in the industrialised countries, and which appears to be irreversible in the long term. It is interesting to note in this respect that gross enrolment ratios in higher education in developed regions had already reached almost 60 per cent by 1995, and in North America 84 per cent. Overall, indeveloping countries, enrolment ratios rose between 1960 and 1995 from 1.8 per cent to 8.9 per cent and teacher numbers in the same period increased by a factor of more than eleven, revealing growth rates much higher than those observed in the developed countries. It should be added in this respect that these figures take only partially into account those adults taking various non-traditional post-secondary courses offered by establishments of higher education and other public or private organisations.

Several factors combine to produce this spectacular development in higher education. The expansion of secondary education is one of the most prominent. Although it has not reached the growth rates of higher education, secondary education is growing at a pace no less significant. Between 1960 and 1995, its student numbers worldwide increased from 91 million to 372 million, and gross enrolment ratios at secondary level doubled, from 29 per cent to 58 per cent. In the developed countries, where enrolment ratios have reached 99 per cent, secondary education has become almost universal. In developing countries during the same period, student numbers were multiplied by 6.7 and gross enrolment ratios have almost tripled. Everywhere, numbers of young graduates of secondary education have increased relentlessly.

However, in very many countries, most students in the secondary sector are concentrated in general subject areas where curriculum content too often continues to be designed solely to prepare students for entry into higher education. This leads many young people, on completion of their secondary studies, to move into higher education simply because they have not been prepared to enter the world of work. Not possessing any other skills, those graduates of secondary education who, for one reason or another, do not enter higher education are confronted with the risk of unemployment.

This situation, the far-reaching changes which changes which higher education needs to undergo and the prospect of lifelong for all (which implies the possibility of lifelong access to higher education at any age, to supplement or bring up to date students's general or specialized skills, and/or to retrain or acquire new skills), create the need to reconsider the overall design of secondary education. The secondary sector must have **a twofold objective:** to prepare for the world of work and at the same time to prepare for the entry into higher education. This twofold objective will enable us to define the spirit and content of secondary education for the twenty-first century, its diversification and the role at this level of education of technical and vocational training.

The combined effect of the expansion of secondary education, the steady increase in the number and the proportion of jobs and professional activities which require high-level knowledge and skills, and the continuing increase in the need for higher studies and advanced learning, for updating knowledge, retraining and redeployment, is that, in the more or less long term according to country, practically everyone will undergo, at some time or other in life and probably more than once, post-secondary higher education in one form or another. In this sense, it is possible to speak of a trend towards the generalisation of higher education, which will be supported and facilitated by a better mastery of information and communication technologies and increasingly broad use of these. This generalisation will not result in a direct transition for all from secondary to higher education. It will be achieved using increasingly diversified methods, at different times in life, through curricula with different purposes, access routes and durations, and which will be increasingly varied, with studies within an institutionalised framework alternating with self-teaching and other forms of learning.

It is with this future in view that access to higher education will be widened, popularised and made more equitable, and efforts will be made to promote equal opportunities for success in higher studies.

The necessary transition of higher education into a space for higher learning in which everyone will be able to enjoy more flexible access at any age for intensive training, updating knowledge and the acquisition of new skills, or for the purposes of redeployment, constitutes one of the main aspects of the democratization and the renovation of higher education and education in general. At the same time, this development will make higher education an ideal meeting-place for the sharing of knowledge and the mutual enrichment of teachers at all levels.

Two other key ideas appear to me to deserve mention at this point: that of **the mission** of higher education, and that of low it should be opened up to the whole of society as a means of promoting **interaction** between the principal social actors and the main sectors of the economy.

As regards the mission of higher education, the debates have shown that it needs to be widened. Beyond its **traditional functions of teaching, training, research and study, all of which remain fundamental,** many heads of delegation made a point of asserting the importance of the educational mission of higher education, which consists in **promoting development of the whole person and training responsible, informed citizens, committed to working for a better society in the future.** Higher education also has **a contribution to make to the solution of the major problems of planetary, regional and local importance** (poverty, homelessness, worsening inequalities, environmental degradation, etc.), and to work to promote development, the sharing of knowledge, solidarity, the universal respect of human rights, democracy, equality of rights between women and men and a culture of peace and non-violence. The Conference stressed very strongly **the cultural and ethical mission** of higher education, which, in the age in which we live, is one of the highest priorities of education in general.

On the vast subject of **the interaction of higher education with society,** I will confine myself hereto mentioning, briefly, three points. The first relates to the relationship between higher education and the State, and society as a whole. The Conference has reaffirmed, as the essential condition enabling higher education to fulfill its mission, that institutional **autonomy** and **academic freedoms** must be guaranteed and respected by the State and society. The **corollary** is the duty placed on institutions of higher education **to account** to society for their activities and the use of the resources placed at their disposal. In this context also, the responsibility of the State for the financing of higher education as an essential public service, as well as the need for society to support it, were strongly reaffirmed by a number of speakers. At the same time, they emphasized the importance for institutions of higher education of securing additional sources of financing, implementing revenue-generating activities, strengthening their management, adopting forward-looking management practices to that end and using their resources in a more rational and more effective way. These positions are clearly emphasised in the Declaration of the Conference. The question of **financing** will clearly be **one of the major challenges** or the years to come.

This problem is particularly acutely felt in many developing countries, and measures aimed solely at reinforcing management and using resources more rationally will not be sufficient to solve it. A revision of national budget priorities also deserves to be envisaged. Other measures are necessary in order to make it possible for developing countries to release additional resources for education and for the solution of many social problems.[2]

Another major point which was widely commented upon relates to the interaction between higher education and **the world of work.** It is important that this interaction be conceived as a **partnership, a relationship of equals,** not as the subordination of one to the other. I would like to quote here Mr. Lionel Jospin, **Prime Minister of France,** who challenged "the mercantile attitude whereby higher education could be market-led. (...) In this field, as in others," he declared, "the market economy is a fact of life within which we act. But it should not form the horizon of society. The market is an instrument; it is not the *raison-d'être* of democracy".

One of the speakers said in his contribution that **student enrolment in the business of higher education** is healthy, even though it may sometimes be "noisy". The Conference heard an **important declaration** from the representative of student organizations. That declaration expressed students' awareness of their responsibility for their studies, but also their responsibility for society and in society. This is good to hear, and we should make the point strongly that their participation, and that of their organisations, in everything that relates to higher education, are essential.

In adopting its Declaration and the Framework for Priority Action, the World Conference has laid the foundations that will **guide the development of national higher education policies** for the next century. The Conference has also promoted the emergence of an alliance between the university and educational communities and their principal partners within society. Parliaments, as the voice of the people, have an important role to play in consolidating this alliance and in making it widely known and effective. The time has now come for action, and I am pleased to note, as I meet with heads of state and government, ministers of education and higher education, and Permanent Delegates to UNESCO, that in their efforts to design and implement higher education reforms, Member States are beginning to draw inspiration from the orientations contained in the texts adopted by the World conference.

Much will now depend on the speed of reaction of all those in the alliance- individuals and institutions- who must work together to promote change in higher education. UNESCO took the initiative of launching the process which led to the World Conference. UNESCO will do its best **to ensure**, in close cooperation with higher education authorities and the IGOs and NGOs concerned, **that the actions now to be undertaken are pursued as effectively as possible**. For my part, I have already taken a series of measures within the Organization to ensure that follow-up action to the World Conference will be given all necessary impetus.

We stand at the beginning of a new century and a new millennium. **It is** symbolic that they should have been preceded by the **International Year for the Culture of Peace,** which will be immediately followed by the International Decade for a Culture of Peace and Non-Violence for the Children of the World (2001-1010), both proclaimed by the General Assembly of the United Nations. In the Declaration adopted by the World Conference, the point is made that "on the threshold of a new millennium, it is the duty of higher education to ensure that the values and the ideals of a culture of peace prevail". It is of the greatest importance that, true to their humanistic traditions and to their vocations, institutions of higher education the world over, their teachers, students and organisations, should be among the most active and the most committed of all those who will mark the Year and the International Decade by their efforts to promote a culture of peace and non-violence. May this Year and this Decade serve in particular to implement long-term programmes of action for solidarity, one of the fundamental values of a culture of peace, to the benefit of the institutions, teachers and students of the developing countries.

Federico Mayor

References

1. "Everyone has the right to education. Education shall be free, at least in the elementary and fundamental stages. Elementary education shall be compulsory. Technical and professional education shall be made generally available *and higher education shall be equally accessible to all on the basis of merit.*" (Article 26 (1)).

2. The resources of many developing countries are to a large extent mortgaged by the burden of debt servicing and repayment. In 27 countries, debt exceeds GDP. Between 1990 and 1995, the countries of sub-Saharan Africa devoted on average 12 billion dollars per annum to debt repayment, whereas their total levels of indebtedness increased by 33 billion dollars. Some of these countries devote to debt repayment amounts practically equivalent to the totality of the government aid they receive for their development. In adopting at its twenty-fifth session the International Development Strategy for the Second Development Decade, the General Assembly of the United Nations fixed the objective for official development assistance by the industrialised countries at 0.70 per cent of their GNP. This objective of solidarity, since then confirmed several times, is far from having been achieved. In an interdependent world, solidarity is not only an ethical requirement. It is also a political necessity.

PREFACE

The World Conference on Higher Education (Paris, 5-9 October 1998) was convened by UNESCO with an objective to lay down fundamental principles for the in-depth reform of higher education systems throughout the world. The Conference was preceded by a widespread mobilisation of partners, of national policy makers, institutional leaders, the professorate and researchers, the student community, the economic and professional sectors and the civil society.

The World Declaration and the Framework for Priority Action, the outcomes of the World Conference on Higher Education, will help set up agenda both for higher education policy making UNESCO Member States and for development strategies to be established or further strengthened by UNESCO and its partners. The long-term outcome of the Conference will be the efficient and effective renovation and renewal of higher education systems and institutions based on the principles of relevance and quality, and with a commitment to enhance international co-operation and academic solidarity. Much now depends on the dynamism of the coalition of all these individuals and institutions involved in the process of change in higher education.

The documents adopted at the World Conference on Higher Education (Paris 1998) and at the Regional Conferences on Higher Education (Havana 1996, Dakar 1997, Tokyo 1997, Beirut 1998, and Palermo 1998) presented in this book in their original form will guide in realising the core missions of higher education—to educate, to train, to undertake research, and to provide services to the community-throughout the world in the twenty first century.

I am thankful to the UNESCO and its associated regional offices for reproducing the documents in preparing this book for the benefit of policy makers, educationists, planners, researchers, teachers and students.

D.B. Rao

INTRODUCTION

In convening the World conference on Higher Education (Paris, 5-9 October 1998), UNESCO's objective was to lay down the fundamental principles for the in-depth reform of higher education system throughout the world. In our complex and rapidly changing global society, higher education must contribute to the building of peace founded on a process of development and predicated on equity, justice, solidarity and liberty. To attain this objective, access on the basis of merit, the renovation of systems and institutions, and service to society, including closer links to the world of work, must be the basis of renewal and renovation in this level of education. This requires that higher education enjoy autonomy and freedom exercised with responsibility.

When calling the Conference, Federico Mayor, the Director-General of UNESCO, had in mind that this initiative should contribute to transforming higher education, in its material and virtual manifestations, into an environment for lifelong learning, for cultural debate, for the affirmation and safeguarding of diversity, and for forging and confirming the values and principles laid down in the constitution of UNESCO for "the intellectual and moral solidarity of mankind".

The analysis made by ministers and heads of delegations during the conference, the positive comments of the Executive Board of UNESCO immediately after the World Conference and the actions being taken all over the world by governments to include the principles of the Declaration in their policy statements and decisions concerning higher education show that the Conference gave the international community a powerful instrument to facilitate the reform of higher education.

The basis for these initiatives lies in the principle that higher education shall be equally accessible to all on the basis of merit, in keeping with Article 26.1 of the Universal Declaration on Human Rights. As accepted by all participants at the conference, no discrimination can be accepted in granting access to higher education on grounds of race, gender, language, religion or economic, cultural or social distinctions, or physical disabilities.

The core missions of higher education - to educate, to train, to undertake research and to provide services to the community - must be preserved, reinforced and further expanded. The World Conference stressed that higher education institutions must seek to educate qualified graduates who are responsible citizens and to provide opportunities for higher learning throughout life. At the end of this century, we can see the devastating effects of a concept of economic developed based on speculation. Thus, the adoption by the international community of a document stating clearly that higher education institutions must preserve their critical functions in the interest of democracy is timely and this must be taken seriously by policy-makers.

Relevance cannot be an abstract concept. As the Conference declared, relevance "should be assessed in terms of the fit between what society expects of institutions and what they do". In particular, relationships with the world of work should be based on long-term orientations and societal aims and needs, as well as on respect for cultures and environmental protection. Relevance means also a better integration of higher education into the whole education system: The Conference insisted on "the reordering of its links with all levels of education, in particular with secondary education" as a priority.

The search for quality is indispensable for a policy based on merit. But quality must be linked in a given context to relevance and to the solution of problems of the community, and assessments of quality should embrace all functions and activities of higher education. In this the role of research is especially essential. This will be the main subject of the World Conference on Science that UNESCO is organising (July 1999, Budapest). Research must be enhanced in all disciplines as an instrument for the advancement of knowledge through approaches reinforcing interdisciplinarity, transdisciplinarity and innovation. In the follow-up of both world conferences, we would like to see the expansion and networking of Centres and Chairs on higher Education and on Science Policy in each region.

The Conference statements regarding the role of staff, in particular teachers, the importance of the involvement of students in the decision process and the measures that should be taken or reinforced to ensure the participation of women in higher education, constitute essential points of these documents and must serve as a guide to policy-makers and to all who have responsibilities in their implementation.

Finally, a key philosophical point but with concrete impact is the statement made by the Conference that higher education should be considered as a public good. Equally important is the affirmation that the international dimension of higher education is an inherent part of its quality. UNESCO gave the example with the launching of the UNITWIN/UNESCO Chairs Programme and its work on the recognition of studies, degrees and diplomas, based on close partnership, solidarity and co-operation among equals.

As stated in the preamble of the Declaration, the second half of this century will go down in the history of higher education as the period of its most spectacular expansion. The analysis of the implications of this reality was made by the *UNESCO Policy Paper for Change and Development in Higher Education* launched in 1995. This document showed also that as we come to the end of the twentieth century, there are still flagrant inequalities in higher education, and a growing gap between the industrialised countries and the so-called developing countries.

In convening the World Conference on Higher Education, UNESCO reaffirmed its strong 50 year-old commitment to fostering the development of higher education and research. The Conference sought to generate a broad debate on higher education to complement other major conferences in the field of education that constitute landmarks in the process of its renewal, notably the World Conference on Education for All (Jomtien, Thailand, 1990), the 45th session of the International Conference on Education on the Role of Teachers in a Changing World (Geneva, 1996) and the International Conference on Adult Education (Hamburg, 1997). In addition, the World Conference reiterated the recommendations relating to the opening up of higher education of the International Commission on Education for the Twenty-first Century, *Learning: The Treasure Within* (1996).

The Conference was preceded by a widespread mobilization of partners, of national policy-makers, institutional leaders, the professorate and researchers, including those involved in the UNITWIN/UNESCO Chairs Programme, the student community, and the economic and professional sectors as well as the civil society, including parliamentarians.

Regional Conferences were held in Havana in November 1996 (Latin America and the Caribbean), Dakar in April 1997 (Africa), Tokyo in July 1997 (Asia and the Pacific), Palermo in September 1997 (Europe) and Beirut in March 1998 (Arab States). The results of these conferences, their declarations and their plans of action were taken into consideration in the preparation of the documents adopted at the World Conference and were included in this report. The findings of these conferences were also utilised for the working documents and constituted the main base for the discussions of the Commissions of the Conference on *relevance, quality, management and financing, and international co-operation.* They confirmed that we are now facing global problems that call for solutions to be applied worldwide, even though in every region there are variations in the economic, social, cultural and political context. UNESCO will publish a series of documents, including one on the work of the Commissions.

The results of the regional conferences were complemented by studies and analyses undertaken by some fifty governmental and non-governmental organizations charged with preparing a series of thematic debates on important issues on higher education at the end of this century. Twelve debates were structured in relation with three main domains:

Higher education and development

- The requirements of the world of work
- Higher education and sustainable human development
- Contributing to national and regional development
- Contributing to national and regional development
- Higher education staff development: a continuing mission

New trends and innovations in higher education

- Higher education for a new society: a student vision
- From traditional to virtual: the new information technologies
- Higher education and research: challenges and opportunities
- The contribution of higher education to the education system as a whole

Higher education, culture and society

- Women and higher education: issues and perspectives
- Promoting a culture of peace
- Mobilising the power of culture
- Autonomy, social responsibility and academic freedom

The Thematic Debates raised a great interest among Conference participants. Their results will be disseminated separately.

In addition to the commissions and thematic debates, a series of special lectures and at plenary sessions speeches from ministers and chiefs of delegation reported on what is happening in their countries in the field of higher education and expressed their position on the themes of the conference. The Ministers addressed the following issues:

- The changing missions of higher education in the twenty-first century
- Interaction of higher education with society
- The impact of the change process of higher education, diversification and increased flexibility of systems, and their promotion of lifelong learning
- Access to higher education

All these contributions were taken into consideration in the final version of the Declaration and Framework for Action as well as the comments of all Member States, intergovernmental and non-governmental organiszations with an interest in higher education, or invited to attend the Conference.

There is no doubt that the documents the participants adopted at the end of the conference the "World Declaration on Higher Education for the Twenty-first Century: Vision and Action" and the "Framework for Priority Action for Change and Development of Higher Education" represent an agreement between all stakeholders concerning the principal and key actions needed for the renewal of higher education in the twenty-first century. Now comes the time for action, for the execution of projects, for developing international co-operation based on solidarity and the building of an equitable society, in particular through research, training of specialists and community projects aiming at eliminating poverty, violence, illiteracy, hunger, intolerance, environmental degradation and disease, and the development of a culture of peace.

The World Declaration and the Framework for Priority Action will help set up the agenda both for higher education policy-making in Member States and for development strategies to be established or further strengthened by UNESCO and its partners.

As a result of the Conference process, a new coalition between the higher education community and its major partners has emerged. Contacts with Chiefs of states, Ministers of Education and Higher Education and delegates to UNESCO showed clearly that they have already started to utilise these documents in the implementation of reforms in higher education.

The long-term outcome of the Conference will be the efficient and effective renovation and renewal of higher education systems and institutions based on the principles of relevance and quality, and with a commitment to enhance international co-operation and academic solidarity.

Much now depends on the dynamism of the coalition of all those-individuals and institutions - involved in the process of change in higher education. UNESCO took the responsibility of launching the process which culminated with the World Conference. UNESCO will make its best efforts to ensure an efficient follow-up, jointly with higher education authorities, intergovernmental organisations and non-governmental organisations interested in higher education.

1

ORAL REPORT

by **Ms Suzy Halimi**, Rapporteur-General,

at the closing ceremony of the
World Conference on Higher Education
(Friday, 9 October 1998)

Distinguished Ministers,
Mr President of the General Conference,
Mr Chairperson of the Executive Board,
Mr Director-General,
Excellencies,
Ladies and Gentlemen,

I have the honour as Rapporteur-General to offer you a synoptic account of the statements and addresses we have heard, of the analyses and critical considerations that have been expressed in the commissions and during the thematic debates, of the expectations and demands that have been formulated, and, finally, of the commitments made regarding the new vision which we have together forged for higher education. Allow me, therefore, to convey my wholehearted gratitude for this token of your trust.

This Conference has been attended by some 4,000 delegates and observers: representatives of Member States, to be sure, but also of a whole range of international organisations, institutions and agencies, as well as by all those who, in civil society, are involved in higher education-universities, academics and students, regional authorities, the private sector, associations, businesses and the world of work. This major international gathering has been the culmination of an ambitious project, of a process which began hesitantly but has continued to harness energies throughout its momentum-gathering course. The stimulating working documents that have been prepared for us, the insights we have contributed during the deliberations, the draft Declaration and draft Framework for Action we have examined and refined during the past week, have enabled us to reach a critical consensus, which is the hallmark of UNESCO. The fact that the Conference has taken place on the very eve of the third millennium, with all the challenges, uncertainties and promises pertaining thereto, can only extend its impact and raise the expectations which have been placed in it.

I should like in particular to highlight the fact that our World Conference has successfully combined policy presentations, in-depth expert reports, democratic participation, and statements reflecting a range of cultural sensibilities around four major topics, namely, relevance, improvement of quality, the management and financing of higher education with a view to ensuring justice and equity, and finally, international co-operation.

Four commissions have focused four critical areas, in order to take stock of the current situation and to assess the latest developments and achievements. Their deliberations have served to enhance approaches, compare viewpoints and consider together a number of priority areas for action. In addition, thematic debates, bringing together various panels, were devised, organised and directed by the main actors involved in higher education and research. Reflected therein was the desire to consolidate dialogue and to strengthen its validity. A number of powerful expectations were expressed, and precise demands were put forward. As a result, the Conference took on the form of an open learning forum, one that proposed, over and above the officially programmed activities, a profusion of initiatives reflecting the sheer multifariousness of higher education on the eve of the third millennium.

In a bid to reflect this profusion of ideas, including the ministers' own statements, I shall first sketch in the context in which this wide-ranging process of mutual consultation took place, then highlight the salient points which emerged from our joint reflection, grouping them together around the four themes that served to structure the whole: relevance, quality, management and international co-operation.

I. THE CONTEXT

The future of higher education cannot be usefully addressed without first taking stock of the national, regional and international context in which it is called upon to fulfil its missions, be they traditional or novel.

A. Globalisation

We must be fully alive to the fact that higher education can no longer be conceived solely in terms of national situations and criteria. Research and training that are worthy of the name cannot hence'orth be conducted in purely local terms.

The general problems that have been itemized, mainly within the framework of the statements by ministers and heads of delegation, reveal that, beyond the various situations specific to a particular country or group of countries, there exists a growing trend for problems to become globalised, a trend characterised by the extreme complexity of the situations involved.

'It may well be that globalisation, despite the differences of opinion which surround it, is today an inescapable fact of life', Prince Talal Bin Abdul Aziz suggested, at the opening meeting of our Conference. It might also, as Mr Portella, President of the General Conference of UNESCO, added, constitute an ethical challenge and a vast arena for international solidarity.

Globalisation, it must be emphasised, means not only economic globalisation; it is also the internationalisation of human exchanges and the circulation of ideas. The present Conference is a living witness thereof, by virtue of the number and the calibre of its participants, as Mr Pál Pataki, Chairperson of the Executive Board, stressed.

Humankind is faced with a series of problems that cannot be solved within the framework of isolated policies. That is what prompted the French Prime Minister to refer to the 'new and stimulating context' in which higher education must today perform its many different functions, and ensure its own transformation.

B. Democratisation

It should also be recalled, as the Director-General of UNESCO reminded us, that higher education is faced with an upsurge of democratiszation and an extension of the rule of law in virtually all societies. The role of education in general, and of higher education in particular, in promoting and preserving democracy, and in educating the young and the less young for democratic citizenship, is now generally acknowledged.

This development is also marked by the prominence won by women in decision-making processes. The struggle being waged for recognition of complete equality is not without its difficulties and even sufferings, but it offers a major challenge for higher education in the twenty-first century. Many speakers raised this issue, notably in the group devoted to the matter, which drew attention to the need to empower women and to adopt measures that would enable them to combine access to positions of responsibility in professional careers with the demands of family life.

C. The progress of science and technology

A further challenge lies in the latest achievements of science, the *sine qua non* of sustainable development, as was stressed in particular by the Islamic Republic of Iran and Switzerland - a situation which should not obscure the fact that the development of individual countries may also be a precondition for the development of science. The ethical issues raised by scientific research and its applications provide higher education with a vast field of study and futurology. These aspects aroused great interest among those taking part in the second thematic debate, who saw in them a means of responding to the complexity and changes typical of the end of the century.

The same is true- as noted by many speakers - of the place acquired by communication technologies in our societies, with the consequences that the invasion of virtual reality has inevitably had on the widening gaps between industrialised and post-industrial countries and developing countries. It would be wise, while taking the measure of the radical disruptions introduced by the new technologies into society and hence into education, to refrain from excessive optimism.

D. The environment

Optimism is equally out of place when it comes to the state of the planet that we shall be bequeathing to future generations. Higher education cannot withdraw into itself and turn a blind eye to the damage being done to the environment, damage that we deplore without managing fully to put right. Population growth and galloping urbanisation are, of course, not unconnected with the serious problem of the ecological future of our planet. These matters were dwelt upon by several delegations, including that of Côte d'voire.

E. Social exclusion

The decline of agriculture and industry- varying from country to country and the progression of the service sector, which were referred to in the debate on 'The requirements of the world of work', give rise to a further challenge relating to the evolution of the economy and the structure of the job market. More and more sectors of the population are having to contend with social exclusion, and young graduates are themselves not spared by unemployment. This is undoubtedly the most acute problem facing us today: indeed, the entire enterprise of democratization and the values of our societies are being undermined by it. We must, as the Director-General of UNESCO urges us, dare to share. Here again, higher education undoubtedly has a role to play in developing new capacities for adapting to economic trends, with a view to ensuring greater social cohesion and strengthening democratic citizenship. If there is to be sharing within countries, as between countries, a number of conditions must be met: there must be a determination to promote and respect basic human rights, the political will to commit resources to human development, a deep sense of solidarity, and the mobilisation of all institutional and financial partners in both the public and private sectors.

F. The brain drain

For many developing countries, the brain drain is a daunting problem. While it is indeed essential to maintain mobility- which is a source of intellectual enrichment- measures must also be taken to encourage nationals to return to their country of origin and to take part in its economic, social and cultural development. The students gave extensive coverage to this dimension during their round table, as well as on the occasion of the thematic debate on their vision of the form that a new society should take.

G. Armed conflicts

Our societies are, alas, plagued by many conflicts, the most serious being regional and national wars. The acts of violence perpetrated in many countries are symptomatic of the difficulty experienced by citizens, including many youngsters, in finding their place in a new society in which most of the old standards have vanished and values are no longer perceptible. As the representatives of Costa Rica and India in particular pointed out, the University has a role to play in bringing about a culture of peace. Having faith in youth, and in particular in students, is a challenge that higher education must meet in all our countries.

Such, then, is the complex context in which we are called upon to work out a new vision for higher education. And a question immediately arises: can higher education take on new functions while remaining as it was before? This issue was raised by Brazil, and formed the focus of Thematic Debate No. 6. What challenges must it meet at the dawn of the third millennium?

II. THE MAJOR CHALLENGES FACING HIGHER EDUCATION IN THE TWENTY-FIRST CENTURY

How could we fail to seize the Opportunity afforded by this great international gathering to pinpoint, in the observations formulated, in the initiatives taken here and there, in the successes as well as in the setbacks, the major issues facing the higher education of today and tomorrow? We here encounter once again the four main lines of inquiry that have been selected to structure this World Conference and the various events that preceded it.

A. Relevance

We are first faced with the task of establishing a mass higher education system integrated into lifelong education. Several of those who took the floor, including the representative of Chile, noted and applauded the general interest shown today in higher education, not least by the major funding agencies—itself a sign of a change in attitude. Higher education is acknowledged to be a factor of development in a knowledge-based society and economy. Of course we still need to be in a position to provide as many young people as possible with relevant and high quality training that gives them access to the job market and enables them subsequently to update their skills and knowledge.

We have just alluded to the need to open higher education to a broader student population. This assumes, as the representative of

Indonesia and several other speakers pointed out, that real opportunities exist to respond to the growing demand for higher education in the different countries of the world. Admittedly, the mass provision of higher education is already a reality in a number of countries. Others have undertaken to move towards this objective, one that calls for co-operation and solidarity. We shall return to the matter in the final section of this report.

Everyone found that the experience of democratizing higher education runs up against the criterion of relevance. The discussions demonstrated that relevance is a dynamic concept, varying according to context and from one target group to another, with particular attention needing to be paid to minority groups. The issue of who decides what is relevant lay at the heart of the discussions in Commission II and was also debated in plenary. The representatives of Canada, Colombia, Egypt and the Islamic Republic of Iran drew particular attention to this dimension. It emerged, in our view, from the deliberations that relevance can only be the outcome of dialogue and consultation among the different partners concerned, including the students themselves.

B. Quality and its evaluation

The quality of higher education is judged mainly by the strength of the ethical and pedagogical principles it embodies. It is riven by a number of conflicts and paradoxes: the contradiction between the explosion and fragmentation of demand on the one hand and the unemployment which affects an ever growing number of graduates on the other; between the duty of equality and justice, and the financial constraints upon the mass extension of this form of education; and finally, the conflict between ethical and moral obligations and the various incitements to misuse knowledge and discoveries. Faced with such tensions and paradoxes, higher education must develop a new vision, take advantage of its adaptability, flexibility and imaginative resources in order to develop problem-solving and forward-looking capacities, equip itself with an ever watchful critical spirit and promote teamwork, without ever jettisoning its role as ethical watchdog.

The issue of quality cannot be dissociated from the quest for excellence and the need to establish evaluation criteria. Many countries are calling for international quality standards. Such criteria and standards should take account of the diversity of situations. The need to develop a culture of evaluation is inseparable from the concept of quality, itself intimately bound up with the successful democratisation of the higher education system.

C. Management and financing

These particular problems were the responsibility of commission III.

Education can no longer be - and in many cases no longer is- confined to an ivory tower. The **sharing of responsibilities** with all partners, both inside and outside the university, is essential.

Within the institution, responsibilities belong to all users, teachers, researchers, students and administrative staff and, more widely, to all who have management and advisory functions. New forms of management which strengthen collective responsibility and transparency must be introduced.

Outside the institution, the multiplicity of partners is now an established fact: business enterprises, regional authorities created by the decentralization process and scientific research establishments independent of the university. Higher education has developed its relations with the economic world; gone are the days when the two camps ignored or found fault with one another. But in this partnership, higher education must be careful not to adopt a mercantile attitude, as firmly pointed out by the Prime Minister of France: the market is of course an inescapable fact of life, but its demands must not be allowed to predominate. This problem seems particularly acute in the countries in transition.

The partnership with industry and other sectors of society can also help to vocationalise higher education. Internships in industry have become routine in many countries, while many business managers are currently involved in higher education. In addition, consultative arrangements under which companies take part in the management of universities can be put in place, research projects can bring universities and businesses closer together and assistance in job seeking can be jointly envisaged. All this calls for a different approach on the part of business enterprises, corresponding to the recognition by universities of the need for change.

In the context of this complex and demanding style of management, the **autonomy of universities** and the exercise of academic freedoms must be respected. At the national level, the growing number of very diverse institutions needed to meet the changing trends in demand cannot be properly managed without flexible mechanisms and some degree of decentralisation.

The supervisory function must be exercised through a policy of encouragement and support rather than restraint. It is the only way of developing forms of higher education that are better adapted to demand: open university, private service providers of various kinds, distance-education systems, virtual campuses, shared multi-site networks, etc.

Of course the thematic debates took up the question of the resources offered by the **new information and communication technologies,** including the possibility of setting up virtual universities such as the United Nations University. The debate on this question was highly instructive and produced a number of interesting proposals. A video conference demonstration illustrated the fundamental changes that are already taking place - and will continue to do so in the future - as a result of the transition from the traditional to the virtual. These changes affect the three main pillars of higher education, namely courses, laboratories and libraries. The speakers drew attention to the impact of these new technologies, without losing sight of the ethical, cultural and geopolitical dimensions involved in access to these tools, in the generation of knowledge and in its dissemination. The establishment of North/South and South/South co-operation was recommended so as to facilitate the access of all to these technologies, to strengthen endogenous capacities and to make universally available the knowledge thus produced.

Technologies cannot solve every problem. As the representative of Algeria stressed, special efforts must be made on behalf of women who, in many countries, are still excluded from higher education and left out of the decision-making processes of society. Technologies can help, but the genuine democratization of higher education also requires the removal of the socio-economic, cultural and political obstacles that hinder women's full access to education and their full social integration.

The **financing** of higher education remains a major problem at the dawn of the twenty-first century. The flexibility sought after—and already largely obtained—by the universities is not a reason for failing to be accountable; a method should be found, according to some speakers, including the representative of Swaziland, that both respects university autonomy and provides accountability; performance-related financing is one of the many ways of achieving that end. Whatever the case, there must be no violation of academic freedoms or of the basic principles underlying them.

In view of the development of higher education, the state cannot hope to be the sole or even the main source of financing for the sector as a whole. This view was shared by several speakers, including the representative of Morocco. But it in no way detracts from the state's responsibility for ensuring that higher education is adequately financed. The contractual system, as practised in France, which links higher education institutions and the ministry responsible for a four-year period, may enable the latter to determine the extent of its financial commitment but does not prevent the institution from seeking other partners. Numerous speakers, such as the representatives of Cape Verde and Mali, were concerned by the withdrawal of the state. Of course, it is obvious that the state alone cannot supply all the requisite financing, so it is advisable to create at the decision-making level an atmosphere conducive to greater diversification of funding sources for higher education. The solutions will be many and varied. In any event, an effort should be made to foster an entrepreneurial spirit in institutions which are striving to raise funds not only by traditional research and training activities but also by commercial or production operations. In yet other cases, we see the ever growing development of a private higher education sector. New ways of diversifying resources, resulting from a variety of pressures and opportunities, are continually emerging; UNESCO and other networks could play a useful role by disseminating them.

All these possibilities of diversification are fraught with dangers that must be avoided. The most serious of all is that of undermining equality of access to higher education. Private education, for instance, while leading to wider access than would otherwise be available, tends to be fee-paying and therefore enrols fewer underprivileged students. Involvement by the state and the retention of a public service are still the best guarantee of equal opportunities and the democratization of higher education.

D. International co-operation

At this stage in the analysis of the major changes in higher education we feel it is necessary-and the texts we are to adopt so invite us - to accord greater importance to international experience, partnership and solidarity, which several delegations, including that of South Africa, supported.

The working documents setting out the experiences of institutions, countries and regions all stress the contribution of co-operation to greater solidarity and genuine peace. This co-operation is necessary not only to reinforce the quality, relevance and internal effectiveness of higher education, but also to build bridges between local and national partners and between nations.

The participants in Commission IV welcomed the ideas in the working document submitted to them and, at the initiative of the International Association of Universities, strongly urged that higher education should include among its primary missions international co-operation and the need to promote plurality of cultures, global awareness of problems and sustainable development throughout the world.

At the international level, the networking of higher education and research institutions under programmes such as the UNITWIN/UNESCO Chairs Programme was highlighted as an innovative approach to national and institutional capacity-building in the developing countries.

The open-doors approach to learning and training which encourages academic mobility appeared to many developing countries, and to some non-governmental organizations and foundations, to be the sole preserve of the industrialised world. The developing countries are suffering from the brain drain, which is a sort of exile of 'intelligence', and from its adverse effects on their ability to strengthen their institutions and shape critical and creative citizens. Without automatically linking those trends, the Conference endorsed this concern and launched an appeal for the promotion of mobility, while assisting countries deprived of their experts to retain and motivate their specialists at home, or encourage them to return, by setting up North/South co-operative links between institutions, and by creating centres of excellence in the developing countries. TOKTEN and TALVEN, which were presented during the proceedings, are interesting examples in this context.

Several speakers backed the idea of launching an 'Academics without Frontiers' initiative, referred to in one of the working documents, and hoped that this possibility would be explored.

In connection with work that could be carried out jointly on quality, it should be recalled that many countries were in favour of drawing up international standards for the evaluation of quality, but with all due respect for the diversity and specificity of individual countries. More generally, noting that six intergovernmental committees are resolutely addressing the question of the recognition of studies, diplomas and degrees in higher education, speakers felt that similar bodies should be set up to look into the evaluation of international co-operation. As pointed out by the representative of Morocco, it is crucial for UNESCO to commission an evaluation report on the forms and practices of such co-operation in relation to the specific needs of each region.

Emphasis should also be given to the task of providing expert advice and assistance in institutional capacity-building that falls to UNESCO in higher education, as in its other fields of competence. In addition, the participants requested UNESCO to continue its work on academic freedom, with particular attention to the follow-up to the Recommendation concerning the Status of Higher-Education Teaching Personnel adopted by the Organisation at its General Conference in 1997. They also raised the question of a permanent study group to draw up a Universal Charter of Academic Freedoms.

Conclusion: a call to action

We have reached the end of the proceedings of the World Conference on Higher Education.

The texts we have just adopted are, for our governments, our higher education institutions, the non-governmental organizations, and all the partners here present, lines of action that we undertake to pursue in each of our countries and in the context of international co-operation.

However, this whole exercise, which has involved manifold consultations and has culminated in this international gathering, will have been in vain if it were to cease this evening.

Our first task will be to explain, and if necessary defend, and then to convince. In order to do so, the Declaration and Framework for Action must be widely distributed to those in charge of higher education, to academics, to all the specialists concerned, and to the many relevant institutions of civil society. In our home countries we will probably have to organize debates and set up working groups to look more deeply into particular aspects of the Declaration and Framework for Action, and to consider how the reforms can be put into practice.

Our texts do not stop there. They call for greater regional and international co-operation and active solidarity with countries that are lagging behind in development. We must make sure that in a few years' time we are not driven to the bitter conclusion that the divisions and gaps have widened even further, that still more skilled personnel from the countries of the South have headed into exile, thus diverting an essential and stimulating mobility from its true purpose, and that higher education in many countries is still unable to make an effective contribution to the development of the education system as a whole and to the quality of basic education.

That is why we must shape a new generation of models of co-operation, based on local needs, taking account of economic and social realities and cultural specificities, and providing advisory services and expertise without imposing conditions and without imposing themselves. Co-operating means working together to carry out co-ordinated action. That is what we are called upon to do.

As the work of this World Conference draws to a close, it is extremely important that the curtain should not fall, without lasting impact, on this vision of higher education in the twenty-first century. The concluding Declaration and Framework for Priority Action that we have adopted are there to call to action all those who have worked so intensely and constructively during this week of October 1998. It is up to them, in their own fields and with their own responsibilities, to make sure that these texts are followed up, so that together we can meet the challenges of the next millennium.

On concluding this report, I should like to thank the drafting group, the members of the UNESCO Secretariat and all those who have worked with me throughout the week. For their commitment, support and the pertinence of their contributions, and for the confidence you have placed in me by entrusting me with the uplifting task of Rapporteur-General of the Conference, may I offer you all my most sincere gratitude.

Suzy Halimi

2

WORLD DECLARATION ON HIGHER EDUCATION FOR THE TWENTY-FIRST CENTURY: VISION AND ACTION

PREAMBLE

On the eve of a new century, there is an **unprecedented demand for and a great diversification in higher education, as well as an increased awareness of its vital importance for sociocultural and economic development,** and for building the future, for which the younger generations will need to be equipped with new skills, knowledge and ideals. Higher education includes 'all types of studies, training or training for research at the post-secondary level, provided by universities or other educational establishments that are approved as institutions of higher education by the competent State authorities'.[1] Everywhere higher education is faced with great challenges and difficulties related to financing, equity of conditions at access into and during the course of studies, improved staff development, skills-based training, enhancement and preservation of quality in teaching, research and services, relevance of programmes, employability of graduates, establishment of efficient co-operation agreements and equitable access to the benefits of international co-operation. At the same time, higher education is being challenged by new opportunities relating to technologies that are improving the ways in which knowledge can be produced, managed, disseminated, accessed and controlled. Equitable access to these technologies should be ensured at all levels of education systems.

The second half of this century will go down in the history of higher education as the period of its most spectacular **expansion:** an over sixfold increase in student enrolments worldwide, from 13 million in 1960 to 82 million in 1995. But it is also the period which has seen the gap between industrially developed, the **developing countries** and **in particular the least developed countries** with regard to access and resources for higher learning and research, already enormous, becoming even wider. It has also been a period of increased socio-economic stratification and greater difference in educational opportunity within countries, including in some of the most developed and wealthiest nations. Without adequate higher education and research institutions providing a critical mass of skilled and educated people, no country can ensure genuine endogenous and sustainable development and, in particular, developing countries and least developed countries cannot reduce the gap separating them from the industrially developed ones. Sharing knowledge, international co-operation and new technologies can offer new opportunities to reduce this gap.

Higher education has given ample proof of its viability over the centuries and of its ability to change and to induce change and progress in society. Owing to the scope and pace of change, society has become increasingly **knowledge-based** so that higher learning and research now act as essential components of cultural, socio-economic and environmentally sustainable development of individuals, communities and nations. Higher education itself is confronted therefore with formidable challenges and must proceed to the most radical **change and renewal it has even been required** to undertake, so that our society, which is currently undergoing a profound crisis of values, can transcend mere economic considerations and incorporate deeper dimensions of morality and spirituality.

It is with the aim of providing solutions to these challenges and of setting in motion a process of in-depth reform in higher education worldwide that UNESCO has convened a World Conference on higher Education in the Twenty-First Century: Vision and Action. In preparation for the Conference, UNESCO issued, in 1995, its *Policy Paper for Change and Development in Higher Education*. Five regional consultations (Havana, November 1996; Dakar, April 1997; Tokyo, July 1997; Palermo, September 1997; and Beirut, March 1998) were subsequently held. The Declarations and Plans of Action adopted by them, each preserving its own specificity, are duly taken into account in the present

Declaration - as is the whole process of reflection undertaken by the preparation of the World Conference - and are annexed to it.

*

* *

We, participants in the World Conference on Higher Education, assembled at UNESCO Headquarters in Paris, from 5 to 9 October 1998,

Recalling the principles of the Charter of the United Nations, the Universal Declaration of Human Rights, the International Covenant on Economic, Social and Cultural Rights, and the International Covenant on Civil and Political Rights,

Recalling also the Universal Declaration of Human Rights which states in Article 26, paragraph 1, that 'Everyone has the right to education' and that 'higher education shall be equally accessible to all on the basis of merit', and **endorsing** the basic principles of the Convention against discrimination in Education (1960), which, by Article 4, commits the States Parties to it to 'make higher education equally accessible to all on the basis of individual capacity',

Taking into account the recommendations concerning higher education of major commissions and conferences, *inter alia*, the international Commission on Education for the Twenty-First Century, the World Commission on Culture and Development, the 44th and 45th sessions of the International Conference on Education (Geneva, 1994 and 1996), the decisions taken at the 27th and 29th sessions of UNESCO's General Conference, in particular regarding the Recommendation concerning the Status of Higher-Education Teaching Personnel, the World Conference on Education for All (Jomtien, Thailand, 1990), the United Nations Conference on Environment and Development (Rio de Janeiro, 1992), the Conference on Academic Freedom and University Autonomy (Sinaia, 1992), the World Conference on Human Rights (Vienna, 1993), the World Summit for Social Development (Copenhagen, 1995), the fourth World Conference on Women (Beijing, 1995), the International Congress on Education and Informatics (Moscow, 1996), the World Congress on Higher Education and Human Resources Development for the Twenty-First Century (Manila, 1997), the fifth International Conference on Adult Education (Hamburg, 1997) and especially the Agenda for the Future under Theme 2 (Improving the conditions and quality of learning) stating: 'We commit ourselves to ... opening schools, colleges and universities to adult learners

.... by calling upon the World Conference on Higher Education (Paris, 1998) to promote the transformation of post-secondary institutions into lifelong learning institutions and to define the role of universities accordingly',

Convinced that education is a fundamental pillar of human rights, democracy, sustainable development and peace, and shall therefore become accessible to all throughout life and that measures are required to ensure co-ordination and co-operation across and between the various sectors, particularly between general, technical and professional secondary and post-secondary education as well as between universities, colleges and technical institutions,

Believing that, in this context, the solution of the problems faced on the eve of the twenty-first century will be determined by the vision of the future society and by the role that is assigned to education in general and to higher education in particular,

Aware that on the threshold of a new millennium it is the duty of higher education to ensure that the values and ideals of a culture of peace prevail and that the intellectual community should be mobilised to that end,

Considering that a substantial change and development of higher education, the enhancement of its quality and relevance, and the solution to the major challenges it faces, require the strong involvement not only of governments and of higher education institutions, but also of all stakeholders, including students and their families, teachers, business and industry, the public and private sectors of the economy, parliaments, the media, the community, professional associations and society as well as a greater responsibility of higher education institutions towards society and accountability in the use of public and private, national or international resources,

Emphasising that higher education systems should enhance their capacity to live with uncertainty, to change and bring about change, and to address social needs and to promote solidarity and equity; should preserve and exercise scientific rigour and originality, in a spirit of impartiality, as a basic prerequisite for attaining and sustaining an indispensable level of quality; and should place students at the centre of their concerns, **within a lifelong perspective,** so as to allow their full integration into the global knowledge society of the coming century,

Also believing that international co-operation and exchange are major avenues for advancing higher education throughout the world,

Proclaim the following:

Missions And Functions Of Higher Education

Article 1. Mission to educate, to train and to undertake research

We affirm that the core missions and values of higher education, in particular the mission to contribute to the sustainable development and improvement of society as a whole, should be preserved, reinforced and further expanded, namely, to:

(a) educate highly qualified graduates and responsible citizens able to meet the needs of all sectors of human activity, by offering relevant qualifications, including professional training, which combine high-level knowledge and skills, using courses and content continually tailored to the present and future needs of society;

(b) provide opportunities (*espace ouvert*) **for higher learning and for learning throughout life**, giving to learners an optimal range of choice and a flexibility of entry and exit points within the system, as well as an opportunity for individual development and social mobility in order **to educate for citizenship and for active participation in society,** with a worldwide vision, for endogenous capacity-building, and for the consolidation of human rights, sustainable development, democracy and peace, in a context of justice;

(c) **advance, create and disseminate knowledge** through research and provide, as part of its service to the community, relevant expertise to assist societies in cultural, social and economic development, promoting and developing scientific and technological research as well as research in the social sciences, the humanities and the creative arts;

(d) help **understand, interpret, preserve, enhance, promote and disseminate national and regional, international and historic cultures,** in a context of cultural pluralism and diversity;

(e) help, protect and enhance **societal values** by training young people in the values which form the basis of democratic citizenship and by providing critical and detached perspectives to assist in the discussion of strategic options and the reinforcement of humanistic perspectives;

(f) contribute to the development and improvement of education at all levels, including through the training of teachers.

Article 2. Ethical role, autonomy, responsibility and anticipatory function

In accordance with the Recommendation concerning the Status of Higher-Education Teaching Personnel approved by the General Conference of UNESCO in November 1997, **higher education institutions and their personnel and students** should:

(a) preserve and develop their crucial functions, through the exercise of ethics and scientific and intellectual rigour in their various activities;

(b) be able to speak out on ethical, cultural and social problems completely independently and in full awareness of their responsibilities, exercising a kind of intellectual authority that society needs to help it to reflect, understand and act;

(c) enhance their critical and forward-looking functions, through continuing analysis of emerging social, economic, cultural and political trends, providing a focus for forecasting, warning and prevention;

(d) exercise their intellectual capacity and their moral prestige to defend and actively disseminate universally accepted values, including peace, justice, freedom, equality and solidarity, as enshrined in UNESCO's Constitution;

(e) enjoy full academic autonomy and freedom, conceived as a set of rights and duties, while being fully responsible and accountable to society;

(f) play a role in helping identify and address issues that affect the well-being of communities, nations and global society.

Shaping A New Vision Of Higher Education

Article 3. Equity of access

(a) In keeping with Article 26.1 of the Universal Declaration of Human Rights, admission to higher education should be based on the merit, capacity, efforts, perseverance and devotion, showed by those seeking access to it, and can take place in a lifelong scheme, at any time, with due recognition of previously acquired skills. As a consequence, no discrimination can be accepted in granting access to higher education on grounds of race, gender, language or religion, or economic, cultural or social distinctions, or physical disabilities.

(b) Equity of access to higher education should begin with the reinforcement and, if need be, the reordering of its links with all other levels of education, particularly with secondary education. Higher education institutions must be viewed as, and must also work within themselves to be a part of and encourage, a seamless system starting with early childhood and primary education and continuing through life. Higher education institutions must work in active partnership with parents, schools, students, socio-economic groups and communities. Secondary education should not only prepare qualified candidates for access to higher education by developing the capacity to learn on a broad basis but also open the way to active life by providing training on a wide range of jobs. However, access to higher education should remain open to those successfully completing secondary school, or its equivalent, or presenting entry qualifications, as far as possible, at any age and without any discrimination.

(c) As a consequence, the rapid and wide-reaching demand for higher education requires, where appropriate, **all policies concerning access to higher education** to give priority in the future to the approach based on the merit of the individual, as defined in Article 3(a) above.

(d) Access to higher education for members of some special target groups, such as indigenous peoples, cultural and linguistic minorities, disadvantaged groups, peoples living under occupation and those who suffer from disabilities, must be actively facilitated, since these groups as collectivities and as individuals may have both experience and talent that can be of great value for the development of societies and nations. Special material help and educational solutions can help overcome the obstacles that these groups face, both in accessing and in continuing higher education.

Article 4. Enhancing participation and promoting the role of women

(a) Although significant progress has been achieved to enhance the **access of women** to higher education, various socio-economic, cultural and political obstacles continue in many places in the world to impede their full access and effective integration. To overcome them remains an urgent priority in the renewal process for ensuring an equitable and non discriminatory system of higher education based on the principle of merit.

(b) Further efforts are required to eliminate all gender stereotyping in higher education, to consider gender aspects in different disciplines and to consolidate women's participation at all levels and in all disciplines, in which they are under-represented and, in particular, to enhance their active involvement in decision-making.

(c) Gender studies (women's studies) should be promoted as a field of knowledge, strategic for the transformation of higher education and society.

(d) Efforts should be made to eliminate political and social barriers whereby women are underrepresented and in particular to enhance their active involvement at policy and decision-making levels within higher education and society.

Article 5. Advancing knowledge through research in science, the arts and humanities and the dissemination of its results

(a) The advancement of knowledge through **research** is an essential function of all **systems** of higher education, which should promote postgraduate studies. **Innovation, interdisciplinary and transdisciplinarity** should be promoted and reinforced in programmes with long-term orientations on social and cultural aims and needs. An appropriate balance should be established between basic and target-oriented research.

(b) Institutions should ensure that all members of the academic community engaged in research are provided with appropriate training, resources and support. The intellectual and cultural rights on the results of research should be used to the benefit of humanity and should be protected so that they cannot be abused.

(c) Research must be enhanced in all disciplines, including the social and human sciences, education (including higher eduction), engineering, natural sciences, mathematics, informatics and the arts within the framework of national, regional and international research and development policies. Of special importance is the enhancement of research capacities in higher education research institutions, as mutual enhancement of quality takes place when higher education and research are conducted at a high level within the same institution. These institutions should find the material and financial support required, from **both public and private sources.**

Article 6. Long-term orientation based on relevance

(a) **Relevance** in higher education should be assessed in terms of the fit between what society expects of institutions and what they do. This requires ethical standards, political impartiality, critical capacities and, at the same time, a better articulation with the problem of society and the world of work, **basing long-term orientations on societal aims and needs, including respect for cultures and environmental protection.** The concern is to provide access to both broad general education and targeted, career-specific education, often interdisciplinary, focusing on skills and aptitudes, both of which equip individuals to live in a variety of changing settings, and to be able to change occupations.

(b) Higher education should **reinforce its role of service to society,** especially its activities aimed at eliminating poverty, intolerance, violence, illiteracy, hunger, environmental degradation and disease, mainly through an **interdisciplinary and transdisciplinary approach** in the analysis of problems and issues.

(c) Higher education should enhance its contribution to **the development of the whole education system,** notably through improved teacher education, curriculum development and educational research.

(d) Ultimately, higher education should aim at the creation of a new society- non-violent and non-exploitative - consisting of highly cultivated, motivated and integrated individuals, inspired by love for humanity and guided by wisdom.

Article 7. Strengthening co-operation with the world of work and analysing and anticipating societal needs

(a) In economies characterised by changes and the emergence of new production paradigms based on knowledge and its application, and on the handling of information, the links between higher education, the world of work and other parts of society should be strengthened and renewed.

(b) Links with the world of work can be strengthened, through the participation of its representatives in the governance of institutions, the increased use of domestic and international apprenticeship/work-study opportunities for students and teachers, the exchange of personnel between the world of work and higher education institutions and revised curricula more closely aligned with working practices.

(c) **As a lifelong source of professional training, updating and recycling,** institutions of higher education should systematically take into account trends in the world of work and in the scientific, technological and economic sectors. In order to respond to the work requirements, higher education systems and the world of work should jointly develop and assess learning processes, bridging programmes and prior learning assessment and recognition programmes, which integrate theory and training on the job. Within the framework of their anticipatory function, higher education institutions could contribute to the creation of new jobs, although that is not their only function.

(d) Developing entrepreneurial skills and initiative should become major concerns of higher education, in order to facilitate employability of graduates who will increasingly be called upon to be not only job seekers but also and able all to become job creators. Higher education institutions should give the opportunity to students to fully develop their own abilities with a sense of social responsibility, educating them to become full participants in democratic society and promoters of changes that will foster equity and justice.

Article 8. Diversification for enhanced equity of opportunity

(a) Diversifying higher education models and recruitment methods and criteria is essential both to meet increasing international demand and to provide access to various delivery modes and to extend access to an ever-wider public, in a lifelong perspective, based on flexible entry and exit points to and from the system of higher education.

(b) More diversified systems of higher education are characterised by new types of tertiary institutions: public, private and non-profit institutions, amongst others. Institutions should be able to offer a wide variety of education and training opportunities: traditional degrees, short courses, part-time study, flexible schedules, modularised courses, supported learning at a distance, etc.

Article 9. Innovative educational approaches: critical thinking and creativity

(a) In a world undergoing rapid changes, there is a perceived need for a new vision and paradigm of higher education, which should be student-oriented, calling in most countries for in-depth reforms and an open access policy so as to cater for ever more diversified categories of people, and of its contents, methods, practices and means of delivery, based on new types of links and partnerships with the community and with the broadest sectors of society.

(b) Higher education institutions should educate students to become well informed and deeply motivated citizens, who can think critically, analyse problems of society, look for solutions to the problems of society, apply them and accept social responsibilities.

(c) To achieve these goals, it may be necessary to recast curricula, using new and appropriate methods, so as to go beyond cognitive mastery of disciplines. New pedagogical and didactical approaches should be accessible and promoted in order to facilitate the acquisition of skills, competences and abilities for communication, creative and critical analysis, **independent thinking and team work in multicultural contexts,** where creativity also involves combining traditional or local knowledge and know-how with advanced science and technology. **These recast curricula should take into account the gender dimension and the specific cultural, historic and economic context of each country.** The teaching of human rights standards and education on the needs of communities in all parts of the world should be reflected in the curricula of all disciplines, particularly those preparing for entrepreneurship. Academic personnel should play a significant role in determining the curriculum.

(d) New methods of education will also imply new types of teaching-learning materials. These have to be coupled with new methods of testing that will promote not only powers of memory but also powers of comprehension, skills for practical work and creativity.

Article 10. Higher education personnel and students as major actors

(a) A vigorous policy of staff development is an essential element for higher education institutions. Clear policies should be established concerning higher education teachers, who nowadays need to focus on teaching students how to learn and how to take initiatives rather than being exclusively founts of knowledge. Adequate provision should be made for research and for updating and improving pedagogical skills, through appropriate staff development programmes, encouraging constant innovation in curriculum, teaching and learning methods, and ensuring appropriate professional and financial status, and **for excellence in research and teaching,** reflecting the corresponding provisions of the **Recommendation concerning the Status of Higher-Education Teaching Personnel approved by the General Conference of UNESCO in November 1997.** To this end, more importance should be attached to international experience. Furthermore, in view of the role of higher education for lifelong learning, experience outside the institutions ought to be considered as a relevant qualification for higher educational staff.

(b) Clear policies should be established by all higher education institutions preparing teachers of early childhood education and for primary and secondary schools, providing stimulus for constant innovation in curriculum, best practices in teaching methods and familiarity with diverse learning styles. It is vital to have appropriately trained administrative and technical personnel.

(c) **National and institutional decision-makers should place students and their needs at the centre of their concerns,** and should consider them as major partners and responsible stakeholders in the renewal of higher education. This should include student involvement in issues that affect that level of education, in evaluation, the renovation of teaching methods and curricula and, in the institutional framework in force, in policy-formulation and institutional management. As students have the right to organize and represent themselves, students' involvement in these issues should be guaranteed.

(d) Guidance and counselling services should be developed, in co-operation with student organizations, in order to assist students in the transition to higher education at whatever age and to take account of the needs of ever more diversified categories of learners. Apart from those entering higher education from schools or further education colleges, they should also take account of the needs of those leaving and returning in a lifelong process. Such support is important in ensuring a good match between student and course, reducing dropout. Students who do drop out should have suitable opportunities to return to higher education if and when appropriate.

From Vision To Action

Article 11. Qualitative evaluation

(a) **Quality in higher education is a multidimensional concept,** which should embrace all its functions, and activities; teaching and academic programmes, research and scholarship, staffing, students, buildings, facilities, equipment, services to the community and the academic environment. Internal self-evaluation and external review, conducted openly by independent specialists, if possible with international expertise, are vital for enhancing quality. Independent national bodies should be established and comparative standards of quality, recognized at international level, should be defined. **Due attention should be paid to specific institutional, national and regional contexts in order to take into account diversity and to avoid uniformity.** Stakeholders should be an integral part of the institutional evaluation process.

(b) Quality also requires that higher education should be characterised by its international dimension: exchange of knowledge, interactive networking, mobility of teachers and students, and international research projects, while taking into account the national cultural values and circumstances.

(c) To attain and sustain national, regional or international quality, certain components are particularly relevant, notably careful selection of staff and continuous staff development, in particular through he promotion of appropriate programmes for academic staff development, including teachings/learning methodology and mobility between countries, between higher education institutions, and between higher education institutions and the world of work, as well as student mobility within and between countries. The new information technologies are an important tool in this process, owing to their impact on the acquisition of knowledge and know-how.

Article 12. The potential and the challenge of technology

The rapid breakthroughs in new information and communication technologies will further change the way knowledge is developed, acquired and delivered. It is also important to note that the new technologies offer opportunities to innovate on course content and teaching methods and to widen access to higher learning. However, it should be borne in mind that new information technology does not reduce the need for teachers but changes their role in relation to the learning process and that the continuous dialogue that converts information into knowledge and understanding becomes fundamental. Higher education institutions should lead in drawing on the advantages and potential of new information and communication technologies, ensuring quality and maintaining high standards for education practices and outcomes in a spirit of openness, equity and international co-operation by:

(a) engaging in networks, technology transfer, capacity-building, developing teaching materials and sharing experience of their application in teaching, training and research, making knowledge accessible to all;

(b) creating new learning environments, ranging from distance education facilities to complete virtual higher education institutions and systems, capable of bridging distances and developing high-quality systems of education, thus serving social and economic advancement and democratisation as well as other relevant priorities of society, while ensuring that these virtual education facilities, based on regional, continental or global networks, function in a way that respects cultural and social identities;

(c) noting that, in making full use of information and communication technology (ICT) for educational purposes, particular attention should be paid to removing the grave inequalities which exist among and also within the countries of the world with regard to access to new information and communication technologies and to the production of the corresponding resources;

(d) adapting ICT to national, regional and local needs and securing technical, educational, management and institutional systems to sustain it;

(e) facilitating, through international co-operation, the identification of the objectives and interests of all countries, particularly the developing countries, equitable access and the strengthening of infrastructures in this field and the dissemination of such technology throughout society;

(f) closely following the evolution of the 'knowledge society' in order to ensure high quality and equitable regulations for access to prevail;

(g) taking the new possibilities created by the use of ICTs into account, while realising that it is, above all, institutions of higher education that are using ICTs in order to modernize their work, and not ICTs transforming institutions of higher education from real to virtual institutions.

Article 13. Strengthening higher education management and financing

(a) The management and financing of higher education require the **development of appropriate planning and policy-analysis capacities** and strategies, based on partnerships established between higher education institutions and state and national planning and co-ordination bodies, so as to secure appropriately streamlined management and the cost-effective use of resources. Higher education institutions should **adopt forward-looking management practices** that respond to the needs of their environments. Managers in higher education must be responsive, competent and able to evaluate regularly by internal and external mechanisms, the effectiveness of procedures and administrative rules.

(b) Higher education institutions must be given autonomy to manage their internal affairs, but with this autonomy must come clear and transparent accountability to the government, parliament, students and the wider society.

(c) The ultimate goal of management should be to enhance the institutional mission by ensuring high-quality teaching, training and research, and services to the community. This objective requires **governance that combines social vision, including understanding of global issues, with efficient managerial skills.** Leadership in higher education is thus a major social responsibility and can be significantly strengthened through dialogue with all stakeholders, especially teachers and students, in higher education. The participation of teaching faculty in the governing bodies of higher education institutions should be taken into account, within the framework of current institutional arrangements, bearing in mind the need to keep the size of these bodies within reasonable bounds.

(d) The promotion of North-South co-operation to ensure the necessary financing for strengthening higher education in the developing countries is essential.

Article 14. Financing of higher education as a public service

The funding of higher education requires both public and private resources. The role of the state remains essential in this regard.

(a) The diversification of funding sources reflects the support that society provides to higher education and must be further strengthened to ensure the development of higher education increase its efficiency and maintain its quality and relevance. **Public support for higher education and research remains essential** to ensure a balanced achievement of educational and social missions.

(b) Society as a whole must support education at all levels, including higher education, given its role in promoting sustainable economic, social and cultural development. **Mobilisation for this purpose depends on public awareness and involvement of the public and private sectors** of the economy, parliaments, the media, governmental and non-governmental organizations, students as well as institutions, families and all the social actors involved with higher education.

Article 15. Sharing knowledge and know-how across borders and continents

(a) The principle of solidarity and true partnership amongst higher education institutions worldwide is crucial for education and training in all fields that encourage an understanding of global issues, the role of democratic governance and skilled human resources in their resolution, and the need for living together with different cultures and values. The practice of multilingualism, faculty and student exchange programmes and institutional linkage to promote intellectual and scientific co operation should be an integral part of all higher education systems.

(b) The principles of international co-operation based on solidarity, recognition and mutual support, true partnership that equitably serves the interests of the partners and the value of sharing knowledge and know-how across borders should govern relationships among higher education institutions in both developed and developing countries and should benefit the least developed countries in particular. Consideration should be given to the need for safeguarding higher education institutional capacities in regions suffering from conflict or natural disasters. Consequently, an international dimension should permeate the curriculum, and the teaching and learning processes.

(c) Regional and international normative instruments for the recognition of studies should be ratified and implemented, including certification of the skills, competences and abilities of graduates, making it easier for students to change courses, in order to facilitate mobility within and between national systems.

Article 16. From 'brain drain' to 'brain gain'

The 'brain drain' has yet to be stemmed, since it continues to deprive the developing countries and those in transition, of the high-level expertise necessary to accelerate their socio-economic progress. International co-operation schemes should be based on long-term partnerships between institutions in the South and the North, and also promote South-South co-operation. Priority should be given to training programmes in the developing countries, in centres of excellence forming regional and international networks, with short periods of specialized and intensive study abroad. Consideration should be given to creating an environment conducive to attracting and retaining skilled human capital, either through national policies or international arrangements to facilitate the return - permanent or temporary - of highly trained scholars and researchers to their countries of origin. At the same time, efforts must be directed towards a process of 'brain gain' through collaboration programmes that, by virtue of their international dimension, enhance the building and strengthening of institutions and facilitate full use of endogenous capacities. Experience gained through the UNITWIN/UNESCO Chairs Programme and the principles enshrined in the regional conventions on the recognition of degrees and diplomas in higher education are of particular importance in this respect.

Article 17. Partnership and alliances

Partnership and alliances amongst stakeholders - national and institutional policy-makers, teaching and **related** staff, researchers and students, and administrative and technical personnel in institutions of higher education, the world of work, community groups - is a powerful force in managing change. Also, non-governmental organisations are key actors in this process. Henceforth, **Partnership, based on common interest, mutual respect and credibility, should be a prime matrix for renewal in higher education.**

We, the participants in the World Conference on Higher Education, adopt this Declaration and reaffirm the right of all people to education and the right of access to higher education based on individual merit and capacity;

We pledge to act together within the frame of our individual and collective responsibilities, by taking all necessary measures in order realise the principles concerning higher education contained in the Universal Declaration of Human Rights and in the Convention against Discrimination in Education;

We solemnly reaffirm our commitment to peace. To that end, we are determined to accord high priority to education for peace and to participate in the celebration of the International Year for the Culture of Peace in the year 2000;

We adopt, therefore, this World Declaration on Higher Education for the Twenty-First Century: Vision and Action. To achieve the goals set forth in this Declaration and, in particular, for immediate action, we agree on the following Framework for Priority action for Change and Development of Higher Education.

Reference

1. Definition approved by the General Conference of UNESCO at its 27th session (November 1993) in the Recommendation on the Recognition of Studies and Qualifications in Higher Education.

3

FRAMEWORK FOR PRIORITY ACTION FOR CHANGE AND DEVELOPMENT OF HIGHER EDUCATION

I. PRIORITY ACTIONS AT NATIONAL LEVEL

1. **States, including their governments, parliaments and other decision-makers,** should:

(a) establish, where appropriate, the legislative, political and financial framework for the reform and further development of higher education, in keeping with the terms of the Universal Declaration of Human Rights, which establishes that **higher education shall be 'acessible to all on the basis of merit'. No discrimination can be accepted,** no one can be excluded from higher education or its study fields, degree levels and types of institutions on grounds of race, gender, language, religion, or age or because of any economic or social distinctions or physical disabilities;

(b) reinforce the links between higher education and research;

(c) consider and use higher education as a catalyst for the entire education system;

(d) develop higher education institutions to include lifelong learning approaches, giving learners an optimal range of choice and a flexibility of entry and exit points within the system, and redefine their role accordingly, which implies the development of open and continuous access to higher learning and the need for bridging programmes and prior learning assessment and recognition;

(e) make efforts, when necessary, to establish close links between higher education and research institutions, taking into account the fact that education and research are two closely related elements in the establishment of knowledge;

(f) develop innovative schemes of collaboration between institutions of higher education and different sectors of society to ensure that higher education and research programmes effectively contribute to local, regional and national development;

(g) fulfill their commitments to higher education and be accountable for the pledges adopted with their concurrence, at several forums, particularly over the past decade, with regard to human, material and financial resources, human development and education in general, and to higher education in particular;

(h) have a policy framework to ensure new partnerships and the involvement of all relevant stakeholders in all aspects of higher education: the evaluation process, including curriculum and pedagogical renewal, and guidance and counselling services; and, in the framework of existing institutional arrangements, policy-making and institutional governance;

(i) **define and implement policies to eliminate all gender stereotyping in higher education** and to consolidate women's participation at all levels and in all disciplines in which they are under-represented at present and, in particular, to enhance their active involvement in decision-making;

(j) **establish clear policies concerning higher education teachers,** as set out in the Recommendation concerning the Status of Higher-Education Teaching Personnel approved by the General Conference of UNESCO in November 1997;

(k) recognise students as the centre of attention of higher education, and one of its stakeholders. They should be involved, by means of adequate institutional structures, in the renewal of their level of education (including curriculum and pedagogical reform), and policy decision, in the framework of existing institutional arrangements;

(l) recognise that students have the right to organise themselves autonomously;

(m) promote and facilitate national and international mobility of teaching staff and students as an essential part of the quality and relevance of higher education;

(n) provide and ensure those conditions necessary for the exercise of academic freedom and institutional autonomy so as to allow institutions of higher education, as well as those individuals engaged in higher education and research, to fulfil their obligations to society.

2. States in which enrolment in higher education is low by internationally accepted comparative standards should strive to ensure a level of higher education adequate for relevant needs in the public and private sectors of society and to establish plans for diversifying and expanding access, particularly benefiting all minorities and disadvantaged groups.

3. The interface with general, technical and professional secondary education should be reviewed in depth, in the context of lifelong learning. Access to higher education in whatever form must remain open to those successfully completing secondary education or its equivalent or meeting entry qualifications at any age, while creating gateways to higher education, especially for older students without any formal secondary education certificates, by attaching more importance to their professional experience. However, **preparation for higher education should not be the sole or primary purpose of secondary education, which should also prepare for the world of work,** with complementary training whenever required, in order to provide knowledge, capacities and skills for a wide range of jobs. The concept of bridging programmes should be promoted to allow those entering the job market to return to studies at a later date.

.4. **Concrete steps should be taken to reduce the widening gap between industrially developed and developing countries, in particular the least developed countries, with regard to higher education and research.** Concrete steps are also needed to encourage increased co-operation between countries at all levels of economic development with regard to higher education and research. Consideration should be given to making budgetary provisions for that purpose, and developing mutually beneficial agreements involving industry, national as well as international, in order to sustain co-operative activities and projects through appropriate incentives and funding in education, research and the development of high-level experts in these countries.

II. PRIORITY ACTIONS AT THE LEVEL OF SYSTEMS AND INSTITUTIONS

5. **Each higher education institution should define its mission according to the present and future needs of society** and base it on an awareness of the fact that higher education is essential for any country or region to reach the necessary level of sustainable and environmentally sound economic and social development, cultural creativity nourished by better knowledge and understanding of the cultural heritage, higher living standards, and internal and international harmony and peace, based on human rights, democracy, tolerance and mutual respect. These missions should incorporate the concept of academic freedom set out in the Recommendation concerning the Status of Higher-Education Teaching Personnel approved by the General Conference of UNESCO in November 1997.

6. In establishing priorities in their programmes and structures, higher education institutions should:

(a) take into account the need to abide by the rules of ethics and scientific and intellectual rigour, and the multidisciplinary and transdisciplinary approach;

(b) be primarily concerned to establish systems of access for the benefit of all persons who have the necessary abilities and motivations;

(c) use their autonomy and high academic standards to contribute to the sustainable development of society and to the resolution of the issues facing the society of the future. They should develop their capacity to give forewarning through the analysis of emerging social, cultural, economic and political trends, approached in a multidisciplinary and transdisciplinary manner, giving particular attention to:

- high quality, a clear sense of the social pertinence of studies and their anticipatory function, based on scientific grounds;

- knowledge of fundamental social questions, in particular related to the elimination of poverty, to sustainable development, to intercultural dialogue and to the shaping of a culture of peace;
- the need for close connection with effective research organisations or institutions that perform well in the sphere of research;
- the development of the whole education system in the perspective of the recommendations and the new goals for education as set out in the 1996 report to UNESCO of the International Commission on Education for the Twenty-first Century;
- fundamentals of human ethics, applied to each profession and to all areas of human endeavour;

(d) ensure, especially in universities and as far as possible, that faculty members participate in teaching, research, tutoring students and steering institutional affairs:

(e) take all necessary measures to reinforce their service to the community, especially their activities aimed at eliminating poverty, intolerance, violence, illiteracy, hunger and disease, through an interdisciplinary and transdisciplinary approach in the analysis of challenges, problems and different subjects;

(f) **set their relations with the world of work on a new basis** involving effective partnerships with all social actors concerned, starting from a reciprocal harmonization of action and the search for solutions to pressing problems of humanity, all this within a framework of responsible autonomy and academic freedoms;

(g) ensure high quality of international standing, **consider accountability** and both internal and external **evaluation,** with due respect for autonomy and academic freedom, **as being normal and inherent in their functioning,** and institutionalise transparent systems, structures or mechanisms specific thereto;

(h) as lifelong education requires academic staff to update and improve their teaching skills and learning methods, even more than in the present system mainly based on short periods of higher teaching, establish appropriate academic staff development structures and/or mechanisms and programmes;

(i) **promote and develop research, which is a necessary feature of all higher education systems,** in all disciplines, including the human and social sciences and arts, given their relevance for development. Also, research on higher education itself should be strengthened through mechanisms such as the UNESCO/UNO Forum on Higher Education and the UNESCO Chairs in Higher Education. Objective, timely studies are needed to ensure continued progress towards such key national objectives as access, equity, quality, relevance and diversification;

(j) remove **gender inequalities and biases in curricula and research,** and take all appropriate measures to ensure balanced representation of both men and women among students and teachers, at all levels of management;

(k) **Provide,** where appropriate, **guidance and counselling, remedial courses, training in how to study and other forms of student support,** including measures to improve student living conditions.

7. While the need for closer links between higher education and the world of work is important worldwide, it is particularly vital for the developing countries and especially the least developed countries, given their low level of economic development. Governments of these countries should take appropriate measures to reach this objective through appropriate measures such as strengthening institutions for higher/professional/vocational education. At the same time, international action is needed in order to help establish joint undertakings between higher education and industry in these countries. It will be necessary to give consideration to ways in which higher education graduates could be supported, through various schemes, following the positive experience of the micro-credit system and other incentives, in order to start small-and medium-size enterprises. At the institutional level, developing entrepreneurial skills and initiative should become a major concern of higher education, in order to facilitate employability of graduates who will increasingly be required not only to be job-seekers but to become job-creators.

8. **The use of new technologies should be generalized to the greatest extent possible** to help higher education institutions, to

reinforce academic development, to widen access, to attain universal scope and to extend knowledge, as well as to facilitate education throughout life. Governments, educational institutions and the private sector should ensure that informatics and communication network infrastructures, computer facilities and human resources training are adequately provided.

9. **Institutions of higher education should be opened to adult learns:**

(a) by developing coherent mechanisms to recognise the outcomes of learning undertaken in different contexts, and to ensure that credit is transferable within and between institutions, sectors and states;

(b) by establishing joint higher education/community research and training partnerships, and by bringing the services of higher education institutions to outside groups;

(c) by carrying out interdisciplinary research in all aspects of adult education and learning with the participation of adult learners themselves;

(d) by creating opportunities for adult learning in flexible, open and creative ways.

III. ACTIONS TO BE TAKEN AT INTERNATIONAL LEVEL AND, IN PARTICULAR, TO BE INITIATED BY UNESCO

10. **Co-operation should be conceived of as an integral part of the institutional missions of higher education institutions and systems.** Intergovernmental organisations, donor agencies and non-governmental organisations should extend their action in order to develop inter-university co-operation projects in particular through twinning institutions, based on solidarity and partnership, as a means of bridging the gap between rich and poor countries in the vital areas of knowledge production and application. Each institution of higher education should envisage the creation of an appropriate structure and/ or mechanism for promoting and managing international co-operation.

11. UNESCO, and other intergovernmental organisations and non-governmental organisations active in higher education, the states through their bilateral and multilateral co-operation programmes, the academic

community and all concerned partners in society should further **promote international academic mobility** as a means to advance knowledge and knowledge-sharing in order to bring about and promote solidarity as a main element of the global knowledge society of tomorrow, including through strong support for the joint work plan (1999-2005) of the six intergovernmental committees in charge of the application of the regional conventions on the recognition of studies, degrees and diplomas in higher education and through large-scale co-operative action involving, *inter alia,* the establishment of an educational credit transfer scheme, with particular emphasis on South-South co-operation, the needs of the least developed countries and of the small states with few higher education institutions or none at all.

12. Institutions of higher education in industrialized countries should strive to make arrangements for international co-operation with sister institutions in developing countries and in particular with those of poor countries. In their co-operation with sister institutions should make efforts to ensure fair and just recognition of studies abroad. UNESCO should take initiatives to develop higher education throughout the world, setting itself clear-cut goals that could lead to tangible results. One method might be to implement projects in different regions renewing efforts towards creating and/or strengthening centres of excellence in developing countries, in particular through the UNITWIN/ UNESCO Chairs Programme, relying on networks of national, regional and international higher education institutions.

13. UNESCO, together with all concerned parts of society, should also undertake action in order to **alleviate the negative effects of 'brain drain' and to shift to a dynamic process of 'brain gain'.** An overall analysis is required in all regions of the world of the causes and effects of brain drain. **A vigorous campaign** should be launched **through the concerted effort of the international community** and on the basis of academic solidarity and should encourage the return to their home country of expatriate academics, as well as the involvement of **university volunteers-** newly retired academics or young academics at the beginning of their career- who wish to teach and undertake research at higher education institutions in developing countries. At the same time it is essential to support the developing countries in their efforts to build and strengthen their won educational capacities.

14. Within this framework, UNESCO should:

(a) **promote better co-ordination among intergovernmental, supranational and non-governmental organisations, agencies and foundations that sponsor existing programmes and projects for international co-operation in higher education.** Furthermore, co-ordination efforts should take place in the context of national priorities. This could be conducive to the pooling and sharing of resources, avoid overlapping and promote better identification of projects, greater impact of action and increased assurance of their validity through collective agreement and review. Programmes aiming at the rapid transfer of knowledge, supporting institutional development and establishing centres of excellence in all areas of knowledge, in particular for peace education, conflict resolution, human rights and democracy, should be supported by institutions and by public and private donors;

(b) jointly with the United Nations University and with National Commissions and various intergovernmental and non-governmental organisations, become a forum of reflection on higher education issues aiming at: (i) preparing update reports on the state of knowledge on higher education issues in all parts of the world; (ii) promoting innovative projects of training and research, intended to enhance the specific role of higher education in lifelong education; (iii) reinforcing international co-operation and emphasising the role of higher education for citizenship education, sustainable development and peace; and (iv) facilitating exchange of information and establishing, when appropriate, a database on successful experiences and innovations that can be consulted by institutions confronted with problems in their reforms of higher education;

(c) take specific action to support institutions of higher education in the least developed parts of the world and in regions suffering the effects of conflict or natural disasters;

(d) make renewed efforts towards creating or/and strengthening centres of excellence in developing countries;

(e) take the initiative to draw up an international instrument on academic freedom, autonomy and social responsibility in connection with the Recommendation concerning the Status of Higher-Education Teaching Personnel;

(f) ensure follow-up to the World Declaration on Higher Education and the Framework for Priority Action, jointly with other intergovernmental and non-governmental organizations and with all higher education stakeholders, including the United Nations University, the NGO Collective Consultation on Higher Education and the UNESCO Student Forum. It should have a crucial role in promoting international co-operation in the field of higher education in implementing this follow-up. Consideration should be given to according priority to this in the development of UNESCO's next draft Programme and Budget.

ANNEX 1

DECLARATION AND ACTION PLAN ON HIGHER EDUCATION IN AFRICA

We, participants at the **African Regional Consultation** preparatory to the World Conference on Higher Education,[1]

1. **Recalling** the Universal Declaration of Human Rights, article 26, of which affirms that, 'Everyone has the right to education'... and that 'higher education shall be accessible to all, on the basis of merit', and further recalling the Convention Against Discrimination in the field of Education, adopted by UNESCO in 1960, which calls on Member States to 'make higher education accessible to all, based on individual abilities';

2. **Taking into account** UNESCO's Constitution, which encourages inter-institutional exchanges in the field of Education;

3. **Adhering to** the conclusions and recommendations of the *Policy Paper on Change and Development in Higher Education* published by UNESCO in 1995, as well as the major conclusions of the International Commission on Education for the Twenty-first Century, which stipulate that, 'Universities in developing countries have a duty to carry out research that should contribute to solving the most serious problems facing these countries';

4. **Taking into account** the desire of the United Nations to improve co-ordination of the actions of organisations of the United Nations system in order to reinforce their impact on the development of the Africa region, by mobilising every effort (in the same vein as the creation of an Africa Department by UNESCO) and allocating necessary funds for in-depth reform of higher education in Africa;

5. **Having taken note of** the conclusions of the Priority Africa seminars on Higher Education in Africa (Accra: November 1991; Dakar: November 1992; Alexandria: April 1993) *summary papers* (such as *Higher Education in Africa: Trends and Challenges for the 21st Century*. Dakar 1992 and publications like *Future Directions for Higher Education in Africa* published by BREDA in 1994 and *Audience of Africa. Social Development. Priorities for Africa, Final Report (1995)* and taken further into account the findings of the Second World Congress on and Education and Informatics organised by UNESCO in Moscow in July 1996, and other reports by various international and African institutions which have also carried out diagnosis and developed guidelines for action;

6. **Observing** that significant but not quite remarkable progress has been made in Africa through the efforts of higher education institutions to wit: progress in implementing democratic structures, improved access to higher education, training of senior management level personnel for the public and the private sectors, development of programmes of African studies, rediscovery and promotion of the historical and cultural heritage, etc.;

7. **Recognising** at the same time, the persistence of problems needing urgent solutions (e.g. poverty, hunger, disease, unemployment, illiteracy, the debt burden, unfavourable trading conditions, inflation, all forms and types of conflicts, environmental degradation, etc.);

8. **Observing** Africa is more seriously affected than the other regions of the world by the deep-seated societal changes of our time, viz:

   - the upsurge of economic liberalism, globalisation, and the prevailing world order which serves the interests of the strongest economic and financial powers, deregulation the African market, the rise of an uncontrolled and perhaps uncontrallable underground economy;

   - outsourcing, which is of little benefit to Africa, in view of the trend for fund managers to associate Africa with political instability and an insufficient of qualified and skilled person;

- structural adjustment policies leading to loss of jobs in the public sector, (loses not fully absorbed by the private sector) and which have tended to devalue the degrees awarded by institutions of higher education;
- an upward demographic surge which has tended to increase the demand for education, uncontrolled urban and an population growth;
- displaced populations, the result of economic difficulties or the trauma of wars - a situation difficult to manage by the countries receiving such displaced persons;
- exponential growth in knowledge, with very little direct contribution from the Africa region;
- rapid development of new information and communications technologies, with the risk of widening the gap between Africa and the other regions of the world;

9. **Pointing out** that the challenges facing the Africa region and the sweeping changes in society make the structural problems of higher educational institutions all the more critical.

The problems include:

- coping with surging numbers of students in the face of declining budgets;
- excessively high student/teacher ratios, which make individual attention to learners difficult;
- undue attention to municipal and social services, which reduces funds available for teaching and research;
- deterioration of infrastructure, due to lack of maintenance;
- insufficient remuneration of academics, leading to loss of motivation, moonlighting and brain drain;
- imblance in students enrolments between science and technology based programmes and the humanities;
- gender inequity at all levels: within the student body, within academic staff, and within the decision-making cadre;
- insufficient attention to, and the insufficient resources for research;

- lack of a long-term vision in the planning and management of teaching and research activities;
- insufficient pedagogical training of teachers in higher education, coupled with a lack of systematic management training for institutional and system-wide managers;
- teaching-learnig procedures often in the form of memorisation and to the neglect of inclucating the analytical and problem solving skills needed for tackling societal problems.

10. **What is therefore needed** is the development of new guidelines focusing on the following key issues: relevance, quality, management/finance, and co-operation.

11. **Relevance** is the number one problem, for, should African higher education institutions and the authorities responsible for them interpret their missions wrongly, they will not be able to take up the above challenges: the institutions could in fact become obstacles to development. First of all, *it is imperative that they adapt their missions to the needs and constraints of the local, national, regional and international environments.* This is one of those external efficiency indicators by which institutions are judged. This entails links with the 'town': promoters of economic activities and all groups and persons working to ensure the reign of equity and better living conditions for Africans, those engaged in promoting responsible citizenship and ensuring a culture of peace and sustainable human development.

    Relevance also requires better articulation with the world of work and with other efforts geared towards improving he contribution of higher education to the entire educational system, especially through teacher training and research in education.

12. **Quality** is the second area needing thought and action. It is closely linked to the issue of relevance but entails the operationalisation of the envisaged outcomes (a clear definition of goals and objectives) of the inputs the institutions will work with (thus a review of admissions criteria) and the processes and procedures for working with the inputs (the way the management system co-ordinates structures, resources and the institutional culture to obtain the required products). *A policy*

of total quality can be implemented through comparisons between observed and intended outcomes (in terms of quantitative and qualitative internal efficiency) and constant analysis of the sources of dysfunction. This will require a culture of *Autonomy* for higher education institutions as well as of their constituent units. It will also require careful attention to the problems of students and teachers and solidarity and responsibility towards the institution as a project for promoting local development and for ensuring a take-off for national and regional development. Thus the need for *accountability*, which is indissociable from the concept of quality.

13. **Management and Funding** constitute the third major concern. An institution could undertake an in-depth analysis on its mission and translate this into product, process and quality indicators. If, however, the institution fails to built quality into its entire *modus operandi*, and if financial resources are inadequate, if is likely to achieve very little and so very unlikely to be able to meet the challenges of Africa's development. We would therefore urge that higher institutions accept the imperative of adopting *forward-looking management* practices which respond to the needs of the environment, as specified in their missions.

14. **Co-operation** at the national, regional and international levels is the fourth key issue. Co-operation projects have often been mere juxtaposition of disparate efforts not sufficiently linked to an *overall strategic plan*, specifying priorities, deadlines and the constraints arising from the relationships between various projects or components of projects. We would expect that the organisation of African institutions into co-operative *networks*, using appropriate products of new technologies, should be a major priority area.

15. **On basis of these observations** we would suggest the following areas of concrete action:

To Improve Relevance:

16. We recommend that Member States *develop educational programmes* capable of meeting the challenges of sweeping societal changes and the principal challenges which Africa is bound to face in the immediate future.

17. We would suggest that *Member States create observatories' to monitor changes in the employment market*, of imminent social changes, of new approaches to research and development related activities. Such observatories would help the process of developing national educational plans, as data would be made available to institutions of higher learning, to improve their capacity to align their missions with national priority areas.

18. We would suggest that national education programmes aim at *diversification* with a greater emphasis on a *regionalisation* of specific disciplines. This could be a means of getting institutions to serve the specific needs of disadvantages areas and groups. These programmes should target specific needs that will generate employment or create jobs; training programmes and structures should be flexible in order to adapt rapidly to changing needs. It would also be necessary to develop (in consultation with appropriate stakeholders) a wider variety of short duration programmes.

19. We feel that appropriate steps ought to be taken to convince Member States that investment in institutions of higher education is worthwhile, as long as the institutions are oriented to meet the needs of society. International organisations like UNESCO will have to make strong moves to sensitise top political and financial authorities on this issue.

20. Institutions of higher education should define their mission statements in the form of overall general guidelines. These should be closely linked with the national education programmes and based on a thorough analysis of needs, in co-operation with the institution's internal and external actors. They should be presented in the form of observable outcomes.

21. It would be more profitable to define educational programmes henceforth in terms of expected outcomes, and not simply in terms of facts to be transmitted and reproduced, or in terms of mere course titles. This will contribute to the evolution of genuine education programmes with special emphasis on analysis of complex situations, teamwork, higher cognitive skills, the inculcation of responsible citizenship and the development of a culture of peace.

22. Institutions of higher education should make special efforts to develop *scientific and technological programmes* to help meet the demands of the accelerated development of new technologies, especially new information and communication technologies. These programmes should be supported by intensive research activities, from which the critical mass of the expertise needed for the region's development as it faces the pressures of globalisation. We suggest that institutions already having expertise in these areas create a network, with the assistance of UNESCO and other organisations.

    Existing potentials on information and communications technologies should be boosted to give rise to virtual universities, which could considerably improve access, while at the same time providing world class educational resources.

23. Higher education institutions should also make special efforts to promote integrated programmes aimed at seeking appropriate solutions to the major problems of the progressive evolution of a culture of peace and promotion of sustainable development oriented towards reducing hunger and protecting the environment. Such programmes should build on the fruits of social research and designed to the promotion of research, the strengthening of expertise and consultancy services.

24. We recommend that research be made to bear a closer relation to the needs of African societies, so that basic research can be more closely linked with applied and development-oriented research stressing genuine partnerships with public and private institutions and the civil society. This would be one way of ensuring the active involvement of higher institutions in societal development efforts.

25. We recommend that higher degree programmes be organised around a quantitative and qualitative critical mass of committed academics, working together in a qualitatively conducive environment on subjects relevant to Africa's development. Doctoral training programmes can be restructured using team work or networking strategies.

26. We would like to stress the importance and urgency of carrying out a series of case studies on Africa's priorities, in which higher

education institutions should play an important role. These include the type of leadership to be promoted, strategic management and planning, systemic interactions between primary, secondary, tertiary and continuing education, revision of programmes of education and training, the relative importance and feasibility of face-to-face and distance teaching programmes, strategies for ensuring improved participation of women in education and in decision making bodies, town and country planning, measures against the security problems of Africa (such as poverty, displaced populations, the trauma of war...) The Association of African Universities could undertake this task, with the assistance support of UNESCO and the possible collaboration of other organisations working in the field of higher education in Africa.

27. To become more responsive to the needs of society, and in order to acquire greater financial autonomy, we recommend that higher education institutions create structures for the development and management of consultancy activities, which are an essential part of their missions. For this to happen, higher institutions should develop an entrepreneurial spirit as a means of strengthening their service functions which are in themselves complementary to their teaching and research functions.

28. We recommend that Member States organise regional conferences of ministers in charge of higher education, heads of institutions, and organisations or associations involved in the development of higher education.

To Improve the Quality:

29. We recommend that each Member State establish a mechanism for evaluating the quality of higher education institutions, building on existing practices in the region. Such a body will be responsible for evaluating training, research and consultancy activities in the light of institutional missions, national education programmes and the needs of changing times. This should be a control rather than a punitive mechanism, and should use a combination of internal and external evaluation strategies.

30. In order to ensure the quality of programmes, institutions of higher education will required to establish minimum teaching-

learning guidelines for each course module. They should explicitly state learners, entry and exist behaviours in terms of skills, values and attitudes, the teaching and evaluation methods, all within a specific time frame. They will constitute a point of reference and a form of moral contract between various internal and external actors.

31. It would be necessary for every institution to develop a data base on the quantitative and qualitative movement of students. This data base should include any information that could be used to evaluate internal (and even external) efficiency, as well as trends in progress or non-progress in terms of the equity of the system. The data base should provide decision-makers at various levels with the information needed for the development of a total quality policy, or with the involvement of all stakeholders.

32. We expect that, with assistance from UNESCO and other regional or international organisations, every higher education institution will establish a teaching-learning resource unit staffed by skilled personnel charged with the task of pedagogical skill development and other forms of teaching-support activities.

33. We also hope that every institution will create appropriate structures for evaluating and controlling the quality of its curricula (including the performance of students), in keeping with agreed guidelines.

34. We recommend that UNESCO call on Member States to improve the living and working conditions and emoluments of academics and, more importantly, to guarantee the autonomy of higher education.

35. We declare our support for the project on the conditions and status of higher education personnel, recently approved by an international committee of intergovernmental experts and which will be at the 29th General Conference of UNESCO (Paris, November 1997).

36. Having observed the undesirable effects of conflicts and strikes in universities, we suggest that institutions should create an enabling climate for dialogue with a strong emphasis on prevention rather than repression.

37. Convinced that research (as a fundamental mission of higher institutions) will need to be reinforced, we call for a substantial increase in the number of academic journals and the implementation of a coherent publications policy at sub-regional and regional levels. UNESCO could call on the organisations which took part in the present Consultation to submit concrete proposals on this issue.

38. Efforts to improve quality in each institution will be facilitated if Member States could develop regional networks for education and training activities as well as for research and consultancy activities. We call on UNESCO to lend its full weight to such networks.

39. We suggest that, at the regional level, existing institutions and organisations (such as CAMES for example) whose aim is to harmonise qualifications and certification procedures be strengthened, so that the potential for mobility is increased for both students and teachers, in line with the practice in other regions.

To Improve Management and Funding:

40. We suggest that Member States guarantee equal rights to higher education based on ability and aptitude (i.e. merit). Member States should take on principal responsibility for funding for higher education. However, since it will be difficult for Member States to bear the entire financial burden, additional sources should be sought using the political and administrative mechanism of each State, whose sovereignty should be respected. We strongly advise that the economic conditions of families be taken into consideration, and that the only criteria for access or non-access should be merit.

41. To improve efficiency and strengthen the management of higher education institutions, it would be necessary to develop appropriate mechanism for regular dialogue between the institutions and their partners, particularly State structures, without compromising the autonomy of the institutions.

42. It is important to build the habit of forward-looking management and planning into higher education institutions in Africa. This

means that appropriate training opportunities should be provided for administrators, whether they occupy a permanent or an elected position. It also means that necessary computer database should be developed as soon as possible to ensure high-quality forward-looking management and planning. The institutions should find either within themselves or through co-operation the necessary skills to create, maintain and develop these data banks. UNESCO should seek support from organisations such as the Association of African Universities, the International Institute of Educational Planning, the Association of Commonwealth Universities, the Commonwealth Secretariat, etc., in this aspect of its work. The goal is for, African universities could be managed like high-performance service businesses able to play a crucial role in solving the problems besetting the Africa region.

43. We believe quality management is not the sole responsibility of top academic authorities. Each sub-system (faculty, department or other structures) should also take on responsibility for forward-looking management and planning. This means that each unit must clearly define its missions to bring them in line with the overall mission of the institution, translate them into observable indicators, and allocate the resources available in accordance with the mission and with a clear order of priority. They should also prepare regular activity reports, which they should be shared with staff and supervising authorities. This mode of management entails a certain degree of autonomy (thus a margin for manoeuve) and full commitment to institutional goals. The culture of evaluation and responsibility must therefore be strengthened, or established in those institutions that still practise the rigid centralisation inherited from certain colonial structures.

44. We feel that, despite the prevailing financial crisis, the management of higher education institutions cannot be reduced to financial management based on purely economic criteria. One should take in account some criterion of equity (such as women's or underprivileged persons' access to higher education) and the criterion of social relevance applied to teaching, research and consultancy activities. We would expect each institution's activity reports to include actions taken towards

this end and the results obtained, in order to promote awareness in the appropriate ministerial authorities and obtain recognition and support for relevant actions.

45. Since WOMEN have a major role to play in the development of the Africa region, we request that international organisations, Member States and higher education institutions develop well-articulated policies, remove gender inequity in education and more importantly promote the advancement of women in the entire society. This should include measures implemented, by the institutions of higher education themselves. We suggest that meaningful affirmative action be taken in all possible directions. Women's associations and networks should be fully supported. A systematic and coherent policy of gender research and case studies should be implemented and their findings widely publicised and ploughed back into the teaching, management and overall development work of higher education institutions.

46. We recommend that measures be taken to double the number of women (students, teachers and decision-makers) in higher education, within the next ten years. Particular attention should be paid to orienting women towards scientific and technological disciplines.

47. We consider that student involvement in decision-making bodies should be given a considerable boost, with greater attention paid to their needs by taking into consideration students' perspectives which are often relevant to the analyses of problems and to the search for viable solutions. Student involvement is also equally a means of inculcating the leadership skills needed in after-school life as workers and as citizens.

48. At the regional level, it would be necessary to organise regular meetings under the aegis of organs like the Association of African Universities, for exchanges on problems related to the management and funding of institutions of higher education. These meetings should be used to improve the operation of the institutions themselves and to develop the capacity for meaningful pressure on ministerial authorities in charge of

higher education. The authorities should themselves be involved in these meetings.

49. We would suggest that, at the regional level, a student association forum be organised as means of mobilising students to contribute to current efforts aimed at making higher education institutions more forceful, more active and more efficient partners, in the promotion of sustainable development in Africa. The conclusions of the forum could form Africa's contribution to the International Students' Forum to be held in Paris in 1998, as part of the commemoration of the fiftieth anniversary of the Declaration on Human Rights and at the World Conference on Higher Education.

To Reinforce Co-operation:

50. We invite existing associations of institutions and of subject specialists as well as national, regional and international organisations to support and co-ordinate actions and projects aimed at establishing or strengthening inter-African and intercontinental networks working to reduce the gap between Africa and other regions by solving key regional development problems. Institutions of higher education should adopt a proactive policy in this connection and invest all their energy into fighting poverty, environmental degradation, discrimination of all kinds, and the ravages of conflicts.

51. We recommend that institutions of higher learning create networks of centres of excellence responding to the most pressing needs of the African continent, in terms of training, research and consultancy. Each institution should focus on an area of expertise in which it is likely to excel, as its contribution to a regional skill-sharing network. Such strategies of solidarity/complementarity could enable Africa to meet some its contemporary challenges.

52. It would be necessary for UNESCO to organise in the near future an exchange and evaluation meeting for all existing networks such as the UNITWIN/UNESCO Chairs programme, UNISPAR, and the Commonwealth Secretariat. The meeting would promote the sharing of experience, reveal the factors responsible to their relative successes or failures, and co-

ordinate and strengthen projects that offer the most viable solution to the problem of the Africa region.

53. The African Regional Convention and the international recommendation on the recognition of studies and diplomas should be strengthened through the promotion of academic and professional mobility of students, and academics. This would support the on-going regional integration process by using culture and education as a basis for political and economic unity. It would be desirable to strengthen associations whose aim is to harmonise the qualification awarded by higher education institutions in Africa (e.g. CAMES). UNESCO should take the lead in mobilising major regional and international organisations to create a region-wide mobility programme for students and academics. This has been done on other regions, one example being RIMA (Réseau International de mobilité Académique or the International network for academic mobility) established by MERCOSUR.

54. We would further suggest that UNESCO works in concert with bilateral and multilateral co-operation agencies like the Commonwealth Secretariat and AUPELF-UREF, etc., for the early creation of priority area networks. These should include a research network on the use of new information and communications technologies, a network of teaching-learning resource units, a network of research units in education devoted to priority areas for Africa development, which could be grouped under UNESCO Chairs in Education. UNESCO should whenever possible, mobilise resources for co-operation on areas of common concern.

55. To respect the right to cultural diversity, we would urge UNESCO to assist in the creation of a network of lusophone institutions of higher education and to intensify its support to the activities of association of Portuguese and Spanish speaking universities as one other means of reinforcing South-South co-operation. The development of graduate programmes in Portuguese-speaking countries should be supported. Other regional networks could contribute their expertise in this area.

56. It goes without saying that the participation of students, teachers and researchers in the meetings and networks depends on

relative ease of procedures for obtaining visas. We urge UNESCO to sensitise its Members States to this particular problem, so that they can simplify existing administrative procedures for obtaining visas.

57. Given these challenges and the expected roles of institutions of higher education, it would be necessary to reinforce the higher education unit of the Regional Office of UNESCO in Dakar (BREDA). The unit should play a more active role in the envisaged regionalisation strategies and also be the key actor in the synergy-building missions described in the above proposals. The Regional Advisory Committee on Co-operation in Education in Africa should include representatives of government organisations and NGOs working in the field of higher education.

58. It is further suggested that, as part of the NGO consultation process, UNESCO/Dakar organise a meeting with the participation of AAU, AUPELF-UREF, ACU, AULP and AIUP, as well as sub-regional organisations and bilateral co-operation and inter-governmental organisations such as CAMES, OAU, ECA, the Commonwealth Secretariat, etc., as a means of facilitating co-ordination into operative action plans as soon as possible.

59. We recommend that, with the assistance of UNESCO, stakeholders and organisations involved in the development of higher education in the region should translate these proposals into operative action plans as soon as possible.

60. We suggest further that the report of the Regional Consultation in Dakar be tabled at the next MINEDAF and the next summit of the OAU.

61. Finally, we request UNESCO to convene a meeting of experts at the end of the year 2001, to evaluate in the implementation of the recommendations of this Regional Consultation.

Adopted in Dakar
4th April 1997
The Regional Consultation

LIST OF ABBREVIATIONS

AAU:	Association of African Universities
AUPELF-UREF:	Agence francophone pour l'enseignement supérieur et la recherche
ACU:	Association of Commonwealth Universities
AULP:	Association of Universities in Portuguese-speaking countries
AIUP:	Association Internationale des Présidents d'Unniversitiés
CAMES:	Conseil Africain et malgache pour l'enseignement supérieur
ECA:	Economic Commission for Africa

Reference

1. Dakar, Senegal, 1-4 April 1997.

ANNEX 2

BEIRUT DECLARATION ON HIGHER EDUCATION IN THE ARAB STATES FOR THE XXIST CENTURY[1]

We, the participants to the Arab States Regional Conference on Higher Education for the XXIst Century, held in Beirut, Lebanon, from 2 to 5 March 1998,

1. Recalling the terms of the Universal Declaration of Human Rights, which states that 'higher education shall be equally accessible to all on the basis of merit' (article 26.1), and that such 'education shall be directed to the full development of the human personality and to the strengthening of respect for human rights and fundamental freedoms' (article 26.2); Ratifying the contents of the Convention on the struggle against discrimination in the field of education (1960), which states that the Signatory States commit themselves 'to ... offer all people alike higher education on the basis of a real equality and to the skills of each individual ... (article IV);

2. Recognizing the importance of the analysis and recommendations of the *UNESCO Policy Paper for Change and Development in Higher Education*, the International Commission on Education for the XXIst Century, and the World Commission on Culture and Development;

3. Pointing out the view of the International Commission on Education for the XXIst Century that education throughout life should be based on four pillars: learning to know, learning to do, learning to live together, and learning to be, and that universities have a duty to carry out research that should contribute to solving the most serious problems facing developing countries;

4. Taking into account the recommendations made in United Nations, via (a) An agenda for peace, that contains principles and suggestions bearing on the preventive measures that will protect peace, as well as effective actions for restoring peace when uncontainable conflicts emerge, and (b) An Agenda for development, that sets the conceptual bases for fostering a sustainable and permanent human development. Also highlighting the need of the Region for a just and comprehensive peace allowing for learning opportunities for all and pacing the way for the attainment of development;
5. Noting that the Arab States share common historical, language and cultural traditions and heritage, yet they show diversity with regard to demography, economic means, and educational traditions;
6. Pointing out that the globalisation of economies and professional services and the rapid growth and in-depth transformation of information and communication technologies have resulted in increased demands for specialised professionals in every endeavour of life capable of sustaining high standards, calling for an increased appreciation of the role of higher education in the development and advancement of societies and for a revision of training and working methods of higher education graduates;
7. Acknowledging that significant progress has been made in recent years in the development and strengthening of higher education in the Arab States, leading to improved student access and more equitable representation of different social groups among graduates;
8. Supporting the initiative taken by H.R.H. Prince Talal bin Abdel-Aziz Al-Saud concerning the establishment of an Open Arab University as a model for unifying Arab efforts in the field of higher education;
9. Emphasising the recommendations of the six ALECSO conferences of Ministers responsible for Higher Education and Scientific Research in Arab States since 1981, and those of the Fifth Regional Conference of Ministers of Education and those Responsible for Economic Planning (Cairo, 1994);

10. Noting that the main issues in higher education in the Arab States encompass the following:

   a. Higher education in the Arab States is under considerable strain, due to high rates of population growth and increasing social demand for higher education, which lead states and institutions to increase student enrolment, often without adequate allocated financial resources;

   b. A number of Arab States are facing blockade, occupation, and external impediments and constraints limiting the expansion and development of higher education;

   c. Although general rate of female enrolment in higher education is close to those observed at the international level, all Arab States look up to increasing this rate;

   d. Management of higher education institutions is still heavily centralised, calling for more flexibility and for the participation in decision-making of all concerned parties;

   e. The lack of close links between higher education institutions and general education and between universities and other post-secondary institutions, and weaknesses in students' orientation into the various streams of higher education on the basis of their skills and interests, have contributed to inflated enrolment in some disciplines and to obvious lower enrolment in applied and technological disciplines, to low internal efficiency, and to low quality of graduates, and led to pressures on institutions to provide remedial programmes in order to improve the quality of enrolled students;

   f. Higher education institutions have, in most cases, not developed adequate programmes and projects to serve local communities and participate in their development;

   g. The development of private and open universities, and of non-university institutions, is recent in most of the Arab States, and, thus far, has not alleviated pressures on public universities in such a manner as to permit the development, the diversification, and the expansion of higher education;

   h. Status and conditions of higher education teaching personnel, while enormously varied among Arab States, do not often match some of the international standards as set in the Recommendation concerning the Status and Conditions of Higher Education Teaching Personnel adopted in 1997 by UNESCO General Conference;

i. Higher education institutions should be more sensitive to students' concerns, taking into account their needs in all endeavours of life during years of study, as to selection curricula, teaching, and transition to working life. These institutions should allow students and their representatives to actively participate in decision-making concerning their academic and social life within the institution;

j. There is a need to promote new teaching and learning processes that better serve the development of scientific thinking skills;

k. As a result of international developments in science and technology, new demands have emerged for teaching personnel and researchers to increase co-operation with industry, and for continuing education of graduates;

l. Lack of highly qualified graduates in some disciplines is often accompanied with unemployment and under-employment of great numbers of graduates in other disciplines, while significant numbers of highly qualified Arab scholars lead academic careers abroad with little impact on higher education and scientific research in the Arab States;

In view of the above, we do hereby declare the following:

1. Higher education is essential for any country to achieve sustainable and global development. It is also essential for the enhancement of citizens' participation in public life, for social mobility, and for the achievement of harmony, justice, and just and comprehensive peace, at both internal and international levels, on the basis of the respect for human rights, active participation of citizens, and mutual respect.

2. Higher education should aim at the following: (a) to educate well-aware, autonomous and responsible citizens committed to national and universal principles, capable of dealing with the challenges of the Century and of lifelong learning, (b) to

provide highly trained professionals to meet the needs of government, the professions, and the productive and service sectors, (c) to provide expertise to assist in economic and social development, and in scientific and technological research, (d) to help conserve and disseminate national and regional cultures, drawing on the contributions from each generation, (e) to provide critical and detached perspectives concerning the strategic options and to contribute to human renewal by active contribution to the production of scientific knowledge, taking into account ethical issues, and addressing planetary challenges (such as population growth, peace, environment, etc.), (f) to undertake research and scholarship which contribute to the understanding, the anticipation and the solving of the most serious problems of the Region.

3. Determined efforts are necessary to further increase access to higher education to all groups of society. Open learning systems and other systems of education relying on modern technology can play a major role in widening access and can contribute to higher cultural achievements of Arab States citizens, if they are provided with the means to ensure quality. Diversification of institutions and programmes can also play a significant role on alleviating the strains put on traditional institutions by the ever growing social demand for higher education due to rapid growth rate of population and appeal of higher education for large sectors of society.

4. Arab States should devote determined efforts to improve general education as to ensure that graduates of this level of education master the essential competencies needed for life, including those necessary for the pursuit of higher education endeavours. Higher education institutions should actively participate in the efforts leading to improvement of pre-university education.

5. Arab States and their higher education institutions should adopt specific national and institutional plans of action in order to increase the participation in higher education of disadvantaged groups at all levels and in all disciplines, particularly females and the citizens under strenuous conditions due to occupation or blockade. They should work in co-operation with regional

and international agencies in order to provide learning opportunities to deprived students and to permit them enrolment in higher education institutions within their countries.

6. All higher education systems and institutions should give a high priority to ensuring the quality of programmes, teaching, and outcomes. Structures, procedures, and standards for quality assurance should be developed at the regional and national levels commensurate with international guidelines while providing for variety according to the specificities of each country, institution, or programme. Further, higher education institutions need appropriate financial and human resources to achieve higher quality of education.

7. Modern information and communications technology (ICT) is already making radical changes in methods of teaching and learning in higher education by both on-campus and distance education students. It has the potential to make positive impact on quality, relevance, access and cost of higher education, if direct access to technical and cultural information resources is provided, and rapid communication among teachers and researchers is facilitated. These technologies allow for the establishment of networks between institutions and scholars and enhance their development and efficiency. They also contribute in the provision of courses and degree-awarding programmes through multiple and advanced means, thus breaking through the traditional barriers of space and time. The virtual capacity of these developments in teaching tools is almost limitless for improving distance, open and life-long learning, if the adequate conditions are ensured.

8. Access to scientific knowledge is an essential element of cultural and intellectual understanding and the further development of higher education institutions. With the increased emergence of digitalisation and the increasing reliance on communication technologies as a means of storage and transfer of scholarly information, open and affordable access to communication networks becomes an important and indispensable element of quality of higher education institutions and programmes. Governments of Arab States should ensure that informatic and communication network infrastructure,

personal computer facilities, and human resources training, now a globally recognised prerequisite for the normal functioning of higher education institutions and research centers, are adequately provided Regional and international co-operation and development organisations are called upon to allocate technical and financial resources to support these developments in the Arab States.

9. While recognising that globalisation is a trend that could not be ignored nor avoided, it should not lead to dominance of some cultures and value systems on some others, nor to the emergence of new forms of hegemony. To this effect, it is of vital importance that every effort should be made to protect and promote the strengths of the Arab and Islamic culture and civilization as part of the major intellectual cultures in the world; at the same time, dialogue and cultural exchanges between the Arab States and the other world states should be maintained.

10. The concept of lifelong learning is of utmost importance. In rapidly changing economies, the labour market will constantly require new and various skills. Hence, mechanisms must be developed at higher education level to allow workforce in all fields to upgrade their skills and develop new competencies at regular intervals throughout their lives. Higher education institutions must offer learning opportunities in response to diverse and new demands and work co-operatively with other agencies and employers to ensure that appropriate and flexible programmes and courses are widely available and accessible to all citizens who need to update their knowledge and skills in order to effectively deal with such matters as population, labour, environment, etc. At the same time, higher education must take a leading role in the evolution of the world of work to better meet sustainable development requirements.

11. The involvement of all key stakeholders in decision-making in higher education institutions is of utmost importance, particularly the academics, the students, and the productive and service sectors, alongside with representatives of governmental agencies. Experience has demonstrated the value of such participation in enlightening the visions necessary for decision-

making and the formulation of balanced higher education policy, both system wide and institutionally.

12. In view of its multiplier effects on social, cultural and economic development, public funding of higher education should be considered as an investment, the return of it being as much important as investment in all sectors. However, better use of allocated resources and other funding sources must be sought after as well as developing partnerships with the private sector and the society.

13. Co-operation among the Arab States, especially in higher education, through academic exchanges, twinning and networking arrangements, can make significant contributions in addressing major higher education policy matters, and facilitating the sharing of pioneering expertise and experiences. Arab co-operation is made easier in view of the common linguistic and cultural heritage of the Arab States. This co-operation should be reinforced especially at graduate studies, scientific research programmes, institutional research and development.

14. Freedom of movement of students and access to academic institutions across Arab States frontiers will strengthen the Arab cultural development and contribute efficiently to Arab integration in higher education.

15. There is a pressing need to develop a plan of action and guidelines to further develop higher education in the Arab States, especially related to the key issues of relevance, quality, management and finance, and co-operation which are defined as follows:

RELEVANCE refers to the fit between what higher education institutions provide and what society expects from them. Relevance requires from higher education to make an enhanced contribution to the development of the society as a whole, encompassing the development of the education system. Relevance also requires reciprocal harmonization with the world of work and the requirements of sustainable global development. Relevance requires higher education to contribute to the preservation, the enlargement, the deepening, and the dissemination of knowledge in such a manner as to help humankind solve the problems it faces. It also requires safeguarding cultural diversity, the quest for just and global peace and respect of human rights.

QUALITY refers to standards of inputs, processes, and outputs of a system, an institution, or a programme. It has no meaning without relevance. Quality is a multi-dimensional concept and embraces all the functions and activities of higher education, i.e. academic programmes, research, and community services, in all their features and components: Infrastructure, equipment, human resources, students, objectives, nature and content of programmes, delivery modes and implementation practices, academic and socio-cultural environment, etc. Quality mechanisms are implemented through continuous assessments and comparisons between observed and intended processes and constant search for the sources of dysfunctions to correct them.

MANAGEMENT AND FINANCE cover, on one hand, issues related to internal management of institutions, funding and resources, and, on the other hand, the relations of higher education institutions with the state, and other stakeholders. Higher education authorities and institutions need to adopt long-term strategies aiming at embodying the institutions in the whole social tissue they serve, i.e. the Governmental bodies, the professions, the education sector, the productive and service sectors, and the socio-cultural environment. As for financing, despite the general trend towards diversifying sources of funding, governmental support for higher education and research remains essential to ensure achievement of educational and social missions of educational institutions. Furthermore, with the extension of private investment in higher education, appropriate mechanisms of accreditation and monitoring should be developed to guarantee access, equity, quality, and the rights of students.

CO-OPERATION at the national, regional, and international levels through advanced methods and mechanisms fit for the XXIst Century is essential for higher education institutions in order for them to adequately fulfill the missions entrusted with them.

PLAN OF ACTION

Based on the principles, observations, and recommendations set out in the Declaration on Higher Education in the Arab States for the XXIst Century adopted by the Conference, and considering the need for the renewal of systems through the adoption of new policies and paradigms for higher education funded on such concepts as globalization of knowledge, lifelong learning, sustainable development, preservation of cultural diversity, transparency and accountability, and involvement of all stakeholders, the following recommendations were adopted by the Conference:

First: The Arab States must fulfill their commitments to higher education and meet the pledges made at regional and international conferences with regard to the provision of adequate structures and human and financial resources as to enable higher education to adequately face the challenges of the XXIst Century. This includes the following:

a) setting up of policies and legislations as well as establishment of effective mechanisms dealing with the overall governance of higher education system and institutions, with due consideration to the promotion of institutional autonomy and the participation of all sectors concerned;

b) establishment of rules and regualtions to ensure the protection, at higher education institutions, of basic rights (e.g., access by merit, equality of treatment, etc.) and freedoms, especially academic freedom;

c) establishment of accountability measures proper to achieve stated goals, and to ensure quality of inputs, processes and outcomes;

d) enabling higher education institutions fulfill their multiple duties towards society;

e) providing for modern communication technology in order to ensure unconditional access to accumulated human knowledge;

f) promoting partnerships with industry, and productive and service sectors, and other governmental or non-governmental relevant institutions.

Second: Higher education institutions must define their missions in harmony with the overall aims and principles as defined by the Declaration and Plan of action approved by the Conference. These missions should be translated into well-defined objectives, with allocation of the required resources, and the establishment of concrete mechanisms proper to ensure adequate monitoring and evaluation of progress and achievements based on observable indicators. A framework for evaluation and monitoring should thus be established and strengthened in all institutions, with proper structures and resources.

Third: Joint Action Plans must be established to ensure the further development of higher education in the Arab countries, optimize efficiency, and prevent duplication of efforts. Co-operation between organizations which promote the development of human resources, particularly within the framework of institutionalized networks, at the global, regional, and national levels, offers great potentials for the enhanced mobilisation of resources. Responsibility for this mobilisation lies on international and regional organisations dealing with inter-university co-operation, as well as the associations of universities and higher education institutions, private and public universities, institutions of research, development organisations and agencies, governmental and non-governmental institutions. Concerned agencies active in the Arab Region, particularly ALECSO, ISESCO, ABEGS, the Association of Arab Universities, the Arab Federation of Councils for Scientific Research, and the Arab Federation for Technical Education, could play an important role in strengthening existing networks and in building new regional networks leading to the solution of pressing problems of higher education and of the societies of the Arab States. The Association of Islamic Universities, and other cross-regional and international organizations could also play a role in finding solutions to problems of common interests. Partnerships with world organizations and institutions are particularly sought after. The mass media should also be called on to support these initiatives.

Fourth: UNESCO, through the joint efforts of Headquarters, Regional Offices, and its centres, institutes or units specialized in higher education in other regions, in co-operation with other UN agencies such as UNDP and the Economic and Social Commission for Western Asia (ESCWA), Higher Education NGOs, and UNESCO Chairs and Networks, must reinforce its programmes of higher education in the Arab States, including its contribution to the development of the whole education system. In particular, UNESCO must reinforce its unit in Higher education at its Beirut Office, so that this may, in conjunction with the other relevant bodies and units:

a) encourage studies, projects and research activities to support the elaboration of public policies and other initiatives related to higher education, and promote public understanding of the value of higher education. In particular, UNESCO should sponsor regional projects aiming at (1) the development and implementation of new ideas concerning the governance of higher education systems and institutions, (2) the development and sustainable implementation of a framework for quality assurance, (3) the implementation of structures dealing with research and institutional development, (4) the elaboration of common understandings as regards to the role, functions and functioning of higher education private institutions, and (5) the elaboration of programmes aiming at establishing close links between social problems and concerns and higher education institutions and support for their implementation;

b) provide managers of higher education with opportunities for the discussion of issues, current problems, and long-term challenges related to higher education;

c) foster training for teaching personnel and mangers of higher education institutions;

d) co-ordinate the implementation of UNESCO/UNITWIN Chairs Programme in the Arab States and, in particular, stimulate the development of centres of excellence, through the creation of specialized networks, with special attention given to networks for distance education, teachers training, the utilisation of information and communication technologies, and institutional development in higher education;

e) work in partnership with regional and international organisations, associations, and networks.

In addition, UNESCO is called upon to reinforce its current programmes, carried out by the UNESCO Cairo Office, for assisting Arab universities in developing their co-operation infrastructure and acquiring the knowledge and skills of information and communication technologies and in-using these technologies for upgrading the quality of their teaching in fundamental and applied sciences.

Member States and donor organisations of the Arab Region are called upon to support UNESCO to enable it carry on the above mentioned programmes and activities for the benefit of all Arab States.

Fifth: The elaboration of decisions and plans taken by all the bodies mentioned above should be based on the principles stated below.

1. RELEVANCE

i. Access to higher education

1. Arab governments must expand and diversity opportunities for every citizen to upgrade his or her qualifications and develop higher-level personal, academic and citizenship competencies such as those provided in higher education institutions. Appropriate strategies should be elaborated and implemented and serious efforts should be made to increase participation rates in higher education, particularly for those already involved in the world of work or dropouts of the educational system, through flexible programmes and schedules, allowing for part-time study and diversified should qualifying or diploma-driven programmes.

2. Distance education and open learning constitute important alternative delivery systems of higher education. Governments should provide the legislative and regulatory frameworks in order for such schemes to be developed. They also should encourage such initiatives and facilitate their operation through easy access to modern communication networks and recognition of the qualifications earned without neglecting the basic requirements for quality assurance and the relevance of outcomes.

ii. The world of work

3. In order to facilitate the elaboration of national educational plans and to improve the capacity of higher education institutions to align their policies with national priorities, governments should create or reinforce planning mechanisms to monitor trends and needs of the labour market, in close, continuous, and interactive partnership with higher education institutions and the productive and service sectors. "Observatories" may be created to monitor short-and long-term trends of the world of work and the harmonization needed between these trends and higher education policies and programmes.

4. Higher education institutions must help shape the labour market by identifying the needs of the social and economic sectors for new professionals and specialists. New disciplines and specialisations should be introduced into the curriculum of

higher education institutions. At the same time, job opportunities should be created for the graduates of these disciplines by a joint effort of governments, enterprises, and the higher education community. Higher education institutions should also provide school dropouts and those already in the workforce flexible opportunities to upgrade their competencies and knowledge levels, as well as to profit from retraining and career-switching.

5. Special attention should be given to the development of study programmes at the professional level, particularly by introducing or expanding higher colleges of technology, and at the graduate level, by expanding master's and Ph.D. programmes, with due regard to designing specializes learning material of specific disciplines of high quality relevant to societal needs and delivered through new information and communication technologies.

6. Curricula should be organised to stimulate the entrepreneurial skills of students, grounded on flexible, innovative, and interdisciplinary approaches, as to break the general trend towards the dependence of most graduates on public employment. Incubator projects which help create new enterprises should be fostered with the support of governments, the productive and service sectors, and local communities. In addition, more industry-based projects and new paradigms of university-industry partnership must be instituted. UNESCO, UNIDO, UNDP, the World Bank, AGFUND, Islamic Development Bank, and other development funding agencies could be sought after to assist in this matter.

iii. Responsibility towards other education levels

7. Higher education must take up its duties towards other levels of education. This is needed not only to ensure that students are better prepared for higher education, but also to ensure that pupils experience less failures, stay longer in schools, and are given educational and guidance services appropriate to their abilities and interests. To this effect, auxiliary educational services should be created at all levels of education and services should be provided to all students who require them. Moreover, in view of the ever increasing rates of illiteracy in some Arab States, of the negative effects of illiteracy on economic and

social development, and of the enormous human potential of the hundred thousands of students enrolled in higher education, higher education community should take a leading role in combating illiteracy, particularly among girls and women.

8. to act on its responsibility and role towards the whole education system, higher education in the Arab States should actively participate (a) in the improvement of the quality of general education, (b) in the renovation of teacher and other educational personnel training schemes aiming at more professionalisation, (c) in conducting research on social and educational variables that may reduce school failure and dropout, and in recommending appropriate educational approaches and policy alternatives, etc., (d) in the development, in close, continuous, and interactive partnership with education authorities and institutions, of activity programmes and direct services to the education community aiming at helping the education system reach the objectives of education for all as set in Jomtien Conference (1990). Networks and Chairs in educational sciences should be created and reinforced as part of the strategy to achieve these ends.

iv. Major social problems

9. Higher education institutions should contribute to the development of students' personal awareness, commitment, and capacity to cope, at the personal as well as at the professional levels, with the major social issues facing humankind, such as population, poverty, illiteracy, public health, protection of the environment, protection of cultural diversity, social participation, human rights and international understanding, etc. All higher education study programmes should include courses dealing with these issues with appropriate concrete applications according to students' fields of specializations.

10. Arab higher education should take active part in facilitating access to and harnessing of modern technology and scientific discoveries by all members of the educational community and by the public at large. It has a special responsibility, alongside with the media, towards the passage of Arab societies to information and communication age. In particular, all higher education teaching, technical, and administrative personnel,

and all students of all disciplines must be provided with the necessary training that enables them to integrate new information and communication technologies into their work.

v. Regional integration

11. Higher education institutions must promote processes aiming at Arab integration, starting at the cultural and educational levels, with the view to attain economic and political integration. The adoption of common standards for quality assessment and recognition of educational and professional qualifications constitutes a step forward towards such an integration, as well as the adoption of common core study programmes in the various professional fields. The implementation of common research projects may constitute another way towards this end. Intensive efforts should be devoted to studying the economic, social, cultural, ecological and political obstacles to integration and the strategies and actions needed to overcome these obstacles.

2. QUALITY

12. Each Arab State should establish a mechanism for evaluating the quality of its higher education at the systemic, institutional, programme, personnel, and outcomes levels. Quality assurance methods may include academic accreditation, institutional evaluations or sector reviews by disciplines and professional areas, performance funding, competency-based approaches to professional education and training.

13. Appropriate emphasis needs to be placed on the renewal of curricula, on continuous assessment of teaching and learning approaches and the adoption of new ones, as well as the promotion of multidisciplinary studies. The utilization of multi-media and the Internet must all be used, with due consideration to promote interaction between students, teachers, and managers.

14. Governments and institutions of higher education must adopt appropriate strategies for the recruitment and training of teaching personnel, for their further professional development and for recognition of their achievements. Legislative bodies, governments, and higher education institutions should take the

necessary measures to implement the Recommendation concerning the Status and Conditions of Higher Education Teaching Personnel, approved by the 29th Session of UNESCO General conference (Paris, 1997).

15. Each higher education institution should establish a center for the professional development and the improvement of the teaching performance of its teaching personnel.

16. Higher education institutions should modernize libraries and take the necessary measures to provide for scientific equipment and guarantee its modernisation within the framework of their long-term plans. In this context, regional and international co-operation should particularly be enhanced as to ensure to students and academics from Arab States adequate access to scientific equipment and information that could not be made available due to limited budgets and resources.

17. Higher education institutions must provide each student with orientation and study skills training, and pave the way for him to play an efficient role in society.

18. Appropriate strategies should be developed in order to strengthen research capacity at higher education institutions, including research aiming at the acquisition, the broadening, and the deepening of knowledge and publishing its results. Conducting such research should be an obligation to all members of the teaching personnel at higher education institutions. States and institutions should provide for proper structures, equipment, and staff, as well as the necessary financial support as to ensure the involvement of teaching personnel in research and publication activities. Co-operative programmes at the national, regional, and international levels should be encouraged, including linking of higher education institutions, centres, and laboratories to government and industry research laboratories.

3. MANAGEMENT AND FINANCIAL RESOURCES

I. Governance and management systems

19. Autonomy of higher education institutions of the Arab States should be fostered. This includes, among other things, the

freedom to select staff and students, to determine the conditions under which they remain in the institution, to determine the curriculum and degree standards, to allocate resources for different activities, and to select research topics. Institutional autonomy should be accompanied by a high level of responsibility and accountability and the widest possible participation of students, faculty, and administration in decision-making.

20. Governments should consider creating or reinforcing agencies that act as buffer between concerned ministries and higher education institutions and provide advice on such matters as organisation, accountability and quality assurance, allocation of resources, and the administration of grants and financial assistance, with due consideration to the fact that higher education implies that its appraisal cannot be restricted to economic quantitative indicators alone.

21. Opportunities should be given, wherever possible, to government, and the professional and productive sectors to participate in decision-making concerning management and organization of higher education.

22. Management capacities in higher education should be strengthened by appropriate training and staff development programmes for all managers, especially those in executive positions, the adoption of clear job descriptions and decision-making channels, the improvement of managerial procedures, and the introduction of computerized management systems.

23. Each higher education institution should establish a unit staffed with experienced qualified personnel with the mandate to conduct the necessary studies and research and to propose strategies and actions aiming at the institutional development and the improvement of management. Its studies can include, inter alia, such matters as planning and management, evaluation of training and service programmes and the introduction of new ones, the development of distance education schemes, the condition of women and the strategies to enhance their participation at the different levels of the institution. To this end, UNESCO Chairs and Networks could be developed and implemented in the Arab States.

ii. Financial resources

24. Arab States must renew the commitments made by them at the social Development Summit in Copenhagen and at other world bodies to "make new and additional resources available" and thus increase their budgets allocated to education in general and to higher education in particular, measured as a percentage of their gross national product.

25. Even though the state should remain the main party responsible for funding higher education, diversification of funding sources, in particular, through cost recovery of extra -academic activities, and encouragement of various income-generating activities, such as contract research, cultural and academic services, short-term courses, etc... should actively be sought after. This could only be achieved by the involvement of all stakeholders, the public and private sectors, local communities, academic associations, and non-governmental organisations. Legislative bodies should play a leading role in the matter by the adoption of appropriate measures to encourage diversification of funding sources with due consideration to ensuring access to higher education according to merit, and equity.

26. In order to assure high-quality research, it is required to adopt adequate systems for public and private support to research undertaken at higher education institutions, as well as to double the existing level of funding.

27. The complementary role of private institutions of higher education must be recognised. Governments should provide a legal framework to regulate private higher education institutions and develop appropriate mechanisms for accreditation, diploma recognition, and licensing, in addition to setting standards for quality assurance and adequacy of the required educational facilities and services.

4. CO-OPERATION

28. Each institution of higher education must envisage the creation of a specialised unit for managing Arab and international co-operation. These units must develop international linages, such as those for the exchange of students and teaching personnel,

and other academic co-operation activities. As well, they must co-operate within the framework of the activities of international organizations and bilateral agreements.

29. International and Regional organizations must support projects aiming at reinforcing co-operation between higher education institutions through the establishment and strengthening of higher education networks, and support to the activities of existing associations, especially the Association of Arab Universities, the Arab Federation of Councils for Scientific Research and the Arab Federation for Technical Education

30. Higher education institutions should strengthen their endogenous and co-operative capacities related to priority issues in the Arab States. Centers of excellence can have a positive impact on the solution of major social problems related to the environment, demographic growth, sustainable development, research on higher education, educational research, institutional management, teaching staff professional development, arabization of higher education provision of communication technologies, technology transfer, the protection of cultural heritage, etc...

31. The exchange of knowledge and experience between higher education institutions in the Arab States must be carried out in a spirit of solidarity and be the basis for co-operation agreements between them. Within their capacity, UNESCO and other international and regional governmental and non-governmental organisations should respond to the request to provide technical assistance to smaller and poor countries.

32. A special effort must be undertaken to re-build the higher education system in Palestine and in occupied territories, to remove the barriers which the military occupation places that prevent the free movement of students and faculty members, and that hinder access to research and study. Concerned parties should endeavour to stop all measures that threaten the safety and security of students and staff of institutions of higher education. At the same time, appropriate pressures must be exerted to remove obstacles to the free exchange of students and academics between Palestine and the Arab States. Finally, Arab institutions of Higher education are urged to continue their policies supporting access of qualified Palestinian students to higher education.

33. The establishment of the Arab Open University must be encouraged in the light of the results of the studies pertaining to it.

34. Regional co-operation projects in the field of teaching staff personnel and their professional development should be reinforced. Arab States are urged to encourage the establishment of the Arab University for Graduate Studies and Scientific Research.

35. A series of actions should be undertaken by governments and higher education systems in the Arab States following the recommendations of the Regional Committee responsible for the application of the Convention on the Recognition of Studies, Diplomas and Degrees of Higher Education in the Arab States; in particular:

   - Exchange of information and documentation with regional committees of other regions;
   - development of inter-regional co-operation among national documentation centers for the recognition of studies and diplomas;
   - development of capacities in view of collection, treatment and dissemination of information in order to facilitate the recognition of studies and diplomas in higher education;
   - development of research aiming at facilitating the recognition of studies and diplomas, on subjects or themes such as academic and professional mobility, recognition of skills and experiences, etc...

36. Within the framework of the Convention on the Recognition of Studies, Diplomas and Degrees of Higher Education, governments, institutions of higher education, professional bodies and international organisations must encourage student, academic and professional mobility to benefit the process of economic, educational, political and cultural integration in the Arab States and to develop mutually accepted standards for the recognition of diplomas. In this action, attention should be paid to incorporate the Arabic dimension as an integral part of teaching and research. Furthermore, all efforts should be made

to remove practical, administrative and legal obstacles to academic exchange at institutional, national and international levels.

5. FINAL RECOMMENDATIONS

37. Governments, higher education institutions, and all stakeholders concerned with the development of higher education in the Arab States must translate the recommendations of this plan of action into operational projects as soon as possible.

38. For improving the systems of co-operation in the Arab States, an evaluation of existing networks, including those established within the framework of UNITWIN/UNESCO Chairs programme, should be carried out.

39. UNESCO, with the support of governments and other organizations, must convene a meeting of experts in 2002 or 2003 to evaluate and follow-up the implementation of the recommendations of Beirut Conference.

Reference

1. Arab Regional Conference on Higher Education, Beirut, Lebanon, 2-5 March 1998.

ANNEX 3

DECLARATION ABOUT HIGHER EDUCATION IN ASIA AND THE PACIFIC

We, participants of the Asia and Pacific Regional Conference on Higher Education National Strategies and Regional Co-operation for the 21st Century,[1]

1. **Recalling,** on one hand, the terms of the Universal Declaration of Human Rights, which states in article 26 that "every person has the right to education"... and that "higher education shall be accessible to all, on the basis of merit", and, on the other hand, the UNESCO Constitution which encourages institutional exchanges in the area of education;
2. **Recognising** the importance of the analysis and recommendations of the Policy Paper on Change and Development in Higher Education launched by UNESCO in 1995 and resulting from a world-wide reflection on the role of higher education in society; the view of the International Commission on Education for the XXI Century that "Universities in developing countries have a duty to carry out research that should contribute to solving the most serious problems facing these countries"; and the conclusion of the World Commission on Culture and Development that development is "a far more complex undertaking than had than had been originally thought" and that it should not be "seen as a single, uniform, linear path, for this would inevitably eliminate cultural diversity and experimentation, and dangerously limit humankind's creative capacities in the face of a treasured past and an unpredictable future'";
3. **Noting** the exceptional diversity of and variety within the Asia

and Pacific region with regard to demography, religion, culture, ethnicity and education, with the most populous nations existing alongside small states, and the region including not only some of the fastest growing and wealthiest economies but also some of the poorest; and further noting that this region has been characterised as the cradle of civilisation, of the world's great religions and philosophies, and the earliest educational systems,

4. **Pointing out** that the rapid growth and in-depth transformation of societies and of key regional economies has resulted in a new appreciation of the role of higher education in technological development and increased demands for specialised professionals, while the increasing use of new information and communications technologies provides exciting possibilities for innovation in course design and delivery, for access to intellectual resources and for building new networks of experts and institutions, thus requiring that the concept and practices of lifelong learning be further developed;

5. **Acknowledging** that as the countries of the region draw closer together through trade, improved transportation and rapid communications into a seemingly common destiny, each one is consciously fostering its own sense of identity and nationhood, and rediscovering its cultural heritage and the value of its languages. In recent years, the region has demonstrated impressive capacity for innovation, especially in the application of science and technology, and exceptionally high rates of economic growth. In 1960, Asia had only 4 per cent of the world-wide GNP, whereas it now accounts for 25 per cent, with this figure being predicted to reach 30 per cent by the year 2000. However, in many professional fields there are on-going serious shortages in the supply of qualified professionals while rapid growth has resulted in major urban and social problems, and serious degradation of the environment.

6. **Observing** that significant progress has been made in recent years in the development and strengthening of higher education within the countries of the region, particularly leading to improved student access, strengthened research and postgraduate programmes, more equitable representation of different social groups among graduates, renewed curricula and adoption of

new teaching and delivery methods, and enhanced institutional management and strategic planning capacity. At the same time, many nations of the region are still far from achieving a desirable number and quality of graduates required by the new economic situation.

7. **Noting** that the main trends in higher education in the region include the following:

- Higher education across the region is under considerable strain. Student enrolments continue to increase resulting in further pressure on public funding for higher education institution; the level of financial resources is often considered inadequate and there is widespread evidence of experimentation to diversity funding sources, including reinforced links with the productive sector;
- Gender inequality, particularly among students, academic staff and senior management, continues to be an issue of considerable concern at all levels in the majority of countries. In a number of countries at the undergraduate level, female participation has approached or exceeded 50 per cent of enrolments, but generally female students are concentrated in "traditional" feminine disciplines. In many countries, women constitute no more than 20 per cent or 30 per cent of academics, while in other instances women are practically excluded from participation in higher education at all;
- In many countries, higher education institutions are heavily concentrated in urban areas, whereas the majority of the population lives in rural areas, thus requiring new mechanisms to address rural disadvantage; other disadvantaged sectors of society, such as those with disabilities, are not adequately served;
- As a result of international developments in science and technology and their impact on both economic development and social life-style, new demands have emerged for researchers, technicians and other specialised professionals and for an increased level of co-operation with industry in R & D. Frequently there are serious mismatches in the demand for and supply of highly trained personnel, especially

in countries undergoing rapid economic growth and indstrialization;

- Dramatic increases have occurred in the number of private higher education institutions, with accompanying diversification in structures, curriculum and teaching methods and management approaches resulting from both internal factors (such as changes in academic disciplines and new instructional methods) and external factors (such as population growth, the need to cater for more diverse clienteles and changing labour market requirements). Particularly important has been the development of non-university institutions and the establishment of open universities and distance learning systems;
- There is increasing concern in many countries with regard to the quality of courses., facilities, staff and graduates and the deterioration of infrastructure (laboratories, buildings and libraries) and a lack of scientific equipment.
- Unemployment of graduates especially in countries undergoing rapid transition, and lack of highly qualified professionals from less developed nations, have unfortunate long-term consequences for a number of countries of the region;
- Many leaders of higher education in the region see that need for better integration of western concepts and values with Eastern philosophy and culture;
- In many countries, teaching and learning procedures are often based largely on memorization and recall, which do not develop analytical and problem-solving skills. Frequently, undue emphasis is placed on the immediate utility of knowledge rather than on fundamental wisdom while the persistence of dogmatic approaches in education seriously hinders the development of enquiring minds;
- The lack of close links, in many countries, between universities and other post-secondary institutions, and between higher education institutions and secondary school is a matter of on-going concern;

8. **Recognizing** the various initiatives taken over the past decade by several governmental and non-governmental organisations

and higher education institutions (e.g. debates in the framework of APEC for the formulation of a regional programme in higher education for human resource development; restoration of the activities of the SEAMEO Regional Institute for Higher Education and Development (RIHED); the recent formation of the Association of Universities of Asia and Pacific (AUAP); establishment of the UMAP University Mobility in Asia and the Pacific Programme (UMAP) which aims at promoting student mobility at undergraduate level; the formation of the UNESCO-supported Asia Pacific Higher Education Network (APHEN) to foster research collaboration; progress with the UNESCO Chairs, UNITWIN and UNISPAR Programmes and the conclusions of various conferences on higher education issues and reforms hosted by different countries of the region;

9. **Taking into account** the conclusions of the Sixth Regional Conference of Ministers of Education and those Responsible for Economic Planning in Asia and the Pacific, organised by UNESCO in co-operation with ESCAP, which called for support for regional and national programmes to encourage mobility, networking and quality monitoring in higher education; Resolution No. 1.6 adopted by the twenty-eighth session of the General Conference of UNESCO in November 1995, which called for the strengthening of regional co-operation in higher education in Asia and the Pacific notably by taking appropriate measures to establish a Regional Programme in Higher Education in UNESCO's Bangkok Office and which invited the Director General to ensure that development of the programme be discussed "in a regional conference on higher education for the preparation of a world conference on higher education planned for 1998"; and the results of various recent major meetings within the region, including those at Armidale, Penang, Tokyo and Xiamen, and the instructional Conference which took place in Manila where a special Declaration was approved;

We, the participants of the Asia and Pacific Regional Conference on National Strategies and Regional Co-operation for the 21st Century, assembled in Tokyo, Japan, from 8 to 10 July 1997, do hereby declare that:

1. Higher education is essential for any country to reach the necessary level of economic and social development and social mobility in order to achieve increased living standards and internal and international harmony and peace based on democracy, tolerance and mutual respect. At the end of the century, we reaffirm that the aims of higher education can be summarised as follows: to educate responsible and committed citizens, to provide highly trained professionals to meet the needs of industry, government and the professions; to provide expertise to assist in economic and social development, and in scientific and technological research; to help conserve and disseminate national and regional cultures, drawing on the contributions from each generation; to help protect values by addressing moral and ethical issues; and to provide critical and detached perspectives to assist in the discussion of strategic options and to contribute to humanistic renewal;

2. All higher education systems and institutions should give a high priority to ensuring the quality of provision and outcomes. However, great care should be taken in making comparisons between the achievement of different higher education systems and institutions since it is not possible to arrive at one set of standards applicable to all countries and institutions and against which institutions can be assessed. Further, higher education institutions need appropriate financial and human resource to achieve quality of provision;

3. Modern information and communications technology provides considerable promise to enhance teaching and learning in higher education by both on-campus and distance education students, and disabled students who tend to be denied access to traditional institutions, provide access to technical and scholarly information resources, and to facilitate communications among researchers and teachers and the establishment and enhancement of networks of institutions and scholars. Already the notion of the virtual university is being actively explored within the region. At the same time, harnessing this technology will require considerable investment in hardware, software and staff development, while deliberate efforts to ensure that the human and social interaction elements of education are not undervalued.

4. Access to scholarly communication is an essential element of cultural understanding and the further development of higher education institutions. With the increased emergence of digitalization and the increasing reliance on telecommunications as a means of scholarly communication, it is important that access to communication be open and affordable. Governments of the region should work to ensure that control of telecommunications links and software infrastructure is widely shared;

5. While recognising that globalisation and internationalisation are irreversible trends, support for these concepts should not lead to dominance or new forms of imperialism by major cultures and value systems from outside the region; rather, it is of vital importance that every effort should be taken to protect and promote the strengths of local cultures and intellectual and scholarly traditions;

6. Regional co-operation among the countries of the region, especially in higher education, can make significant contributions in addressing major policy problems, strengthening national capacity in economic and social development, and facilitating the sharing of important expertise and experience. Regional co-operation is especially desirable in view of the adversity of the region and the potential for dynamic collaboration. In addition, higher education institutions should explore opportunites to promtoe processses aiming at regional integration without losing diversity;

7. Involvement in decision-making by all key stakeholders of higher education institutions is of utmost importance. Experience has demonstrated the value of such participation in bringing to decision-making a variety of different perspectives.

8. The concept of lifelong learning is of utmost importance. In rapidly changing economies, the labour market will constantly require new and different skills and so mechanisms must be enhanced to allow professionals to upgrade their skills at regular intervals and develop new competencies. People's needs of lifelong learning have expanded in all countries of the region. Higher education institutions thus must offer learning opportunities in response to diverse demands and work co-

operatively with other agencies and employers to ensure that appropriate courses are widely available. Ready access and flexibility in timing are of utmost importance.

9. Determined efforts are necessary to increase access to higher education, especially for groups currently poorly represented. Distance education and open learning can play a major role in widening access.

10. There is an urgent need to develop a plan of action and accompanying guidelines for co-operation especially related to the key issues of relevance, quality, management and finance, and co-operation which are summarised as follows:

Relevance refers to the fit between what higher education institutions do and what society expects of them. Relevance requires higher education to make an enhanced contribution to the development of the whole education system, notably through improved teacher education and educational research, and through reinforcement of its community service functions, including activities to eliminate poverty, hunger and disease. Relevance requires better articulation with the world of work and democratization of access to higher education, wider opportunities for participation during the various stages of life as well as the full involvement of the higher education community in the search for solutions to pressing human problems, such as population control, environmental degradation, and the quest for peace, international understanding, democracy and human rights. Academic freedom and responsible institutional autonomy particularly in the core academic functions are crucial for the achievement of the goal of relevance.

Quality refers to standards of resourcing and provision, and the achievements or outputs of an institution or system. Quality is a multi-dimensional concept and it is not possible to arrive at one set of quality standards applicable to all countries and against which institutions can be assessed. Quality embraces all the main functions and activities of higher education: teaching and academic programmes, research and scholarship, staffing, students, infrastructure and the academic environment. It can be implemented through comparisons between observed and intended outcomes and constant analysis of the sources of dysfunction. Both internal self evaluation and external review are vital components of any well developed quality assurance system. The concept of accountability is closely allied with quality. No system of higher education can fulfil its mission unless it demands the highest quality of itself. Continuous and permanent assessment is necessary to reach this objective. At the same time, it must be acknowledged that great care must be exercised in making quality assessments since it involves matters of judgement, academic values and cultural understanding.

Management and Finance covers both internal institutional management, funding and resource issues, as well as relations of higher education institutions with the state and national planning and co-ordination. Higher education institutions need to adopt forward-looking management practices which respond to the needs of their environments and which are articulated in their missions. Today, despite the general trend towards diversified sources of funding, public support for higher education and research remains essential to ensure achievement of educational and social missions. Both institutions and national agencies can develop appropriate strategies to strengthen management, planning and policy analysis capacities.

Co-operation at the national, regional and international levels is essential as, today, no institution can realistically expect to attain the highest standard in every field by itself. Furthermore, the steady advance of information and communication technologies must facilitate inter-university co-operation. Society as a whole must in a democratic system support education at all levels. Moblization for this purpose depends on the awareness and involvement of Parliaments, the media and governmental and non-government organisations.

PLAN OF ACTION

Based on the principles, observations and recommendations set out in the Declaration of Higher Education approved by the Conference, and considering that strong support is needed for the renewal of systems through new policies and new paradigms for higher education founded on such concepts as sustainable development, lifelong education, globalisation of knowledge, continuity of the reform process, anticipatory capacity, transparency and accountability, involvement of Parliaments and the media, and preservation of cultural identity and values, the following is recommended:

Joint Action Plans must be established, in order to prevent duplicated efforts, to optimize efficiency and to ensure the further development of higher education through the enhanced mobilisation of additional resources, but international and regional organisations dealing with inter-university co-operation and strengthening of global networks, by all regional, sub-regional and national associations of universities and higher education institutions, by the representatives of private and public universities, by networks of institutions for research and teaching, as well as by development organisations and agencies, governmental and non-governmental organisations. The United Nations University and, in particular, the Institute of Advanced Studies in Tokyo, should co-operate with higher education institutions of the region in strengthening networks and in building global networks leading to the solution of pressing global problems of human survival and welfare. The mass media of the region should be called on to support these initiatives.

Governments and Parliaments must fulfil their commitments to higher education and be accountable for pledges made at regional and world conferences over the past decade with regard tot he provision of human and financial resources. This includes, inter alia, the establishment of effective new mechanisms to deal with policy and legislation, appropriate follow-up activities, monitoring and evaluation of progress towards the achievement of stated goals and the promotion of institutional autonomy.

Each higher education institution must define its mission in harmony with the overall goals of the sector itself, translate this mission into observable indicators and allocate the required resources. The culture of evaluation should thus be established or strengthened in all institutions. These plans of actions should be based on the principles mentioned above and on the principles and considerations of the Declaration approved by this conference and on the proposals stated in this plan of action.

UNESCO, though the joint efforts of Headquarters, PROAP and other regional offices in Asia and the Pacific and specialised agencies such as the International Institute for Educational Planning (IIEP), and in co-operation with other UN agencies such as the Economic and Social council of Asia and the Pacific (ESCAP), must reinforce the programmes of higher education in Asia and the Pacific, including its contribution to the development of the whole education system, and, in particular, must reinforce its Unit in Higher Education at its Bangkok Office, so that this may:

- carry out studies, analyses, projects and research activities to support the elaboration of public polices and other initiatives related to higher education in the region. In particular, UNESCO should sponsor a regional process to explore the possibility of developing a framework for quality assessment to feed into the 1998 UNESCO World Conference on Higher Education in Paris;
- provide a venue for the discussion of issues, current problems, long-term challenges and opportunities related to higher education in the region;
- foster training for leaders and senior managers of higher education institutions in the region;
- function as information centre that supports both the work of research groups and of the academic community in the field of higher education in Asia and the Pacific, as well as that of civil society, the state and the productive sector.
- co-ordinate the implementation of the UNITWIN/UNESCO Chairs Programme in the region and, in particular, to stimulate the development of regional centres of excellence, through the creation of thematic or geographical networks (with special attention given to networks for innovation, for the utilisation of new technologies and for distance education and also for studies on higher education issues);
- work in partnership with regional institutions, associations and networks;
- act as a regional clearing house for inter-country information on huger education institutions and systems in Asia and the Pacific.

The elaboration of plans and decisions taken by the organisations mentioned above should be based on the principles stated below:

RELEVANCE

Major social problems of humankind

1. Higher education must give every student the philosophical, historical, psychological and anthropological foundations of

knowledge with regard to humankind, its environment and its different societies. In addition, the motivations, aspirations, transactions and achievements of different peoples, within the context of their respective histories and cultures must be communicated.

2. Higher education must support research and pilot curriculum projects which provide expertise to facilitate access to modern technology and scientific discoveries, but which also lead to the understanding, appreciation, internationalisation and dissemination of human and societal values, with special attention to the goals of peace and democracy and the protection of the environment.

Responsibility towards other education levels

3. Higher education must act on its responsibility and role towards other levels of education. This is needed not only to ensure that students are better prepared for higher education, but also to bring to bear the resources and expertise of the higher education community to the tasks of teacher training, socio-economic research on such education variables as school retention and repetition, appropriate pedagogies, and educational policy alternatives, thereby improving education at all levels.

Regional integration

4. Higher education institutions must promote processes aimed at regional integration. Furthermore, cultural and educational integration should be the bases for political and economic integration. In a global environment, higher education institutions must approach their studies on regional integration in the light of the specific economic, social, cultural, ecological and political aspects involved.

Access

5. Governments must expand and diversify opportunities for every citizen to benefit from higher level skills, training, knowledge and information which are the qualifications for entry into the world of work. Serious efforts should be made to increase participation rates in higher education. Appropriate strategies

should be taken for increasing the participation of disadvantaged groups, including women, who must be encouraged to undertake higher degrees and enter academic and graduate employment. Similar efforts are also needed to encourage the participation of ethnic minorities.

The world of work

6. Higher education institutions should promote continuous and interactive partnerships with the productive sector using both reactive and proactive approaches. They must adjust the curriculum to meet the needs of the workplace and ensure that new disciplines and specialisations are incorporated into its content. Also, they must help shape the labour market on one hand by identifying, independently of conjunctural interests of enterprises, new local and regional needs, and on the other hand by designing mechanisms for retraining and career switching. Curricula should be organised to stimulate the entrepreneurial skills of students. This requires flexible, innovative and interdisciplinary approaches.

7. Countries should create 'observatories' to monitor changes in the labour market in order to facilitate the elaboration of national educational plans and to improve the capacity of higher education institutions to align their policies with national priorities. Special attention needs to be given to career prospects and job conditions of students in course areas of high skills such as engineering and technology for long term development.

8. Governments, the productive sector and local communities should, based on experience gained within and outside the region, encourage institutions of higher education to foster incubator projects which help create new enterprises. Governments, in particular, should provide incentives for the creation of micro-enterprises and fostering of university-industry links.

9. Greater emphasis should be given to the regionalisation of specific disciplines, through programmes which target specific needs that will generate employment. In addition, more industry-based projects and new paradigm of university-industry partnership must be instituted, specially in developing countries.

UNESCO, UNIDO, UNDP, World Bank, other regional development banks and other funding agencies must be sought in these activities.

10. Innovative approaches such as those of community colleges need to be encouraged. In countries with a large affiliated college system, specific attention needs to be given to strategies for improvement of colleges. Special efforts are needed to strengthen programmes to assist under-privileged groups in society.

Autonomy

11. Responsible institutional autonomy should be stimulated in the region. This principle upholds the freedom to select staff and students, to determine the conditions under which they remain in the university and select research topics. Freedom to determine the curriculum and degree standards and to allocate funds (within the amounts available) across different categories of expenditure are other aspects to be respected. At the same time, institutional autonomy should be accompanied by a high level of responsibility and accountability.

Quality

12. Appropriate, and if so required, greater emphasis needs to be placed on the renewal of the curriculum, on new approaches to both classroom and distance education teaching, on interdisciplinary and multidisciplinary studies and on vocational education programmes as alternatives to traditional university courses. Innovative approaches to higher education, such as community colleges, international collaboration, and twinning arrangements, need to be encouraged as appropriate.

13. The experience of certain countries regarding the creation of co-operative research centres linking higher education institutions, government research laboratories and industry should be the subject of case studies, the results of which should be available to all countries in the region.

14. Pedagogical programmes should be established to encourage students to be more entrepreneurial and initiative-oriented.

15. UNESCO along with other intergovernmental and non-governmental organisations specialised in higher education must carry out a series of case studies on the region's priorities in the field of higher education. These can include, inter alia, strategic management and planning, interaction among all levels of education, the revision of programmes and training, strategies to enhance the participation of women in higher education and in decision-making bodies, and the development of distance education schemes. Distance education and Open Learning provide important alternative mechanisms of higher education access and learning. In particular, such approaches provide opportunities for those already in the work-force to upgrade their competencies and knowledge levels. The possibilities of these approaches for school leavers, however, needs further analysis and experimentation.

16. Each country of the region should establish a mechanism for evaluating the quality of its higher education institutions. Countries must introduce quality assurance methods at both institutional and systemic levels. These may include academic accreditation, academic adults and institutional evaluations, performance funding, review of disciplines and professional areas, qualifications frameworks and competency-based approaches to vocational education and training.

17. Each higher education institution should establish a teaching and learning resource unit staffed by qualified personnel and charged with the development of pedagogical skills and other forms of teaching-support activities.

18. Countries and institutions must stimulate, through the creation of networks, the development of regional postgraduate studies.

19. Governments and institutions of higher education must adopt appropriate strategies for the recruitment of staff, for their further professional development and for the recognition of their achievements. Governments, Parliaments and institutions of higher education should pay particular attention to the draft Recommendation concerning the Status and Conditions of Higher Education Teaching Personnel, approved recently by a governmental experts meeting, which will be submitted to the General Conference of UNESCO in November 1997.

20. Higher education institutions must provide orientation and counselling, remedial courses, study skills training and other forms of student support, including measures to improve their living conditions.

21. Higher education institutions must modernise libraries and scientific equipment and include measures for the purchase and replacement of scientific equipment in their long-term management plans.

22. Higher education institutions must adopt new approaches for the packaging of information, for course delivery, and for rethinking traditional approaches to teaching and learning. The utilisation of multi-media, CD-ROM, the internet and interactive video is necessary to promote interaction between students and their lecturers. Agreements should be stimulated among regional institutions to exchange programmes and to organise joint debates and symposia.

23. Teachers, professors and technical and administrative staff must be given training that enables them to integrate new information and communication technologies (NICTs) into their teaching programmes, and to examine the multiplier effect with regard to their use. Frequently, the staff development needs of technical and administrative staff are not properly approached.

Management and Finance

24. Governments must formulate national action plans to enhance both access to and the relevance and quality of higher education institutions. As a consequence, institutional management should improve. The concept of higher education as a public asset implies that its appraisal cannot be restricted to economic quantitative indicators alone. These plans must foresee a diversification of funding sources through, in particular, the encouragement of various income-generating activities, such as contract research, a broad range of academic and cultural services, short-term courses and, if so appropriate, the operation of scientific and technology enterprises. Public support to higher education remains essential to ensure its educational, social and institutional missions. Therefore, the state should take the main responsibility for funding this sector. But, since the challenges

for higher education concern society as a whole, the solution to this problem must involve not only the state but all stakeholders - students, parents, the public and private sectors, local and national communications, authorities and academic association, as well as regional and international organisations.

25. Where appropriate, governments should consider creating, or reinforcing, agencies to act as a buffer between ministries and higher education institutions and to provide advice on resource needs and allocation, regulatory frameworks and the administration of grants and financial assistance.

26. In countries where privatisation is accepted, governments should provide a legal framework to regulate institutions, to develop appropriate accreditation and monitoring mechanisms, and to ensure academic freedom and maximum autonomy. The complementary and supportive role of private universities and colleges must be recognised.

27. Management capacities should be strengthened by, inter alia, the recruitment of new senior staff with specialised expertise, appropriate training and staff development programmes for all line managers (and especially for those in executive positions), the introduction of greater clarity in job descriptions and reporting channels, improved management procedures, and the introduction and enhancement of computerised management systems.

28. At the regional level, an association or forum should be created to mobilise the contribution of student organisations to current efforts aimed at making higher education institutions more forceful, active and efficient partners in the promotion of sustainable development in Asia and the Pacific.

29. Staff involvement in decision-making bodies should be considerably strengthened through greater recognition of their needs and by taking into consideration their perspectives, which are often relevant to the analysis of problems and to the search for viable solutions. In the case of students, appropriate consultation is of great importance.

30. Countries of the region must renew the commitments made by them at the Social Development Summit in Copenhagen and

at other world bodies to “make new and additional resources available’ and thus effectively increase their budgets allocated to education in general and to higher education in particular, measured as a significant percentage of their gross national product.

Co-operation

31. Individual institutions must develop international linkages, such as those for the exchange of staff and students and for academic co-operation. As well, they must support the activities of international organisations and bilateral agreements between countries within the region.

32. International and regional organisations should support projects aiming at establishing or strengthening university networks. For their part, institutions of higher education - with the support of national, regional and international organisations dealing with inter-university co-operation- should network centres of excellence which respond to the most pressing training and research needs of the Asia and Pacific region. The transfer and exchange of knowledge and experience between higher education institutions, carried out in a spirit of solidarity, should be the basis for these initiatives. It is recommended to establish an evaluation of existing networks in the region, including those covered by the UNITWIN/UNESCO Chairs Programme.

33. In the framework of the Regional Convention on the Recognition of Studies, Diplomas and Degrees in Higher Education in Asia and the Pacific and the International Recommendation on Recognition of Studies and Qualifications in Higher Education, there is a need to encourage student, academic and professional mobility to benefit the process of economic, educational, political and cultural integration within the region and to develop mutually accepted standards for the recognition of credentials. This will need collective effort by governments, professional bodies and international organisations;

34. Each institution of higher education, as well as all professional associations, must envisage the creation of specialised units for managing international co-operation.

35. Higher education institutions should strengthen their endogenous and co-operative capacities related to priority issues in the region. In particular, centres of excellence can have a positive impact on the solution of major social problems related to the environment and sustainable development, on research in higher education institutions, on educational research in general, on institutional leadership, staff development and teacher training, on the diffusion of new communication and information technologies, on human rights and democracy, on technology transfer, on patents and intellectual property and on the protection of cultural heritage, as well as on the strengthening of education for all and of social development in general.

36. Attempts should be made to develop under the leadership of the Asia and the Pacific distance and multi-media education network under AUAP a general pool of programmes of study for Asia and the Pacific region to cut the cost of distance education.

37. Within their capacity, UNESCO and other international and interregional governmental and non-governmental organisations should respond to the requests to provide technical assistance to smaller and poorer countries in the region, in particular those of island nations, and to collaborate with them in the preparation of joint plans of action with a view to the development of higher education institutions.

Reference

1. **Tokyo, Japan, 8-10 July 1997**

ANNEX 4

A EUROPEAN AGENDA FOR CHANGE FOR HIGHER EDUCATION IN THE XXIST CENTURY : RESULTS OF THE EUROPEAN REGIONAL FORUM AS A CONTRIBUTION TO THE UNESCO WORLD CONFERENCE ON HIGHER EDUCATION

(Palermo, Italy, 24-27 September 1998)

PREAMBLE

In the framework of the preparation of the 1998 UNESCO World Conference on Higher Education, the Association of European Universities (CRE) and UNESCO's European Centre for Higher Education (CEPSES) organised the European Regional Forum in Palermo that brought together almost 400 university leaders, teacher representatives and students, representatives of public authorities and the world of work, and intergovernmental and non-governmental organisations interested in higher education and its development. The Conference was prepared on the basis of twenty case studies of how European higher education institutions of different types and from different regions are addressing the issues of teaching and learning, preparation for the world of work, advancement of knowledge through research, and the transmission of cultural values in a European and a global context, as well as of how they intend to deal with these issues in the future.

A further input for the discussions was provided by a comparative analysis of these case studies. The keynote address entitled "Europe in a Period of Mutation and Change - The Role of Higher Education" focused on the future role of higher education from the point of view of a large industrial concern underlining the importance of lifelong learning and the importance of graduates with both professional skills and broad personal competencies. A panel of stakeholders added its comments.

The discussions were based on these various inputs organised around the four case study themes while taking into account the four main dimensions of the World Conference on Higher Education, namely relevance, quality, internationalisation, and finance and management.

European Agenda for Change—Main Directions

I. Mission

No chain being stronger than its weakest link, higher education should be a strong part of a strong educational system, as well as play a key role in opening new futures by contributing, in close collaboration with other partners, to the innovation chain. Similarly, higher education institutions have a key role to play in European society by contributing to equitable and sustainable development and to the culture of peace. They should act critically and objectively on the basis of rigour and merit, actively promoting intellectual and moral solidarity by serving individual needs. In a world of in-depth transformations, higher education institutions are expected to act responsibly and responsively. They are to foresee, anticipate, and influence changes in all quarters of society and be prepared and able to differentiate and to adapt accordingly.

II. Teaching and Learning

General Assumptions

Given the growing individual demand for higher learning and the resulting pressures on higher education institutions, there is a need for ever more institutional diversification, for new policies of access to higher education, and for a structured development of lifelong learning. In order to better respond to the needs of diversification, a wider and more imaginative institutional profiling is expected to occur within higher education systems, thus leaving less room for categorisation of institutions. At the same time, more programmatic diversification within the institutions is required.

Lifelong learning for personal and professional development, for career change, transferable skills, and matching supply and demand for highly trained personnel is essential. Higher education institutions must be able to offer corresponding courses in continuing education and in alliance with employers and other social partners so as to ensure that they are widely available and contribute to a coherent system of higher education. Thus it is essential to define the links in the overall "educational chain" and the relations between them so that individuals can independently manage their learning at whatever level.

In response to this increasingly differentiated demand, coherence means flexibility with regard to access, content, breadth, depth, and duration of programmes, means of delivery, examination, and validation. Thus, new policies of access should be designed on the basis of merit and equal opportunities, expanding student profiles, and reaching out to hitherto underprivileged groups of society.

Higher education institutions should pay increased attention to promoting strategies for the conceptualisation and the management of educational innovation, particularly with reference to organisation of contents, learning materials, teaching methods, and graduates' personal profiles as a response to the multiple challenges of their environments.

Required Action

The shift from teaching to learning implies self-managed learning, a coaching role for the teacher, professional support services, investment in new delivery, and quality assurance mechanisms, especially in off-campus operations. It should also lead to a new definition of scholarship balancing discovery and transmission as well as the integration and application of knowledge. A crucial level for change is a creative and well-defined personnel policy which opens up teaching as a career, supported by appropriate staff development programmes. Particular attention should be paid to the promotion of opportunities for women, including in top positions in higher education.

It also involves a new approach to curriculum development taking into account multi- and interdisciplinarity and flexibility of choice, but in a coherent system which allows for modularisation, credit transfer, the validation of work experience, and the organisation of the academic year in semesters both at national and international level.

Modern information and communication technologies have major implications for the provision of education and training and require a fundamental restructuring of the ways in which teaching and learning objectives are delivered. Higher education institutions have a key role to play in exploiting, for themselves and together with other partners, the potential of innovative information and communication technologies for academic development.

Given the increased demand for higher education and its democratisation, there is a pressing need to share good practice and to ensure academic quality standards by incorporating a culture of quality and the instruments for quality assurance at both systemic and institutional level.

The new roles both of the teachers and of the students as well as the changing relationship to government and world of work imply the definition of a new and explicit "educational contract" between the different partners, setting out rights and responsibilities for all concerned. It will be especially important to ensure that the voice of the students is heard at all stages of the learning process.

The paradigmatic shift from teaching to learning requires an investigation of the desirability of establishing a European Centre for Teaching and Learning to act as an observatory of good practice and innovation bringing together higher education institutions and their stakeholders at local, national, and international level.

III. Research

General Assumptions

Research, seen as the process leading to the systematic development of new knowledge, is central to the effectiveness of all higher education, while the type of research and the resources and time allocated to its promotion may vary according to the mission statement of the institution and its position within a coherent system of higher education. Accordingly, uniformity of research missions should give way to defferentiated institutional policies focused on achievable and competitive performances.

Research is important for the contribution of higher education to the innovation chain, by a strategic mobilisation of multilateral co-operation between city and regional governments, higher education institutions, industry, and business. In addition, it contributes to a constant supply of qualified young researchers. At the same time, a strong link between research and teaching opens opportunities for involving good researchers in the teaching process.

Multi- and interdisciplinary research is required more and more to solve pressing societal problems, thus also contributing to sustainable human development. There is, however, increasing concern about the ability of the public purse to provide adequate finances to meet these escalating needs.

Required Action

To ensure continued high quality research, governments need to provide adequate funding for basic research infrastructure, but within a competitive framework. Research funding allocations should be based on quality criteria and transparent auditing procedures. Care should be taken to avoid a mismatch between stakeholders' needs for interdisciplinary research and governmental/peer processes of research, adult, and funding, which may be focused on single disciplines. Research in the social sciences and the humanities should not be neglected.

Support mechanisms at national and international level to stimulate and sustain research groups in less developed systems of higher education should be strengthened in order to support institutional development rather than exacerbating brain drain phenomena.

Institutions are encouraged to develop Codes of Practice together with their partners for resolving questions of intellectual property regarding the results of externally funded research. Similarly, Codes of Ethics for the choice and conduct of research projects should be elaborated.

Strategies for diversifying funding sources should be actively sought. Institutions attracting research funding in this way should ensure that their services are realistically costed and priced and that a percentage of this extra income is used to build up an internal development fund for emerging projects or poorly funded areas.

Networking with corporate laboratories, multinational corporations, especially at regional, level, has a particular role to play in enhancing the quality and scope of institutional research as well as its resource base.

IV. World of Work

General Assumptions

In a labour market which is dynamic and heterogeneous, universities should not base their long-term orientations on labour market or manpower planning, but on social demand. They therefore have to prepare their students for meeting the challenges of an intrinsically uncertain labour market. In addition to their professional qualifications, graduates require a broad set of attributes in terms of personal and transferable skills and competencies in order to increase their employability in a knowledge society.

Required Action

To sustain a well-rounded individual development, full participation of stakeholders, in particular representatives of students, teachers, the world of work, and public authorities in higher education policy formation, and curriculum development is essential. As intelligent providers, higher education institutions need to develop their knowledge of markets, anticipate needs, be aware of competition, and invest in processes of quality assurance.

Students have to prepare for an increasingly diversified market, from employment in large industrial concerns to small enterprises, from working in the public sector to the service sector, and not forgetting individual entrepreneurship. There is a special need for the promotion of more constructive relations of higher education institutions to the world of small and medium size enterprises as the sector employing the largest number of graduates.

Higher education institutions should provide systematic information in schools and enterprises to guide student choices, provide placements as an integral part of degree courses, and offer research training in a work environment, as well as career guidance services at all times.

V. Transmission of Cultural Values in a European and Global Context

General Assumptions

Higher education institutions are as much concerned with the creation as with the transmission of cultural values. Although it is misleading to speak of "European" values *per se*, in the specific European context and in terms of the European university tradition, a framework does exist in terms of cultural unity through diversity. This means agreeing to disagree in order to pursue open, critical, and constructive dialogue.

As a consequence, higher education institutions have a key role to play, not only as centres, but also as incubators of cultural diversity and of multiracial harmony and understanding. This means they have a particularly important role to play in creating a civil society and in preparing young people for shaping and living in a democratic society, a place where higher education plays an active role in public debate on ethical and policy questions.

Required Action

These values should permeate all higher education curricula; their transmission, especially as far as ethical considerations are concerned, should not be limited to special courses. Special emphasis should be placed on language training, multi-disciplinarity, and independent and critical learning associated with teamwork. With the help of higher education institutions, this process should start in primary and secondary education.

Attention should be paid to incorporating the European dimension as an integral part of teaching and research and of sustaining the diversity of the learning experience through student and staff mobility. This means strengthening existing provision for the recognition of degrees and diplomas, in particular through the implementation of the UNESCO/ Council of Europe Joint Convention, and supporting the further development of a coherent credit transfer system. Furthermore, all efforts should be made to remove practical, administrative, and legal obstacles to academic exchange at institutional, national, and international level. In this respect, the importance of networking and true international partnerships for co-operation in teaching, research, or service is paramount.

VI. Organisational Change and Development

A constructive partnership between government, business and industry, and higher education institutions is a critical element in the implementation of an Agenda for Change in Higher Education. The role of government is expected to shift from bureaucratic control to policy steering, stable funding formulae, quality monitoring, project-based investment, and providing a cushion against the wider excesses of the demands of the free market. Business and industry should be encouraged to define more clearly their needs as clients and to work together with higher education institutions as training providers. Higher education institutions should be entrusted with a greater institutional autonomy, thus enhancing their capacity for change, for acting responsibly, effectively, and entrepreneurially as "learning organisations", while making them more accountable in terms of performance. Inter-institutional alliances should be a substantial lever for institutional change and development.

In view of the common assumptions on trends affecting future university development in Europe, the growing systematisation of institutional management is a welcome development as is the corresponding awareness of the need for internal strategic planning and rethinking, both for intrinsic reasons and in response to initiatives from national higher education planners.

ANNEX 5

DECLARATION ABOUT HIGHER EDUCAITON IN LATIN AMERICA AND THE CARIBBEAN[1]

Ratifying **the terms of the *Universal Declaration of Human Rights*, which states in its article 26, paragraph 1 that 'every person has the right to education' ... and that 'the access to higher education studies will be equal for all, on the basis of their corresponding merits'. Ratifying in turn, the contents of the Convention against Discrimination in Education (1960), which states in its article IV, that the signatory States commit themselves 'to ... offer all people alike higher education on the basis of a real equality and pursuant to the skills of each individual...'**

Starting by assuming **the trends identified in the Policy Paper for Change and Development of Higher Education, published by UNESCO in 1995. And on the bases of the studies, debates and reflections on that document that have been performed since that date in the region, which have set forth the recommendation of strengthening equity, quality, relevance and internationalisation of higher education.**

Taking into account **the fact that as we enter the XXI century, and faced with the growth of unemployment, poverty and misery, mankind must actively address the following issues: growth with equity, the protection of the environment and the peace-building process. Furthermore, following the recommendations made by the United Nations, via: (a) the Programme for Peace, that contains principles and suggestions bearing on the preventive measures that will protect peace, as well as effective actions for restoring peace when uncontainable conflicts emerge, and (b) the Programme for Development, that sets forth the conceptual bases for fostering a sustainable and permanent human development.**

Highlighting that human development, democracy and peace are inseparable elements-as stated in the medium-term strategy of UNESCO (1996-2001), that aims the higher education programmes of the Organisation at three objectives: expanding access to higher education with no discrimination whatsoever, as well as expanding permanence in the system and the possibilities of having success; improving its management and strengthening the links with the labour work; while at the same time contributing to build peace and foster a development founded on justice, equity, solidarity and freedom.

Taking up the report submitted to UNESCO by the International Commission on Education for the Twenty-first Century. The latter, in fact, does not only reaffirm the above mentioned options. It also sets forth that the universities of developing countries have the obligation of carrying out a research that can help solve the most serious problems that those countries are suffering. This is due to the fact that 'they are the ones that should propose new approaches for development, so that they can build a better future and do so in a more effective manner.'

Acknowledging that economic and social development highly depend on training a highly skilled staff, specifically in this most special stage in history, characterised by the emergence of a new production paradigm based on the power of knowledge and the adequate handling of information. Acknowledging, in turn, that it depends on the potential to create a knowledge that satisfies the specific needs and lacks of the region, and that the latter is derived almost solely from higher education institutions-the knowledge instances that generate, criticise and disseminate it.

Accepting, on the one hand, that the gap that is currently setting aside the countries of the region from the developed nations, is evidenced - among other aspects- in the following elements: education (rates of third-level schooling), technological research and development (size of the scientific and technical staff, investment in R&D), as well as information and communications. In fact, these aspects are set forth in the Report on Human Development of the United Nations Development Programme, that was published in 1996. Likewise, accepting, on the other hand, that the source of R&D in almost all the countries in the region is public and that the highest percentage to research units operates within the framework of universities, as set forth in the World Report on Science published by UNESCO in 1993.

Warning that, without adequate higher education and research institutions, developing countries can not except to adopt and apply the most recent development. And warning, likewise, that it would be even less feasible for them to make contributions of their own to development and to close the gap that keeps them away from industrialised nations.

Taking due note of the fact that higher education in the region evidences the following trends: (a) an outstanding expansion of the student roll; (b) a persistence of inequalities and difficulties when attempts are made at democratising knowledge; (c) a relative restriction of public investments in this sector; (d) a fast-paced increase and diversification of institutions that work in the field of third-level education; and, (e) a growing participation of the private sector in the composition of the education offer.

Estimating that efforts have been made by higher education institutions, the governments of some Latin American and Caribbean countries, or else, the societies themselves of several countries that make up the region, aimed at increasing the rates of post secondary education. And further estimating that despite those efforts, many of these nations are still far from achieving the coverage and quality required by globalisation, regionalisation and economic opening processes, as well as from achieving a real democratisation of knowledge.

Specifying that these trends are also evidenced at an international level. And, further, specifying that they coincide with simultaneous, though sometimes contradictory processes, namely, internationalisation, regionalisation, polarisation, democratisation, isolation and fragmentation, that have an effect on the development of higher education. And specifying, in turn, that the burden of the foreign debt, the increase in the value of imports of goods and services, the drop in the share of world trade, are elements evidenced in the region leading to a situation of social inequality. Furthermore, specifying that the countries of the area make attempts at facing the latter problems with regional and sub-regional groups and implementing several social policies.

Highlighting that, in these times of economic, political or social change- both positive and negative in nature - higher education is called to take up a leading role and to critically study these changes, while at the same time making prospective efforts aimed at predicting and even conducting them via the creation and dissemination of the pertinent knowledge. And, further highlighting that, to this end, higher education must take up its own transformation with the help of society as a whole, not only that of the education sector alone.

Reminding that in the case of Latin America, the Cordoba Reform (1918) - though responding to the needs of a society that was completely different from our own- was characterised by its clear support to the movement of university democratisation. Reminding, in turn, that it insisted on the need to create solid and diversified links between university activities and the needs of society - a process that is currently re-emerging to guide the process of transformation of higher education that is underway in the region. And, further reminding that the latter is seen as a continuous phenomenon aimed at designing an original institutional scheme adapted to satisfy the current and future needs of their countries.

Pointing out that any attempt at improving the quality and relevance of higher education requires a significant transformation of the education system as a whole. Furthermore, pointing out that the solution of the financial problems faced by higher education in Latin America and the Caribbean will not stem from redistributing the scarce resources that are allocated to the different levels in this sector. Likewise, pointing out that, on the contrary, they will be the result of transferring resources of other sectors that are not a real priority, while at the same time improving the distribution of income and diversifying financing sources. Pointing out, in turn, that all this has to be the result of a search undertaken with the participation of the State, the civil society, professional and business communities in order to respond-jointly and equitably- to the needs of the different sectors that make up society.

The participants of the Regional Conference of UNESCO on Policies and strategies for the transformation of higher education in Latin America and the Caribbean, coming from 26 countries, and assembled in Havana, Cuba, from November 18 to 22, 1996, do hereby declare that

1. Education, in general, and higher education, in particular, are essential instruments for facing up with success the challenges posed by the modern world and for educating citizens that can thus build a more open and fair society. It will be a society based on solidarity, respect for human rights and the shared use knowledge and information. At the same time, higher education is an unavoidable element for social development,

production, economic growth, strengthening the cultural identity, maintaining social coherence, continuing the struggle against poverty and the promotion of the culture of peace.

2. Knowledge is a social asset that can only be generated, transmitted, critised and recreated for the benefit of society, in plural and free institutions that have a full autonomy and academic freedom. However, the latter must also have a clear awareness of their responsibility and a will of service that cannot be turned down. Hence, they will be prepared to search for solutions to the demands, needs and lacks of society. This is indeed a society it should be accountable to - as a requirement - in order to exercise fully its autonomy. Higher education will be able to fulfil this important task only if it demands itself the highest quality. In this respect, a continuous and permanent assessment is indeed a most valuable instrument.

3. Higher education must strengthen its capacity to perform a critical analysis, to anticipate and to have a prospective vision. It must do so in order to prepare alternate development proposals and face the emerging problems of a reality undergoing a process of continuous and rapid transformation, in a long term horizon.

4. Higher education institutions must adopt organisational structures and education strategies that render them highly dynamic and flexible, thus enabling them to respond with both the timeliness and anticipation needed to creatively and efficiently face an uncertain future. They are called to facilitate an exchange of students between institutions and between different degree courses of the same institution. They will have to take up-without any further delays the paradigm of permanent education. They will have to turn into pertinent centres for facilitating professionals to be up to date, duly retrained and reconverted. Hence, they will have to offer a solid training in the basic disciplines, along with a wide diversification of programmes and studies, intermediate diplomas and links between courses and subjects. Likewise, they must endeavour to ensure that the activities of extension and dissemination are an important element of the academic life.

5. The nature itself of contemporary knowledge -in a process of

constant renewal and most sudden and dramatic growth - fully agrees with the current notion of permanent education. This must be an indissoluble supplement of studies aimed at obtaining degrees and titles. They offer graduates the possibility of taking refresher courses and of adapting to changing realities that are very difficult to anticipate. Besides, permanent education should also enable any person- at whatever stage of his/her life- to go back to the classrooms and to find in them the opportunity to be a part of the academic life once again. In this way, people are allowed to attain new levels of professional training. In fact, the competence acquired has a value in itself that goes beyond the mere credential.

6. Higher education must implement pedagogical methods based on knowledge, in order to train graduates that learn how to learn and how to undertake. In this way, they will be better prepared to generate their own jobs. They might even be able to create production entities that can help combat the scourge of unemployment. There is a clear need for promoting the spirit of inquiry. Hence, the student will have the tools to search for knowledge in a permanent and systematic manner. In turn, this implies revising the pedagogical methods that are currently in effect and the emphasis now placed on the transmission of knowledge will switch to the process for generating it. In this way, students will count on the instruments they require in order to learn how to learn, how to know, how to live together and how to be.

7. A changing society demands people to have a comprehensive, general and professional education. The latter must encourage the development of a person as a whole and should favour his/her personal growth, autonomy, socialisation and the skills to turn the assets that perfect it into elements having real value.

8. A higher education system will be fulfilling its responsibility and conscientiously carry out its mission - thus turning into a profitable social element - if a part of its teaching staff and institutions also performs intellectual creation (scientific, technical and humanistic) activities. The latter, in turn must be in agreement with the specific objectives of the institution, its teaching capabilities and its material resources.

9. It is absolutely necessary to introduce a solid culture of information in the higher education systems of the region. The adequate combination of information and communication redefines the need to update pedagogical practices at a university level. Besides, its players need to participate in the major academic networks and have access to the pertinent exchange with all the related institutions. Likewise, they must increase their degree of opening and their interactions with the international academic community. At the same time, higher education institutions must take up the main task of preserving and strengthening the cultural identity of the region. In this way, the above mentioned opening will not endanger the cultural values that are typical of Latin America and the Caribbean.

10. Among the challenges posed by this turn of the century, higher education is now facing the need to participate resolutely in the qualitative improvement of all the levels of the education system. Its most concrete contributions can be made a reality via: training teachers; transforming students into active agents of their training; promoting socio-educational research into problems as could be the case of early school drop-out and repeating; and ensuring its contribution to the design of State policies in the field of education. Every higher education policy must be comprehensive and must address and take into due account all the components of the education system. Most specifically, it must do so under the umbrella of an 'education for all', as set forth in the Conference of Jomtien (Thailand, 1990) - at a world scale-and in the Main education project for Latin America and the Caribbean - at a regional level.

11. Higher education institutions of our region must instil in their graduates the awareness that they really belong to the community of Latin American and Caribbean nations. Hence, they must promote processes aimed at regional integration. Furthermore, cultural and educational integration should be the bases for political and economic integration. Faced with the formation of new economic spaces within the current framework of globalisation and regionalisation, higher education institutions must address their studies of Latin American integration in the light of their economic, social, cultural, ecological and

political aspects, among others. This will be their main task and they should address the problems with an interdisciplinary approach.

12. Founded on the Regional convention and the international recommendation on validation of studies, degrees and diplomas, there is a need to encourage academic and professional mobility. The purpose is no other than that of favouring the process of economic, educational, political and cultural integration of the region.

13. Both the transfer and the exchange of experiences between higher education institutions - key elements of the UNITWIN/UNESCO Chairs programme - are indispensable for promoting knowledge and ensuring that the latter is applied to encourage development. Interuniversity co-operation can be further facilitated by the constant progress evidenced in the field of information and communication technologies. In turn, it can be strengthened by the current economic and political integration processes, as well as by the growing need for a real inter-cultural understanding.

14. The considerable expansion of different types of networks and other instruments and mechanisms for linking up institutions, professors and students is a key issue in the collective search for equity, quality and relevance in higher education. This is specifically the case now, when no institution can hope to master all the areas of knowledge.

15. Public support for higher education is still indispensable. The challenges face by higher education are also challenges for society as a whole. They include governments, the production sector, the labour world, the organised civil society, academic associations, along with regional and international organisations that are responsible for the training, research, development or financing programmes.

16. On account of all the considerations above, all the social players must combine efforts and start acting so as to foster the process of in-depth transformation of higher education. To this end, they must be based on a new 'social consensus' that enables higher education institutions to be better positioned and thus

have respond to current and future needs for a sustainable human development in the immediate future, this aspiration will gradually turn more concrete, as the action plan designed in this Conference will be executed.

PLAN OF ACTION FOR THE TRANSFORMATION OF HIGHER EDUCATION IN LATIN AMERICA AND THE CARIBBEAN

Introduction

Any attempt to transform the Latin American and Caribbean higher education systems and institutions (HEIs) must take into account the fact that due to their origins, history, location and fundamental objectives, they present a great diversity which must be recognised and dealt with. Hence, the institutions require particular strategies in accordance with their stage of development and their future goals. Consequently, the process furthered by UNESCO since 1994 through its Regional Centre for Higher Education in Latin America and the Caribbean (CRESALC) has focused on the promotion of comparative research, the provision of spaces of dialogue, reflection and debate among the principal actors of higher education in Latin America and the Caribbean, and the gradual achievement of a consensus as regards strategic guidelines and regional objectives which can help the institutions in the management of their particular transformation.

Among the activities carried out by UNESCO particularly worthy of note is the Regional Conference on Policies and Strategies for the Transformation of Higher Education in Latin America and the Caribbean, held in Havana, Cuba, in November 1996. In its preparatory phase over 4,000 persons connected with higher education and government of the region were mobilised, by holding 36 meetings at the national and subregional level. The wealth of documents generated both by the preparatory seminars and by the Conference itself, which was attended by 688 individuals, constitutes the most important source of information available on the problems, challenges and possibilities of higher education in Latin America and the Caribbean today.

The principal documents stemming from that Conference - the 'Final Report', the 'Declaration on higher education in Latin America and the Caribbean' and the 'Guide for the formulation of a Plan of Action'- emphasise and discuss the nature of higher education as a social asset; highlighting its nature as on instrument which is 'irreplaceable for human development, production, economic growth, the strengthening of cultural identity the maintenance of social cohesion, the struggle against poverty and the promotion of a culture of peace'; and assume most of the principles defended by UNESCO in its 'Policy Paper for Change and Development in Higher Education' (1995) and in the General Introduction to the Regional Conference drafted by CRESALC (1996).

The participants in the Regional Conference requested CRESALC to prepare a Plan of Action for the transformation of higher education in the region, which must include common aspects of the national plans and promote inter-institutional interaction and collaboration at the regional and subregional level. The Plan of Action must serve as on instrument of facilitation and catalysis which can bring together in a coherent way the studies and experiences carried out in the HEIs of Latin America and the Caribbean.

The document presented here is the result of a process of consultation and concerted action which CRESALC launched to fulfil that mission. It incorporates the recommendations of the Regional Conference of Havana and contains the input of several workshops held after said Conference, which were attended by government officials responsible for higher education policies, experts in this field and representatives of the non-governmental organisations (NGOs) of the region. It also received the contribution of the professionals of CRESALC and of the UNESCO-Caracas Office, the Director of the Department of Higher Education of UNESCO and the members of the Advisory Group of CRESALC.

Its basic purpose is to outline guidelines which can help to integrate the multiple activities carried out in the region and promote co-operation between institutions in order to increase their efficacy and efficiency, avoid unnecessary duplication of efforts and raise new financial resources. Likewise, the assistance of the various actors and institutions is sought for furthering the changes to meet the challenges posed by adjustment policies, the opening of the economies, the globalisation and regionalisation processes, increasing poverty; human migrations, vulnerability of democracies, and the collapse of ethical values, which appear as distinctive signs of the end of the millennium in the region.

In order that this be feasible, it is necessary to achieve the operative and concerted action of governments, parliaments, HEIs and their constituencies, the majority of social actors (workers, entrepreneurs, NGOs) and international organisations interested in improving the capacity of the societies of the region to cope with the aforementioned challenges. The Member States of UNESCO, through their governments and parliaments, with the active participation of the HEIs and within the framework of the new dialogue which we propose, must help to formulate and strengthen educational projects aimed at coping with the needs and challenges identified in their respective countries, ensuring the necessary human, material and financial resources for their uninterrupted execution.

Higher education needs to be considered as an integrated system, comprising various sub-systems in constant interaction. Among these, one has to acknowledge the existence of a constellation of university institutions and other HEIs (technological institutes, polytechnic schools, institutes of high studies, technical-professional centres, institutes for the training of teachers, etc.). Each institution must define its mission in harmony with the objectives of sustainable human development, and fulfil its substantive functions using the available resources as efficiently as possible. At the same time, it must provide students with a professional training with a sound ethical and general basis.

It is expected that this Plan will also help to orient action on the part of the international co-operation in order to strengthen the regions capacity to understand and overcome the principal problems of higher education.

I. Fundamental Aspects

Latin American and Caribbean countries are undergoing rapid processes of change which have led to important modifications in their political, economic and social structures. Extraordinary advances are taking place today in terms of technological, scientific and productive capacity, but at the same time, profound inequalities are observed in the levels of progress and development in the various regions of the world.

An international context marked by what has been called globalisation has given rise to both opportunities and difficulties for Latin American and Caribbean countries. In the past few years they managed to improve their economic growth rates, control inflation, achieve a certain monetary stability, adjust their fiscal accounts and establish democratic regimes. But on the whole, they were unable to occupy a larger space in international trade, nor were they able to achieve a significant reduction of the persistent levels of poverty and social inequality. Hence new strategies are sought today to cope with the challenge of a really sustainable and socially equitable economic development in which priority is assigned to the maximisation of the capacities of all human beings.

The region is not alone in this quest, for the benefits of development seem to be concentrated more and more in a limited sector of the world's population, and profound and growing gaps are witnessed in terms of the standard of living and access to the economic and cultural assets between the different social strata, both in the industrialised and the developing countries.

HEIs can be of the utmost importance for the achievement of a new strategy of economic and social development. There is a broad consensus that the future of countries will depend to a large extent on their capacity to maximise the generation of new knowledge. The capacity to create, adapt and adopt new technologies constitutes a strategic element for the achievement of greater collective well being, as well as increased competitiveness of the region and the improvement of its possibilities of insertion in the world economy. Hence the expectations to which universities, technical and professional institutes and other tertiary institutions are subject today require the redefinition of policies, plans, programmes, guidelines, curricula, management capacity and, above all, a commitment to innovation and profound broad-scope transformation.

Knowledge-generated mainly from academic spaces - and technological/productive innovation are of fundamental importance for the achievement of a new stage of economic development, productivity and competitiveness. In order to achieve a better integration between the programmes of higher education and those of science and technology, both in research and in the transfer of knowledge, it will be necessary to reorganise academic and scientific research structures in all areas and at all levels and eliminate the present isolation and fragmentation. It will also be indispensable to allow for scholarly exchange between disciplines and link the projects of transformation of higher education to the needs of the whole society, including those of the social and private productive apparatus. Likewise, the series of demands and needs arising in the region will call for a true reappraisal by the HEIs of the institutional contents, methods and forms, enabling greater flexibility and capacity to respond to the challenges of regional and subregional integration, and to the overgrowing higher education demand.

It is also necessary to reappraise the dialogue between the State and the HEIs, particularly universities, in terms of the emergence of other important actors and of processes which impair excellence in higher education. Only a consensual strategy, in which each entity commits resources and efforts, will enable the necessary transformations. The transformation is more likely to be successful. If it is generated from within the HEIs themselves than if it is imposed or simplistically based on alien institutional models. The challenge lies in the reinvention of institutions in order that they satisfy the demand and deficiencies of Latin American and Caribbean societies, preserving the wealth of traditions, the cultural values and the great diversity and creativeness of their people.

It is important to emphasise that the debate on the transformation of higher education requires a framework, conditions and guarantees, as well as a creative and plural environment to share ideas and reach a consensus as regards strategies of change. In this respect, responsible autonomy is a necessary condition which must be ensured and increased. This condition requires an adequate level of financing by the State, enabling, as a counterpart, the fulfillment of the purposes and objectives of each institution. Within this framework, access to a higher education of quality and its permanence must be ensured for meritorious individuals coming from the less privileged social sectors; In this way the HEIs would be contributing to the achievement of greater social equity. To achieve these objectives remedial or adequate policies could be required to correct the eventual deficiencies of certain social groups.

II. Conception And Objectives

This Plan provides a frame of reference for varies types of actions and is aimed at achieving general objectives common to the region. Five major programmes are suggested here, defined on the basis of the main subjects studies in the Havana Regional Conference on Higher Education.

For each Programme, general and specific objectives are identified and principal lines of action are suggested which will enable the development of specific projects by the HEIs, NGOs, international organisations, and governments - key actors in the process of transformation - which will be responsible for taking these proposals to a more specific and operational level.

The objectives and strategic lines of action contained in this Plan will be inserted in the preparations, discussions and follow-up of the World Conference on Higher Education, convened by UNESCO for the month of October 1998.

A. General objective

To achieve a profound transformation of higher education in Latin America and the Caribbean, in order that it become an effective promoter of a culture of peace, based on a sustainable human development founded on justice, equity, democracy and liberty, improving, at the same time, the relevance and quality of its teaching, research and extension, functions, offering equal opportunities to all by means of a permanent education without frontiers, in which merit is the basic criterion for access, within the framework of a new regional and international co-operation.

B. Specific objectives

1. To generate the bases and conditions for the higher education of the region, in these times of cultural, economic, political and social changes, to assume a leading role in the critical analysis of those changes and in the effort of prevision and even conduction, by means of the creation and transmission of relevant knowledge, assigning, this end, priority to its own transformation and development.

2. To contribute to the transformation and improvement of the conceptions, methodology and practices related to: (i) the social relevance of higher education; (ii) quality, evaluation and accreditation; (iii) management and financing; (iv) the knowledge and use of the new information and communication technologies, and (v) international co-operation, at the institutional, national, subregional and regional level, in all the functions, and areas of activity of higher education.

III. Programmes

In accordance with its specific objectives, the Plan, as a general framework of operational reference, must implement the following programmes progressively:

A. Improvement of relevance.

B. Improvement of quality.

C. Improvement of management and financing.

D. Academic management of the new information and communication technologies.

E. Reorientation of international co-operation.

This set of programmes takes fully into account the fact that the 'Declaration on Higher Education in Latin America and the Caribbean' (Havana, November 1996) stipulated the following: 'All the social actors must unite their efforts and undertake the process of profound transformations of higher education, based on the establishment of a new 'social consensus' which places the HEIs in a better position to respond to the present and future needs of sustainable human. Development, which process would at once begin with the implementation of the Plan of Action conceived in this Conference'. The next meetings to be held in the Caribbean sub-region will in all likelihood serve to further enrich the programme proposed in this document.

The following description is based on the proposals contained in the 'Guide for the formulation of a Plan of Action' (Havana, November 1996), those stemming from the Consultation Meeting with the Non-governmental Higher Education Organisations of Latin America and the Caribbean (Caracas, April 1997) and the workshop of experts convened by CRESALC on 28 and 29 January 1998, specifically to discus the preliminary version of the Plan and polish it. Furthermore, the developments in the region in the field of higher education in the period between the Regional Conference (November 1996) and the drafting of the present Plan of Action (February 1998) were taken into account. Evidently, many of the strategic guidelines to which priority has been assigned in this Plan for a programme can overlap with those of other programmes. The intention is, precisely, to stimulate initiatives which have a greater capacity to disseminate and create systemic synergy in favour of an integrated process of transformation.

These programmes will serve as frameworks of action for each of the agents interested in the transformation of higher education in the region to identify the respective projects.

A. *Programme of improvement of relevance*

According to the contents of the Policy Paper for Change and Development in Higher Education (UNESCO, 1995), 'Relevance is considered particularly in terms of the role of higher educational as a system and of each of its institutions towards society, as well as in terms of the latter's expectations with regard to higher education'. The relevance of higher education refers to the capacity of the educational systems and of the institutions to respond to the needs of their locality, region or country and to the demands of the new world order, with diverse outlooks, instruments and modalities. In this plan of action the institutions are called upon to make the necessary changes to ensure greater relevance of higher education.

1. General objectives

To guarantee that education in general, and higher education in particular, will be essential, instruments, of strategic value, to cope successfully with the challenges of the modern world and to form citizens capable of building a fairer and more open society based on solidarity, the respect of human rights and the shared use of knowledge and information.

To ensure that higher education will constitute an effective, and at the same time an irreplaceable element for social development, production and economic growth, and for the strengthening of cultural identity,, the maintenance of social cohesion, the struggle against poverty and the promotion of a culture of peace.

2. Specific objectives

In order to achieve these aims, projects and activities will have to be designed and implemented which will lead to the achievement of the following specific objectives:

To guarantee that higher education institutions can become or be consolidated as plural and free entities which, in accordance with the respective national legal systems, enjoy full autonomy, and which, deeply aware of their responsibility, show an unwaivable will to serve in the search for solutions to the demands, needs and deficiencies of the society; to which they must account, as a necessary condition for the full exercise of autonomy.

To facilitate the capacity of the higher education institutions for critical, anticipatory, and prospective analysis, enabling them to cope, from. a long-term. horizon, with the challenges of a reality subject to rapid and continuous transformation.

To make changes in the organisational structures and in the educational strategies in order to achieve a high degree of renovation and flexibility in the curricular offer, teaching programmes and methods, providing students with a permanent education of excellence, borderline research, the spirit of investigation, intellectual creation and integral training.

To include the region's higher education institutions to take up the challenge of participating resolutely in the qualitative improvement of the educational system at all levels, resorting, among other measures, to the training of teachers; the transformation of students into active agents of their own training; the promotion of socio-educational research, and the contribution to the formulation of State policies in the educational field.

To help higher education institutions to stimulate in their graduates an awareness of belonging to the community of Latin American and Caribbean nations, promoting the processes which lead to regional integration, and making cultural and educational integration a founding block of political and economic integration.

To promote research and interdisciplinary studies on the processes of globalisation, regionalisation, Latin American and Caribbean integration in their economic, social, cultural, ecological and political aspects, as the basis of programmes of inter-institutional co-operation and collaboration at the regional level.

3. Strategic line of action

To promote studies, provide permanent follow-up and propose a solution to the problem of access and drop-out on the part of the poorer sectors.

To design instruments to increase the linkage between pre-school, elementary and secondary education and higher education, and between, the different sub-systems.

To promote innovations in the teaching systems, the programmes and curricula, enabling the active participation, personal transformation and full development of the potential of each student.

To stimulate research and the exchange of experiences related to educational innovations, enabling the accumulation and evaluation of experiences.

To implement new study programmes which in the medium term ensure a universal post-secondary education of quality. It is proposed that short careers be designed which increase the possibilities of insertion in the labour market and which, with a view to updating skills education, enable the continuity of studies.

To encourage the creation of postgraduate courses, programmes of non-formal education and updating courses which make lifelong education a reality.

To design plans for the dissemination of results and experiences of the HEIs, showing clearly the social and economic benefits which they contribute, for the purpose of facilitating their evaluation by society and promoting support from new social actors.

B. Programme of improvement of quality

According to the aforementioned UNESCO Policy Paper (1995), 'quality embraces all its main functions and activities: quality of teaching, training and research, which means the quality of its staff and programmes and quality of learning as a corollary of teaching and research.... the search for quality... It therefore also implies attention to questions pertaining to the quality of students and of the infrastructures and academic environment.. Finally it is essential to indicate that the principal objective of 'quality assessment' is to achieve institutional as well as system-wide improvement'.

1. General objective

To guarantee the complete and prompt adaptation of higher education to what it must be, bearing in mind that the quality of higher education is a multidimensional concept, which includes universal and particular characteristics related to the nature of the institutions and of knowledge, and to the problems which arise with regard to the different social contexts within the framework of national, regional and local priorities.

2. Specific objective

In order to achieve this general objective, projects and activities will have to be designed and implemented enabling the achievement of the following specific objectives:

To ensure that the quality of the systems, institutions and programmes of higher education is essentially linked to social relevance, to the preparation and commitment of professors and researchers, to the social responsibility involved in the work of the institutions, and to their accountability vis-à-vis the society with regard to their global performance.

To identify mechanisms to ensure that higher education recovers its roots as an indomitable patrimony, in a globalised world in which the mass media affect the national, subregional and regional cultural identities.

To initiate forms of interconnection between higher education and the other subsystems, in order that they cope jointly with their problems and to collaborate in the design and implementation of solutions, in the understanding that the quality of higher education is, moreover, contingent upon the rest of the educational system with which it interacts.

To construct the quality of teaching fundamentally on the basis of the improvement of academic training and an integrated training in the design and development of curricula, in order to provide creative, thoughtful, polyfunctional and enterprising graduates, within the framework of systems of advanced, continuous, open and critical training, in which the students assume their role as active subjects, actors of their own learning, and managers of their life project.

To further the consolidation of common multinational academic spaces for the development of subregional or regional postgraduate studies, the implementation of co-operative research, and the edition of joint publications.

To achieve a culture of evaluation of performance which, by means of different strategies ranging from self-evaluation and self-regulation to state accreditation, will enable the systems and institutions to achieve their fundamental objectives and strengthen responsible autonomy.

To promote the creation of mechanisms enabling, on the one hand, the financing of the costs of evaluations and, on the other hand, the allocation of the necessary resources to solve the problems detected in the feasible projects presented by the institutions themselves as a result of evaluation.

To obtain, in the short, medium and long term, an improvement of the educational service by assimilating the technologies of computer science, telematics and distance education and by placing the merits of the teaching activity on the same footing as those of research and extension.

3. Strategic lines of action

To promote regional postgraduate studies, in particular around issues of strategic value to the region.

To facilitate the exchange of students and the insertion of graduates of different specialities in the labour market, based on the results of the accreditation experiences of each country.

To promote integral plans for the training of teachers and researchers, ensuring their full dedication to academic life and institutional development.

To make a great effort to introduce the culture of evaluation, ensuring the most extensive participation of the academic community and the dissemination of results in order to reflect, and guide the institutional policies, and to guarantee the fulfilment of objectives and goals of each institutional programme.

To maintain the principle of voluntary support of the process of evaluation in the institutions which enjoy autonomy.

To promote evaluations of a formative nature, both in the institutional aspect and in the tasks performed by students and teachers, in order to improve the quality of their academic performance.

To consider the international aspect in the processes of evaluation, taking into account the needs and possibilities of co-operation between institutions.

To create mechanisms for financing cots of evaluations and to overcome the deficiencies identified, in the event that such deficiencies exit.

To increase the use of the new technologies of computer science for innovation and pedagogic experimentation and the strengthening of access to information and documentation resources.

C. Programme of improvement of management and financing

In order to achieve the objectives of relevance, quality and equity of this Plan of Action, a significant improvement of the managerial capacity and the level of financing of the HEIs will be required, within the framework of a joint effort on the part of the whole society. At present, the management of an HEI, particularly that of the most complex ones, encompasses not only the administrative aspect, but also the governmental and academic aspects. Since the investment in education in the region is below the level agreed upon by governments themselves, and in view of the current requirements of an education of excellence, measures must be taken to increase the level of resources, diversify their origin, achieve a better distribution among institutions, and increase the efficiency of expenditures.

1. General objectives

Bearing in mind the unavoidable responsibility of the State in the financing of public higher education, to contribute to the improvement and transformation of management capacity of higher education by means of the adoption of appropriate policies and the diversification of its sources of financing. Strategies to this end are needed in all areas and levels of activity, supported by research on higher education.

To develop strategies aimed at stressing the importance of higher education as a key sector for the economic and social development of Latin America and the Caribbean, helping higher education institutions to obtain official support in the quest for sources in addition to public financing and achieving greater flexibility in the use of public funds in accordance with the objectives of the respective allocations.

To produce the necessary orientations for the strategic and anticipatory management of higher education institutions to help the system fully identify the current changes and future trends and adapt to the speed with which the phenomena occur in different areas.

2. Specific objectives

To promote comparative studies and research on management and financing of higher education experiences at the national, subregional and regional level, in order that the institutions establish and finalise explicit policies in this field.

To favour the formulation of models of allocation of resources which take into account specific objectives such as quality, equity and balanced regional development from the point of view of the actors of the programmes of higher education and to validate their use in negotiations with multilateral development and financing organisations and with national financial institutions.

To design and propose new systems of financing of the HEIs via the national financial institutions.

To formulate new models of management of systems, institutions and financial resources for higher education in the region and establish a permanent action of formation and intensive training of directors and administrators to contribute to the adoption of flexible and transparent management practices.

To ensure that the new models of academic management combine research and postgraduate activities with undergraduate ones, in order to facilitate social integration, extension and transfer of knowledge.

3. Strategic lines of action

To favour a State policy for the distribution of incremental resources based on specific programmes or projects presented by the institutions which can be financed, bearing in mind the need to ensure transparency in the allocation, control, verification, and dissemination of results.

To achieve commitment on the part of the State to pluri-annual programmes of financing of higher education, ensuring the fulfillment of goals and objectives.

To identify, in accordance with the respective national legislation, possible complementary sources of funding, which can be obtained by means of new taxes, incentives to donations to the HEIs or taxation of certain financial transactions. The institutions themselves must carry out studies and research to quantify the potentiality and viability of these proposals.

To promote by adequate means the marketing of the products, services and technological developments generated by the HEIs, protecting intellectual property and collaborating in the management of patents and certificates.

To design flexible systems to facilitate collaboration and the sale of the services of HEIs to public and private organisations in projects destined to overcome needs, deficiencies and demands of the society.

To promote an efficient management of national and international co-operation in order to take better advantage of operating capacities.

To further new mechanisms of student scholarships and/or loans, particularly to poor ones, in order to facilitate their academic performance.

To favour the creation of various types of incentives to reward excellence and productivity of both teachers and officials.

To introduce new administrative techniques which increase rationality in decision-making, including the preparation of budgets, allocation of resources and the implementation practices, in order to increase the transparency and control of management. To develop training programmes and monitoring to that end.

To promote flexible administrative entities in order to ensure the concept of lifelong education, in programmes of non-formal education, training, re-skilling of workers, teaching of adults, and co-operation with trade unions, among others.

D. Programme of academic management of new information and communication technologies

The new telematic technologies are opening up extraordinary possibilities for higher education but they also raise serious questions regarding the very functioning of the institutions. The possibilities of immediate interaction and exposure to vast sources of information which they open, necessarily modify the inputs, processes, and products of higher education as we have known them. Hence it is essential that a perfect understanding be achieved of how the region can use, generate and adapt the new technologies to improve the quality, relevance of, and access to higher education without running the risk of generating an even greater difference between social sectors and between countries, in terms of the capacity to handle these new tools.

1. General objectives

To produce pertinent policies and strategies to base the social and economic development of the countries on, among other factors, knowledge and use of the new information and communication technologies (NICT).

To induce the region to make the necessary investments for an adequate infrastructure of telecommunications and teleinformatics, enabling flexible and cheap connections to the global networks for the HEIs, favouring access to INTERNET, and the promotion of INTRANETS.

To achieve the integration of the new technologies by the HEIs in all the areas of their work.

2 Specific objectives

To formulate polices which assert the right to information and communication as a central element of an education for all, without exclusions.

To achieve the development of a Latin American network for higher education and the consolidation of the national university networks.

To strengthen a culture of exchange, collaboration and academic work by means of electronic networks and to succeed in having these serve as a vehicle to disseminate the cultural values of Latin America and the Caribbean.

To moderise higher education in all its aspects-contents, methodology, management, and administration- by the rational use of the NICTs. Likewise, that the HEIs consider these new technologies as an object of study, research and development.

3. Strategic lines of action

To establish national and regional systems of information, with data bases and statistics regarding the priority areas of common academic interest, taking into account especially the particular needs of the Caribbean region.

To organise presential and virtual training for teachers, researchers, students, and administrators, in order to ensure the full utilisation of the NICTs in higher education.

To explore the creation of postgraduate studies of excellence on priority subjects by means of collaborative consortia among institutions of the region, making use of the possibilities offered by work in networks and distance education.

To further the creation, via the NICTs, of HEI consortia in the region for major research projects which require resources and critical mass beyond the capacities of one single institution.

To promote the creation of centres of excellence in the production of multimedia for teaching activities, information services and the preservation and dissemination of the Caribbean and Latin American cultural patrimony.

To strengthen the academic networks and other mechanisms of liaison between institutions, professors, and students, since few institutions can dominate all the areas of knowledge, for the collective quest for equity, quality and relevance for higher education.

To identify the centres of excellence in NICT, stimulate their work through a network, and help to disseminate their experiences.

E. Programme of international co-operation

International co-operation has been an important mainstay of the Latin American and Caribbean HEIs. Nevertheless, it has also served sometimes to support foreign models of generation of knowledge, curricular construction, views, methodology and work styles. On the other hand, there has been an evident flow of financial resources from the South to the North and, in many cases, instead of contributing significantly to the strengthening of the systems of education and of science and technology of the region, the co-operation has brought about an important and sustained emigration of professionals and scientists with high levels of academic training from the region to the industrialised countries. In this new historical context, it is important to promote relations of mutual learning and greater horizontality. Many institutions of the region have accumulated valuable experiences which can be transferred to other institutions via new systems of international co-operation, seeking to reduce the existing asymmetries.

1. General objectives

To redirect international co-operation to the strengthening and maximisation of the intellectual, cultural, scientific, technological, humanistic and social capacities of the region by means of the development of higher education and science and technology.

To overcome the existing asymmetries, within a new framework of collaboration, assigning priority to a logic of solidary integration which overcomes the differences and leads to work in priority areas with shared resources and proactive horizontal structures enabling the launching of innovative programmes of research, teaching and social projection.

2. Specific objectives

To ensure that inter-institutional co-operation is facilitated by the constant progress of the information and communication technologies and strengthened by he current processes of economic and political integration, and by the growing need for intercultural understanding.

To ensure the transfer and exchange of information and experiences between HEIs - essential elements of the UNITWIN/UNESCO Chairs - in order to promote knowledge in favour of sustainable human development in the countries of the region.

To ensure support of governments, HEIs, NGOs connected with postsecondary education, and the Latin American and Caribbean inter-university networks, to the UNESCO International Institute of Higher education for Latin America and the Caribbean which is being established.

To stimulate academic and professional mobility in favour of the economic, educational, political and cultural integration of Latin America and the Caribbean, based on the Regional Agreement and the International Recommendation on the accreditation of studies, degrees and diplomas.

To increase the presence of higher education within the framework of UNESCO's activities in the region and strengthen the links in this field between Latin America and the Caribbean.

To promote the learning and use of the different languages of the region in order to, improve the quality of academic and cultural exchange.

3. Strategic lines of action

To design a system whereby information regarding the total operating capacity of human, scientific and managerial resources in the Latin American and Caribbean HEIs is easily available, which can serve as a basis of programmes of regional inter-institutional co-operation, and to keep it permanently up to date.

To strengthen the entities of exchange of information and experiences between HEIs in terms of the ideal of regional integration.

To extend and help to consolidate the work of the networks of horizontal co-operation in higher education already existing in the region, as well as that of others which may emerge, and to promote exchange between them and other regions of the world.

To facilitate academic mobility (teachers, researchers and students), emphasising the recognition of partial studies, degrees, diplomas, based on flexible mechanisms of accreditation.

To favour the launching of specific horizontal co-operation projects and the signing of agreements enabling better use of the physical resources and the human capital.

To create postgraduate networks enabling the training of teaching and scientific personnel in the HEIs which do not have this type of infrastructure and the reformulation of shared programmes recognised at the regional level.

To form new university networks like the AUGM in other subregions as soon as possible, and a programmes of scientific and technological academic strengthening by launching megaprojects like those of the European Union.

To prepare personnel specialised in the management of horizontal co-operation with the support of international organisations and experts.

To make rational use of the financial resources available in development agencies and organisations, and in the HEIs themselves.

To create in CRESALC a focal point for the Caribbean community with a view to an advantageous integration of Latin America and the Caribbean.

To promote and sustain a programme of development of skills in the use of the languages of the region within the higher education communities, both academic and institutional.

In the course of the different stages of the process of consultation which resulted in this plan of Action, the eminent persons who took part in it, members of both the academic and the governmental domain, deemed it advisable to recommend that CRESALC, as a regional centre of UNESCO, adopt this Plan of Action and that it dedicate all its experience, capacity, creativity and commitment to the progress of higher education to the fulfilment of the objectives and strategic lines of action set forth in this document, making it an instrument for the guiding of its own activity and the orientation of co-operation with the governments and with HEIs in the Latin American and Caribbean region.

Reference

1. Regional Conference on Policies and Strategies for the Transformation of Higher Education in Latin America and the Caribbean, Havana, Cuba, 18-22 November 1996.

BUREAU OF THE CONFERENCE

President.
Mr André Sonko (Senegal)

Vice-president and Rapporteur General
Ms Suzy Halimi (France)

Vice-presidents
Mr Andrei Marga (Romania)
Mr Fernando Vecino Alegret (Cuba)
Mr Yu Fuzeng (China)
Mr Khalid M. Al-Ankary (Saudi Arabia)

Drafting Group
President of the Drafting Group and Rapporteur General
Ms Suzy Halimi (France)

Members
Algeria (Mr Mohamed Adel Samet)
Australia (Ms Shelagh Whittleston)
Belarus (Mr Alexandre Kozulin/ Dr Michael Dziamchuk
Chile (Mr Raúl Allard)
Costa Rica (Mr Gabriel Macaya)
Democratic Republic of the Congo (Prof. Mutambue-Shango)
Germany (Dr Werner V. Trutzschler)
Italy (Ms Antonella Cammisa/ Mr Giovanni Puglisi)
Japan (Mr Wataru Iwamoto)
Nigeria (Prof. Munzali Jibril)
Saudi Arabia (Prof. Mohammad Sh. Khateeb)
Slovakia (Prof. Ludovit Molnar)
Syrian Arab Republic (Ms Nabila Chaalan/Dr. Mohamed A. Hourieh
Education International (Ms Monique Fouilhoux)
International Association of Universities
(Ms Eva Egron-Polak)

Assistance to Drafting Group
President of the Advisory Group
Prof. Georges Haddad
Members of Regional groups
Africa: Mr Ah Lamine Ndiaya
Arab States: Mr I. Abu-Lughod
Asia and the Pacific: Mr Grant Harman
Europe: Mr John Davies
Latin America and the Caribbean: Mr Jorge Brovetto

Secretary General of the Conference
Mr Colin N. Power, Deputy Director-General for Education

Assistants
Mr Marco Antonio R. Dias, Director, Division of Higher Education
Prof. Jean-Marie De Ketele

Speeches/Lectures (in order of delivery)

Mr Eduardo Portella, President of the General Conference of UNESCO

Mr Pál Pataki, Chairperson of UNESCO's Executive Board

Mr Federico Mayor, Director-General of UNESCO

H.R.H. Prince Talal Bin Abdul Aziz Al Saud,

President of the Arab Gulf Programme for United Nations Development Organisations (AGFUND)

M. Lionel Jospin, Prime Minister of the French Republic

H.E. Mr Olli-pekka Heinonen, Minister of Education of Finland

H.E. Ms Chen Zhi Li, Minister of Education of the People's Republic of China

Mr Ricardo Díez-Hochleitner, President of the Club of Rome

Ms Céline Saint-Pierre, President of the Conseil supérieur de l'éducation, Gouvernement du Québec, Canada

Mr Jorge Brovetto, Rector, Universidad de la Republica, and Executive Secretary of the Montevideo Group of Universities (AUGM)

Ms Kathrine Vangen, National Unions of Students in Europe

Mr Wataru Mori, President of the International Association of Universities

Mr Donald Gerth, President of the International Association of University Presidents

Mr Hans Van Ginkel, Rector of the United Nations University

Mr Claire Jourdan, 1998 President of the International Conference of NGOs

ADVISORY GROUP ON HIGHER EDUCATION*

For UNESCO

Federico Mayor
Director-General

Colin N. Power
Deputy Director-General for Education,
Secretary-General for Education,
Secretary-General of the World Conference on Higher Education

Executive Secretariat of the Steering Committee: Division of Higher Education

Professor Marco Antonio R. Dias
Director

Members of the Advisory group on higher education

Professor Georges Haddad
Chairman
Honorary President, University of Paris 1, Panthéon-Sorbonne

Professor Ibrahim Abu Lughod
Professor of Political Science
Vice-President of Birzeit University (1993-1995),
Palestinian Authority

Professor Jorge Brovetto
President of the Unión de Universidades de America Latina (UDUAL) and of the Montevideo Group of Universities, Uruguay

Professor Donald Gerth
President, International Association of University Presidents (IAUP)
President, Califormia State University at Sacramento, USA

Professor Grant Harman
Pro Vice-Chancellor (Research), University of New England, Australia

Professor Valadimir Kinelev
Former Minister of General and Professional Education of the Russion Federation

Professor Gottfried Leibbrandt
Former Chairman of CEPES Advisory Board

Professor Lydia Makhubu
Vice-Chancellor, University of Swaziland

Professor Narciso Matos
Secretary-General, Association of African Universities, Accra-North, Ghana

Professor Péter Medgyes
Former Deputy State Secretary, Ministry of Culture and Education, Hungary

Professor Yasunori Nishijima
Former Chairman, Japanese National Commission for UNESCO

Professor Eunice Ribeiro Durham
University of Sao Paulo, Brazil

Professor José Sarukhán Kermez
Former Rector, National Autonomous University of Mexico (UNAM)

Professor M.D. Charas Suwanwela
Former President and Adviser, Chulalongkom University, Thailand

Professor Marisa Tejedor Salguero
Former Rector, University of La Laguna, Tenerife, Canaries, Spain

Professor Justin Thorens
Honorary President, International Association of Universities

H.E. Mr Bakary Tio-Touré
Ambassador Extraordinary and Plenipotentiary, Permanent Delegate of Côte d'Ivoire to UNESCO

Professor Carlos Tunnermann Bernheim
Chairman of CRESALC Advisory Group

Professor Hans van Ginkel
Rector, United Nations University, Japan

With the collaboration of

Professor Heitor Gurgulino de Souza
Former Rector, United Nations University, Japan

Professor Alfonso Borrero Cabal
Former Executive Director of the Colombian Association of Universities

---

* *Italic indicates members of the Steering Committee.*

GROUP I

ETATS PARTICIPANTS
PARTICIPATING STATES

AFRIOUE DU SUD/ SOUTH AFRICA

H.E. Porf. Sibusiso Bengu
Minister of Education
(Head of Delegation)

Ms Nasima Badsha
Deputy Director-General
Department of Education

Prof. Wiseman Nkuhlu
Chairman
Council on Higher Education

Dr Teboho Audrey Moja
Ministerial Special Advisor
Ministry of Education

Ms Piyaushi Kotecha
Chief Excecutive Officer
South African Universities

Mr Brian Figanji
Vice Chancellor
Peninsula Technikon/CTP

Mr Basil May
Executive Director
Committee of College of Education
Rectors of South Africa
(CCERSA)

Mr Tshilidzi Ratshitanga
Secretary General
South African Students Congress

Dr Bothale Tema
Secretary-General
South African National
Commission for UNESCO

Associate Professor M. Saleem
Badat
Director
Education Policy Unit-University of
Western Cape

Permanent Delegation of South
Africa to UNESCO

H.E. Mrs Barbara Masekela
Ambassador Extraordinary and
Plenipotentiary of South Africa in
France
Perianent Delegate to UNESCO

Ms Natalie Africa
Deputy Permanent Delegate of
South Africa to UNESCO

Mr Devandhran Moodley
Third Secretary

ALBANIE/ALBANIA

S. Exc. M. Et'them Ruka
Ministre de l'éducation et de la science
(Chef de la délégation)

S. Exc. M. Jusúf Vrioni
Ambassadeur
Delégué permanent de l'Albanie
auprés de l'UNESCO

M. Edmond Hajdëri
Directeur de Département de
l'enseignement supérieur
Ministére de l'éducation et de la
science

ALGERIE/ALGERIA

S. Exc. M. Amar Tou
Ministre de l'enseignement
supérieur et de la recherche
Scientifique
(chef de la délégation)

S. Exc. M. Mohamed Ghoualmi
Ambassadeur Extraordinaire et
plénipotentiaire d'Algérie en France
Délégué permanent auprés de
l'UNESO
(Chef adjoint de la délégation)

Mme Faouzia Boumaiza
Délégué permanent adjoint

M. Mohamed-Adel Samet
Conseiller auprés de la Délégation
permanente

M. Mokhtar Attar
Conseiller culturel
Ambassade d'Algérie en France

Mme Naziha Kersri
Professeur de physique USTHB
(Alger)

M. Arezki Amokrane
Professeur de physique USTHB
(Alger)

M. Abdelhamid Mira
Professeur en médecine

M. Hamid Kherbachi
Professeur en sciences économiques

M. Ahmed Bouyacoub
Professeur en sciences économiques

M. Elhaoues Messaoudi
Professeur en linguistique

M. Hafid Aourag
Professeur en sciences physiques

M. Ibrahim Mahfoud
Directeur du Protocole

ALLEMAGNE/GERMANY

H.E. Mr Helmut Schafer
Minister of State
Federal Foreign Office
(Head of Delegation)

H.E. Mrs Gabriele Behler
Minister for Schools, further
Education, Science and Research
of North-Rhine/Westphalia
(Alternate Head of Delegation)

Dr Abert Spiegel
Federal Foreign Office
(Deputy Head of Delegation)

H.E. Dr Christoph Derix
Ambassador Extraordinary and
Plenipotentiary
Permanent Delegate of Germany to
UNESCO

Mrs Prof. Dr Erika Schuchardt
Member of the Federal Parliament
(Deutscher Bundestag)

Dr. Werner von Trützschler
Ministry for Culture of Thuringia

Dr Reimund Scheuermann
Federal Ministry for Education,
Science, Research and Technology

Mr Hubert Linhart
Federal Ministry for Economic Cooperation and Development

Dr Herbert Krumbein
Federal Ministry for Economic Cooperation and Development

Mr Hans-Josef Over
Federal Foreign Office

Mr Roland Thierfelder
Permanent Conference of Ministers for Culture

Prof. Dr Klaus Hüfner
President of the German Commission for UNESCO

Mrs Dr Christiane Deussen
Deputy Secretary-General
German Commission for UNESCO

ANDORRE/ANDORRA

Professeur Daniel Bastida Obiols
coordinateur
Université d'Andorre
(Chef de la délegation)

Mme Anna Insa Canet
Directrice
Ecole universitaire d'infirmerie

S. Exc. Mme Isabel Escudé
Ambassadeur extraordinaire et plénipotentiaire
Délégué permanent de la Principauté d' Andorre auprés de l'UNESCO

Melle Eva Meduiña
Délégation permanente de la Principauté d' Andorre

ANGOLA

S. Exc. M. Pinda Simào
Vice-Ministre de l'éducation pour la réforme éducative
(Chef de la délegation)

S. Exc. M. Dionisio Swindifonia
Vice-Ministre de la jeunesse et sport

S. Exc. M. Domingos Van-Dunem
Ambassadeur
Délégué permanent de l'Angola auprés de l'UNESCO
M. Manuel Teodoro Quarta
Secrétaire permanent
Commission nationale angolaise pour l'UNESCO

M. le Professeur Victor Kajibanga
Vice-Recteur
Université Agostinho Neto

Mme Manuela Sande
Directrice pour la formation et la coopération
Ministére de la science et technologie

M. Pedro Feliserto Bondo
Directeur
Institut supérieur des sciences de l'éducation

M. le Professeur Pedro Nsingui-Barros
Conseiller
Délégation permanente de l'Angola auprés de l'UNESCO

M. le Professeur Carlinhos Zassala
Secrétaire général
Syndicat des professeurs de l'enseignement supérieur

M. Lopes Raúl
Membre du secrétariat de l'union natinale des étudiants

Mme Djalma Maria da Conceicao Mala
Troisiétaire Secrétaire
Délégation permanente de l'Angola auprés de l'UNESCO

Mme Isabel Daniel Balça
Attaché
Délégation permanente de l'Angola auprés de l'UNESCO

ANTILLES NEERLANDAISES/ NETHERLANDS ANTILLES

H.E. Dr Philip A.E. Nieuw
Minister of Education
(Head of Delegation)

Dr Stanley M. Lamp
Director
Ministry of Education

Dr Roland Ch Antonius
Secretary
University of the Netherlands Antilles

Mme Dr. S. Isabella

ARABIE SAOUDITE/SAUDI ARABIA

H.E. Dr Khalid Al-Ankary
Minister of Higher Education
(Head of Delegation)

H.E. Dr. Abdullah Al-Faysal
Rector
King Saud Univesity

H.E. Dr Suhail Qadhi
Rector
Um-Al-Qura University

H.E. Dr Yousef Al-Jandan
Rector
King Faysal University

H.E. Dr Abdullah ai-Rashed
Vice Minister of Higher Education for Educational Affairs

Dr Mohammed SH. H. Al--Khateeb
Dean of the Education Faculty
King Saud University

H.E. Dr Abdulaziz S. Bin Salamah
Permanent Delegate of the Kingdom of Saudi Arabia to UNESCO

Dr Othman Y. Al-Rawaf
Faculty Member
king Saud University

Dr Abdulrahman Sulaiman Al-Trairy
Faculty Member
King Saud University

Dr Saad A.B. al-Zahrani
Faculty of Education
Um-Al-Qura University

Dr Khaled S. Al-Sultan
Acting Deputy Minister for Educational Affairs
President of the Commission on recognition of Studies, Diplomas and Degrees in Higher Education

Dr Ibrahim Moubarak Al-Juwair
Member of the Faculty of Imam Muhammad Bin Saud Islamic University
Member of the Advisory Council at the Office of H.E. the Minister of Higher Education

ARGENTINE/ARGENTINA

Excma. Sra. susana Decibe
Ministra de Cultura y Education
(Jefe de la delegación)

Lic. Eduardo Sánchez Martínez
Secretario de Estado de Politícas
Universitarias
(Jefe adjunto de la delegación)

Lic. Carlos Marquis
Director Eiecutivo
Fondo para el Mejoramiento de la
Calidad Universitaria-FOMEC

Dr Juan Pugliese
Comisión de Evaluación y
Acreditación Universitaria-
CONEAU

Dr Juan Alejandro Tobias
Presidente
Consejo de Rectores de
Universidades Privadas
(CONEAU)

Lic. José Francisco Martin
Rector
Universidad Nacional de Cuyo
(CIN)

Arq. Hugo Storero
Rector
Universidad Nacional del Litoral
(CONEAU)

Sr. Pablo Javkin
Presidente
Federación Universitaria Argentina

Ing. José Molina
Secretario General
Consejo Nacional de Docentes
Universitarios - CONADU

Sr. Hector Cesar Sauret
Secretario General
Consejo de Rectores de las
Universidades Privadas
(CRUP)

Delegación Permanente de la
República Argentina ante la
UNESCO

Excmo. Sr. Carlos A, Floria
Embajador Extraordinario y
Plenipotenciario
Delegado Permanente
Ministro María Susana Pataro
Delegado Permanente adjunto

Sr. Gustavo A. Arambarri
Secretario

AUSTRALIE/AUSTRALIA

Ms Jennifer ledgar
Assistant Secretary, National
Office Overseas Skills Recognition
(NOOSR)
Department of Employment,
Education, Training and Youth
Affairs
(Head of Delegation)

Mrs Shelagh Whittleston
Counsellor, Education
Australian Embassy
(Deputy Head of Delegation)

Prof. David Robinson
Vice Chancellor and President
Monash University

Prof. David Robinson
Vice Chancellor and President
Central Queensland University

Mr Peter Shannon
Permanent Delegate of Australia to
UNESCO

Prof. Zbys Klich
Pro Vice Chancellor
Southern Cross University

Prof. Chris Duke
Deputy Vice Chancellor and President
University of Western Sydney, Nepean

Dr Marion Myhill
Education Standing Committee
Convenor
Australian Federation of University Women

Ms Anne Siwicki
Australian Permanent Delegation to UNESCO

AUTRICHE/AUSTRIA

M. Sigurd Höllinger
Directeur général
Ministére fédéral des sciences et du transport
(Chef de la délégation)

Mme Elsa Hackl
Directeur, Ministère fédéral des sciences et du transport
(Suppléant du chef de la délégation)

Mme Eva Knollmayer
Ministère fédéral des sciences et du transport

Mme Barbara Weitgruber
Ministèr fédéral des sciences et du transport

Mme Christine Schneider
Ministère fédéral des sciences et du transport

Mme Ulrike Felt
Professeur
Université de Vienne
Mme Gerlinde Hergovich
Conférence des effictifs scientifiques et artistiques

M. Günther Schelling
Conseil sur le système des "Fachhochschulen"

M. Uwe Trummer
Syndicat d'étudiants

Mme Brigitte Winklehner
Professeur
Université de Salzourg
S. Exc. M. Tassilo F. Ogrinz
Ambassadeur extraordinaire et plénipotentiaire
Délégié permanent de l'Autriche auprés de l'UNESCO

M. Gerhard Maynhardt
Ministre Conseiller
Délégué permanent adjoint de l'Autriche auprés de l'UNESCO

Mr Josef Höchtl
Member of the Austrain Parliament
Head of the Parliamentary Committee on Education

Mr Woolfgang Nedobity
Austrian Conference of Heads of Universities

AZERBAIDJAN/AZERBAIJAN

Prof. Gorkhmaz Gouliyev
Rector
Azerbaijan Institute of Languages
(Head of Delegation)

M. Elman Amiraslanov
Recteur
Université de médecine

M. Siyavouch Karaev
Recteur
Académie nationale du pétrole

M. Mamedtagi Safarov
Rector
Azerbaidjan State Academy of Agriculture

M. Hamlet Isahanly
Recteur
Université de "Khazar"

M. Mahir Aliev
Chef de la Direction des relations internationales et de coordination
Ministére de l'éducation

Mr Rasul Mouradov
Dean
Baku State University-faculty of Physics
Délégation permanente de la République azerbaïdjanaise auprés de l'UNESCO

S. Exc. Mme Eleonora Husseynova
Ambassadeur
Délégué permanent de la République azerbaïdjanaise auprès de l'UNESCO

M. Zaour Kessamanly

Mlle Guliara Moustafabeyli

BAHAMAS (LES)/THE BAHAMAS

The Honourable Dion foulkes
Minister of State for Education
(Head of Delegation)

H.E. Mr Arthur Foulkes
The Bahamas High Commissioner to London

Dr Davidson Heppburn
Chairperson
Bahamas National Commission for UNESCO

Dr Leon Higgs
President
Coolege of The Bahamas

Mrs Paula Sweeting-Davis
Assistant Director of Education
Ministry of Education
Tertiary/Scholarships)

Dr Pandora Johnson
Vice-President
Research, Planning & Development - College of The Bahamas

Dr. Rhonda Chipman-Johnson
Vice-President
Academic Affairs - College of The Bahamas

BAHREIN/BAHRAIN

H.E. Dr Ali Fakhro
Ambassador Extraordinary and Plenipotentiary of Bahrain in France
Permanent Delegate of Bahrain to UNESCO
(Head of Delegation)

Mr Ahmed Harmas
Deputy Permanent Delegate of Bahrain to UNESCO

Mr Mohamed Fezea
Second Secretary
Permanent Delegation of Bahrain to UNESCO

BANGLADESH

All Thatiar M. Chowdhury
Acting Permanent Delegate to UNESCO
(Head of Delegation)

Mr. Md. Mustafizur Rahman'
Second Secretary
Permanent Delegation of Bangladesh to UNESCO

Mr Kazi Rakibuddin Ahmad
Secretary
Ministry of Education

BARBADE/BARBADOS

Hon. Mia Amor Mottley
Minister of Education, Youth Affairs and Culture
(Head of Delegation)

Ms Lolita Applewhaite
Permanent Secretary
Ministry of Education, Youth Affairs and Culture

H E. Mr Michael King
Ambassador Extraordinary and Plenipotentiary of Barbados in Belgium
Permanent Delegate to UNESCO

Mrs Barbara Parris
Acting Principal
Barbados Teachers' College

Miss Hyacinth Kirton
Secretary-General
Barbados National Commission for UNESCO

BELARUS

H.E. Mr Vasiliy Strazhev
Minister of Education
(Head of Delegation)

H.E. Mr Vladimir Senko
Ambassador Extraordinary and Plenipotentiary of the Republic of Belarus in France
Permanent Delegate to UNESCO
(Deputy Head of Delegation)

Mr Victor Gaisyonok
Chairperson
State Committee on Science and Technologies

Mr Alexander Kozulin
Rector
Belarusian State University

Mr Igor Volotovskiy
Vice President National Academy of Sciences of Belarus

Mr Vladimir Pavlovich
Deputy Permanent Delegate, Counsellor
Permanent Delegation of the Republic of Belarus to UNESCO

Mr Victar Shykh
Counsellor
Permanent Delegation of the Republic of Belarus to UNESCO

Mr Roman Ramanovsky
Third Secretary, Expert
Permanent Delegation of the Republic of Belarus to UNESCO

Mr Nakalai Minkevich
Exp.

BELGOUE/BELGIUM

S.E.M. Willaim Ancion
Ministre de l'enseignement superieur, de la recherche scienti. fique, des relations Internationales et du sport.
Gouvernement de la Communaut•é française de Belgique
(Chef de la delegation)

S. Exc. le Baron Hubert van Houtte
Ambassadeur
Représentant permanent de la Belgioue auprè de l'UNESCO
(Cheif adjoint de la délégation)

Communauté française de Belgique

M. John-Luc Horward
Direteur du Cabinet adjoint de Monseur le Ministre

M.C. Carette
Conseiller
Cabinet de Monsieur le Ministre

M. Philippart
Directeur générale de
l'enseignement supérieur

Mme C. Kaufmann
Conseillére
Direction générale de
l'enseignement supérieur

M.D. Chasse
President
Conseil général (F) des Hautes écoles

M.J.P. Frére
Vice-Président
Conseil général (F) des Hautes écoles

M. Willy Legros
Recteur
Université de Liège

Communauté flamande de
Belgique

Mme Ria Cabus
Conseiller
Cabinet du Monistre de
l'enseignement

Dr Marie-Anne Persons
Adjoint du Directeur général
Administration enseignement
supérieur et recherche scientifique

M. Jan Geens
Directeur, Relations internationales
Conseil des écoles supérieures

M Jef Van den Perre
Secrétaire général
Conseil interuniversitaire flammand
(VLIR)

Délégation permanente de la
Belgique auprès de l'UNESCO

M. Philippe Cantraine
Conseiller

Mme Rita Stubbe

BELIZE/BELICE

S. Exc. M. Bassam Said Freiha
Ambassadeur extraordinaire et
plénipotentiaire
Délégué permanent du Belize
Auprès de l'UNESCO
(Chef de la délégation)
Mrs Mireille Cailbault
Permanent Delegation of Belize to
UNESCO

BENIN

S. Exc. 4. Damien Zinzou
Modérali Allahassa
Minister de l'éducation nationale et
de la researche scientifique
(Chef de la délégation)

M. André-Guy Ologoudou
Délégué permanent a.i. de la
République du Bénin auprés de
l'UNESCO
(Chef adjoint de la délégation)

M. Osséni Kemoko Bagnan
Recteur
Université nationale du Bénin

M. Taofiki Aminou
Vice-Recteur
Université Nationale du Bénin

M. Rigobert Kpanipa Kouagou
Secrétaire général
Commission nationale béninoise
pour l'UNESCO

M. Albert Nouhouayi
Doyen de la facult•é des lettres, arts
et sciences humaines
Université nationale du Bénin

M. Isidore Monsi
Premier Conseiller
Délégation permanente de la
République du Bénin auprés de
l'UNESCO

M. Marcellin Laourou
Président du bureau exécutif
Fédération nationale des étudiants du Béin, Université nationale du Bénin

BHOUTAN/BHUTAN

Mr Nima Wangdi
Director of Education Division
Secretary-General of Bhutan National Commission for UNESCO
(Head of Delegation)

BOLIVIE/BOLIVIA

Excmo. Sr. Dr. Tito Hoz de Vila Q.
Ministro de Edución, Cultura y Deportes
(Jefe de la delegación)

Lic. Ramóon Daza
Asesor del Ministro en Educación Superior
(Jefe adjunto de la delegación)

Dr Juan Cuevas
Secretario Ejecutivo Nacional del Comité Ejecutivo de la Universidad Boliviana

Ing. Alberto Rodríguez
Rector
Universidad Mayor San Simon
(Cochabamba)

Dr Jorge Orellana
Rector de Universidad Gabriel René Moreno
(Santa Cruz de la Sierra)

Ing. Ramiro Bustamante
Presidente
Associón Nacional de Universidades Privadas

Dr Antonio Gómez Pereira
Asesor del Ministro en Educación Superior

Ing. José Luis Tellería Geíger
Secretario Nacional de Investigación, Ciencia y Tecnología
Comité Ejecutivo de la Universidad Boliviana

Sr. Eduardo Lorini Tapia
Delegado Permanente adjunto de Bolivia en la UNESCO

Sr. Fenando Laredo
Delegado Suplente ante el Consejo Ejecutivo
Delegación Permanente de Bolivia en la UNESCO

Sra. Silvia Roca Bruno
Segundo Secretario
Delegación Permanente de Bolivia en la UNESCO

Mlle Estelle Laurent
Assistante de la Deuxième Secrétaire
Délégation permanente de Bolivie auprés de l'UNESCO

BOSNIE-HERZEGOVINE/BOSNIA AND HERZEGOVINA

H.E. Mr nenad Suzic
Minister of Education
(Head of Delegation)

Mira Grbic
Consultant to the Minister

H.E. Dr Nikola Kovac
Ambassador of Bosnia and Herzegovina to France

Mr Zeljko Jerkic
Permanent Delegation of Bosnia and Herzegovina to UNESCO

BOTSWANA

The Honourable Dr Gaositwe K.T. Chiepe
Minister
(Head of Delegation)

Mr Philemon T. Ramatsui
Permanent Secretary
Ministry of Education

Prof. Sharon Siverts
Vice Chancellor
University of Botswana

Dr Thabo T. Mokoena
Head of Chemistry Department
University of Botswana

Mr Sophiston Nthobatsang
Deputy Principal
Lobatse College of Education

Mr Lloyd G. Mothusi
Secretary-General
Botswana National Commission for UNESCO

H.E. Mr. S. George
Ambassador from Brussels

Mr. T.G. Ramodimossi
Counsellor from Brussels

BRESIL/BRAZIL

Prof. Efrem de Aguiar Maranhào
Président du Conseil national d'éducation
(Chef de la délégation)

Prof. José Ivonildo do Rego
Président
Association nationale des Dirigeants des institutions fédérales de l'enseignement supérieur
ANDIFES

Prof. antonio Celso Alves Pereira
Vice-Président
Conseil de recteurs des universités brésiliennes (CRUB)

Dr Tancredo Maia Filho
Directeur
Institut national d'études et recherches en éducation

Dr Luiz Roberto Liza Curi
Directeur du Secrétariat de l'éducation supérieur
Ministère de l'éducation

Dr Eduardo Krieger
Président
Académie bréilienne des sciences

Prof. Renato de Oliviera
Président
Association nationale des professeurs de l'enseignement supérieur - ANDES - Syndicat national

M. Ricardo Alonso Bastos
Premier Secrétaire
Délégation permanente du Brésil auprés de l'UNESCO

M. Isnard de Freitas
Délégation permanente du Brési auprés de l'UNESCO

Prof. Célia Brandão Alvarenga Cordeiro
Vice-Président de l' Association brésilienne d'universités communautaires (ANRUC)

BULGARIE/BULGARIA

Ass.Prof. Anna-Maria Totomanova
Vice-Minister for Education and Science
(Head of Delegation)

Ass. Prof. Roumen Prantchov
Head of Department
Ministry of Education and Science
Permanent Delegation of Bulgaria to UNESCO

H.E. Mr Stéphane Tafrov
Ambassador Extraordinary and Plenipotentiary of Bulgaria in France
Permanent Delegate to UNESCO

Mrs Alexandra Veleva
First Secretary
Sector of Education and Culture

BURKINA FASO

S. Exc. M. Christophe Dabire
Ministre des enseignements secondaire, supérieur et de la recherche scientifique
(Chef de la délégation)

S. Exc. M. Filippe Savadogo
Ambassadeur extraordinaire et plénipotentiaire du Burkina Faso en Fance
Délégué permanent auprés de l'UNESCO

M. Robert Foro
Conseiller technique

M. Ambroise Zagre
Directeur général de l'enseignement supérieur et de la recherche scientifique

M. Filiga Michel Sawadogo
Recteur
Université de Ouagodougou

M. Moussa Quattara
Recteur
Université polytechnique de Bobo-Dioulasso

M.R. Mathieu Ouedraogo
Directeur général
Ecole normale supérieure de Koudougo

Dr Boubacar Doukoure
Membre du conseil exécutif
ISESCO

M. Moussa Ernest Ouedraogo
Secrétaire général
Commission nationale burkinabé pour l'UNESCO

M. Mamadou Sawadogo
Délégué permanent adjoint du Burkina Faso auprés de l'UNESCO

M. John B. Kaboré
Conseiller
Délégation permanente du Burkina Faso auprés de l'UNESCO

BURUNDI

S. Exc. M. Jean-Baptiste Mbonyingingo
Ambassadeur extraordinaire et plénipotentiaire du Burundi en France
Délégué permanent auprés de l'UNESCO
(Chef de la délégation)

M. Lazare Naniwe
Premier Conseiller
Délégué permanent adjoint du Burundi auprés de l'UNESCO

Mr Venant Nyobewe
Conseiller
Commission nationale du Burundi pour l'UNESCO

CAMBODGE/CAMBODIA

S. Exc. M. Pich Sophoan
Directeur général de
l'enseignement supérieur,
technique et professionnel
Ministère de l'éducation, de la
jeunesse et des sports
(chef de la délégation)

S.A.R. le Prince Norodom
Sihamoni
Ministre d'Etat
Ambassadeur extraordinaire et
plénipotentiaire, Délégué
permanent auprés de l'UNESCO

M. David Measketh
Deuxiéme Secrétaire
Délégation permanente du
Royaume du Cambodge auprés de
l'UNESCO

Mille Dara Mang
Troisiéme Secrétaire
Délégation permanente du
Royauma du Cambodge auprés de
l'UNESCO

CAMEROUN/CAMEROON

S. Exc. M. Atangana Mebara
Ministre de l'enseignement
supérieur
(Chef de la délégation)

S. Exc. M. Charles Etoundi
Ministre d'Etat chargé de
l'éducation nationale

S. Exc. M. Henri Hogbe Nlend
Ministre de la recherche
scientifique et technique

M. Guillaume Bwele
Inspecteur general n 1
Ministere de l'enseignement
superieur

M. Yaya Yakouba
Directeur de l'education de base

M. Barthelemy Mvondo Nyina
Secretaire general
Commission nationale de la
Republique du Cameroun pur
l'UNESCO

M.Joseph Noah Ngamveng
Recteur
Universite de Ngaoundere

Mme Dorothy Njeuma
Recteur
Universite de BUEA

M. Francios Xavier Etoa

M. Lekene Dongfack

Mme Isabelle Tokpanou
Representante
ONG FAWE, CAM

Miss Henriette Wakona Langmi
Etudiante

M. Annicet Kouomou Choupo
Etudiant

Délégation permanente du
Cameroun aupres de l'UNESCO

S. Exc. M. Pascal Biloa Tang
Ambassadeur extraordinaire et
plenipotentiaire du Cameroun en
france
Délégué permanent aupres de
l'UNESCO

M. Jean Marcel Cluzelle
Conseiller culturel

M. Charles Assamba Ongodo
Deuxieme Secretaire

CANADA

The Honourable Andrew Petter
Minister of Advanced Education, Training and Technology
British Columbia
(Head of Delegation)

Mme Pauline Marois
Ministre de l'education, Quebec
(Chef adjoint de la delegation)

H.E. Mr Jacques Demers
Ambassador
Permanent Delegate of Canada to UNESCO

Mr Gerry Armstrong
Deputy Minister of Advanced Education, Training and Technology
British Columbia

Mme Pauline Champoux-Lesage
Sous Ministre de l'education, Quebec

Dr Susan Clark
Executive Director
Nova Scotia Council on Higher Education

Dr. Paul Cappon
Director General
Council of Ministers of Education, Canada

Ms Marilyn Blaeser
Senior Policy Advisor, Education
Canadian International Development Agency

Ms Marla Waltman Daschko
Manager, Learning and Literacy Directorate
Human Resources Development

Prof. Jacques Proulx
President
Sous Commission de l'education, Commission canadienne pour l'UNESCO

Ms Sheila Molloy
International Desk Officer
Council of Ministers of Education, Canada (Alternate Delegate)

M. Richard Martin
Senior Programme Manager, International Aademic Relations Division
Department of Foreign Affairs and International Trade
(Alternate Delegate)

Mme Diane Laberge
Chargée Programme, éducation
Commission canadienne pour l'UNESCO (déléguée suppléante)

Mme Nicole Stafford
Directrice du Cabinet du Ministre De l'education
(déléguée suppléante)

M. Pierre Brodeur
Directeur des addaires internationales
Ministere de l'education
(deleguee suppleant)

CAP-VERT/CAPE VERDE

S. Exc. M. Jose Luis Livramento Monteiro de Brito
Ministre de l'education, de la science, de la jeunesse et du sport
(Chef de la delegation)

M. Mario Ferreira Lopes Camoes
Charge d'Affaires a.i.
Delegue permanent adjoint du Cap Vert aupres de l'UNESCO

Mme Elizabeth Coutinho
Assesseur de S.E.M. le Ministre de l'education, de la science, de la jeunesse et du sport

Mme Claudina Dupret
Secretaire permanente
Commission nationale cap-verdienne pour l'UNESCO

CHILI/CHILE

Excmo, Sr. Jaime Lavados
Embajador
Delegation Permanente de Chile ante la UNESCO
(Jefe de la delegacion)

Sr. Raúl Allard
Jefe de la División de Edcuatión Superior
Ministerio de Educatión

Sr. Samuel Fernandez
Representante Permanente

Sra. Maria Jose Lemaitre
Secretaria Ejectiva del Consejo Superior de Educaión

Sra. Ana Maria Maza
Secretaria Ejecutiva Adjunta
Commision Nacional de Cooperacion con UNESCO

Sr. Juan Andres Music
Rector
Universidad Católica del Norte

Sr. Jaime Pozo
Rector
Universidad de la Serena

Sr. Hugo Zunino
Prorrector
Universidad de Chile

Sr. Mario Albornoz
Rector
Universidad de Las Americas

Sr. Marcel Young
Consejero
Mision Permanente

Srta. Marisol Prado
presidenta
federacion de Estudiantes de la Universidad de chile

Sr. Roberto Yevenes
Presidente
Federacion de Estudiantes de la Universidad de Concepcion

Sra. Beatriz Rioseco
Encargada de Cultura y de Prensa
Delegación Permanente de Chile ante la UNESCO

Sra. Sylvia Beausang
Attache civil
Delegación Permanente de Chile ante la UNESCO

CHINE/CHINA

H.E. Ms Zhili Chen
Minister of Education
(Head of Delegation)

Mr Fuzeng Yu
Secretary-General
National Commission of the People's Republic of China for UNESCO

H.E. Mr Chongli Zhang
Ambassador
Permanent Delegate to UNESCO

Mr Dongxiang Li
Director-General
Department of Foreign Affairs-Ministry of Education

Mr Binglin Zhong
Director General
Department of Higher Eduction
Ministry of Education

Mr Boacheng Ji
Director-General
Ministry of Education
Department of Develoment Planning

Mr Mokai Chen
Director
Education Commission of Jilin Province

Mr Qingshi Zhu
President
University of Science and Technology of China

Mr Shusheng Jiang
Presient
Nanjing University

Mr Weigang Min
Vice President
Peking University

Mr Cuidi Dong
Director of Division
General Office, Ministry of Education

Mr Yue Du
Director, Division of Special Fields Cooperation
National Commission of the people's Republic of China for UNESCO

Mr Yang Shen
Director, Division of European Affairs
Department of Foreign Affairs, Ministry of Education

Ms Jianhong Dong
Second Secretary
Permanent Delegation of the People's Republic of China to UNESCO

Mr Gang Wang
Programme Officer
National Commission of the People's Republic of China for UNESCO

CHYPRE/CYPRUS

H.E. Mr Lykourgos Kappas
Minister of Education and Culture
(Head of Delegation)

H.E. Mr Constantinos Leventis
Ambassador
Permanent Delegate of the Republic of Cyprus to UNESCO

Prof. Milton Chacholiades
Rector
University of Cyprus

Mr Tryphon Pneumaticos
Chief Education Officer
Department of Higher and tertiary Education, Ministry of Education and Culture

Mr Christos Cassimatis
Deputy Permanent Delegate of the Republic of Cyprus to UNESCO

COLOMBIE/COLOMBIA

Excmo. Sr. Dr. German Bula Escobar
Ministro de Educcion National
(Jefe de la delegacion)

Dr Victor Manuel Moneayo
Rector
Universidad National

Dr. Jaime Restrepo Cuartas
Rector
Universidad de Antioquia

Padre Gerardo Arango Puerta
Rector
Pontificia Universidad Javeriana

Dr Fermando Hinestroza
Rector
Universidad Extemado de Colombia

Dr Guillermo Salah Zuleta
Rector
Universidad del Rosario

Dr Luis Carlos Villegas
Presidente
Asociacion Nacional de
Industriales - ANDI

Dr Pedro Hemnandez
Presidente'
Asociación de Profesores
Universitarios - ASPU

Sr. Felipe Carrillo
Representante de los Estudiantes
ante el Consejo Nacional de
Educación Superior

Delegatión Permanente de
Colombia ante la UNESCO

Excmo. Sr. Pablo Gabriel Obregón
Santodomingo
Embajador Extraordinario y
Plenipotenciario
Representante Permanente de
Colombia ante la UNESCO

Dra. Natalia Martin Leyes
Consejero

Dr. Pablo Llinás
Primer Secretario

COMORES/COMOROS

Mme Moinaecha Cheikh
Directrice de Cabinet
Ministere de l'education nationale,
de la sante publique, de la jeunesse
et des sports
(chef de la délégation)

Mme Thoueybat Said Omar
Ambassadeur
Delegue permanent des Comores
aupres de l'UNESCO

Mme Fellouze Taki
Delegue permanent adjoint aupres
de l'UNESCO

M. Idarousse Attoumane
Directeur general
ISFR

CONGO

S.Exc. Prof. Francois Lumwamu
Ministre de l'enseignement
superieur et de la recherche
scientifique
(Chef de la delegation)

Prof. Charles Gombe Mbalawa
Recteur
Universite Marien Nagouabi

M. Elenga Camara
Conseiller a l' enseignement
superieur
Ministere de l'enseignement
superieur et de la recherche
scientifique

M. Francois Sita
Directeur de la cooperation
Universite Marien Ngouabi

Mme Dorothee Mobonda
Directrice des affaires academiques
Universite Marien Ngouabi

M. Daniel Tombet
Delegue permanent adjoint de la
Republique du Congo aupres de
l'UNESCO

M. Jean -Marie Adoua
Secretaire general
Commission nationale congolaise
pour l'UNESCO

M. Henri Ossebi
Conseiller du President de la
Republique a l'education nationale
et aux resources humaines

M. Gaspard Mbemba
Directeur
Ecole normale superieure

M. Cisco Nouroumby
Delegation permanente de la Republique du Congo aupres de l'UNESCO

COSTARICA

Sr. Gabriel Macaya Trejos
Rector, Universidad de Costa Rica
Presidente del Consejo Nacional de Rectores
(jefe de la delegacion)

Excma. Sra. Iris Leiva de Billaut
Embajador, Representante Alterno de Costa Rica ante la UNESCO
(Jefe alterno de Delegacion)

Sra. Sonia Marta Mora
Vicerrectora Academica
Universidad Nacional

Sra. Alicia Guardian
Directora
Instituto de Investigaciones para el Mejoramiento de la Educacion Costarricense

Sr. Henning Jensen
Decano
Facultad de Ciencias Sociales,
Universidad de Costa Rica

Sra. Olimpia Lopez.
Directora de la Maestria en Administracion Universitaria
Universidad de Costa Rica.

Sra. Maria Salvadora Ortiz
Directora
Centro de Investigacion en Identidad y Culturas Latinoamericanas-Universidad de Costa Rica

Mrs. Alejandrina Mata
Decana
Facultad de Education
Universitaria de Costa Rica

Sra. Susana Trejos
Miembro del Consejo Universitario
Universidad Nacional

Sr. Marco Tulio Fallas
Miembro del Consejo Universitario
Universidad Nacional

Observadores

Excma. Sra. Gabriela Castillo
Ministro Consejero
Mision de Costa Rica ante la UNESCO

S. Esteban Arias Monge
Presidente de la Federation de Estdiantes
Universidad de Costa Rica

COTE-D'IVOIRE

S.D. M. Francis Wodie
Minare de i'enseignement superur et de la recherche Scientifique
(Cheise la delegation).

S.E. M. Bakary Tio-Toure
Ammsssadeur extraordinaire et plenpotentiaire
Delegue permanent de Cote d'Ivorcaupres de I'UNESCO

Mme Anna Manouan
Secretaire generale
Commission nationale ivoirienne pour I'UNESCO

Mme Denise Houphouet-Boigny
Directeur des enseignements superieurs
Ministere de I'enseignement superieur, de la recherche et de I'innovation technologique

Prof. Daouda Aidara
President
Universite d'Abobo-Adjame

Prof. Francios Kouakou novo
President
Universite de Bouaké

M. Nahounou Bobouo
Directeur general
Institut national polytechnique
Felix Houphouet-Boigny de
Yammoussoukro

M. Niamkkey Jacques Adom
Directeur de la cooperation et de l'information scientfique et technique
Ministere de l'enseignement superieur et de la recherche scientifique

M. Allouko Pierre Aka
Conseiller
Delegation permanente de la Cote d'Ivoire aupres de l'UNESCO

M. Kouassi Balo
Conseiller
Delegation permanente de la Cote d'Ivoire aupres de l'UNESCO

CROATIE/CROATIA

H.E. Mr Ivica Kostovic
Deputy Prime Minister
Minister of Scinece and Technology, Ph.D.
(Head of Delegation)

Prof. Ivica Mandic
Deputy Minister
Ministry of Science and Technology, Ph.D.

H.E. Mr Vesna Girardi-Jurkic
Ambasador Extraordinary and Plenipotentiary
Permanent Delegation of the Republic of Croatio to UNESCO, M.A.

Mr Josip Butkovic
Representative
Zagreb University Students Association

Prof. Ivo Babic
Rector
University of Split. Ph.D.

Mrs Helena Jasna Mencer
Deputy Rector
Zagreb University

Mrs Tanja Milatic
Deputy Head of International Department
Ministry of Science and Technology

Mr Dino Milinovic
Secretary-General
Croatian National Commission for UNESCO

Mr Vilim Ribic
President
Independant Union of Research and Higher Education of Croatia

Prof. Zvonimir Sikic
President
Independant Union of Research and Higher Education of Croatia. Ph.D.

CUBA

Excmo. Sr. Fernado Vecino Alegret
Ministro de Educacion Superior
(Jefe de la delegacion)

Dr Juan Vela Valdes
Rector
Universidad de la Habana

Dr Antonio Romillo Tarke
Rector
Instituto Superior Politecnico "Jose A. Echeverria"

Dr Julian Rodriguez Rodriguez
Rector
Instituto Superior de Ciencias
Agropecuarias de La Habana

Dr Juan Carrizo Estevez
Rector
Instituto Superior de Ciencias
Medicas de La Habana

Prof. Alfredo Mateo Diaz Fuentes
Rector
Instituto Superior Pedagogico
"Enrique Jose Varona"

Sr. Luis Abreu Mejias
Secretario General
Sindicato Nacional de
Trabajadores de la Educacion, la
Ciencia y la Cultura

Sr. Carlos Valenciaga
Presidente
Federacion de Estudiantes
Universitarios

Dr Fernando Vazquez Castro
Director de Relaciones
Internacionales
Ministro de Educacion Superior

Lic. Elpidio Tomas Alvarez Vichot
Especialista del Programa de
Educacion
Comision Nacional Cubana de la
UNESCO

Delegacion Permanente de Cuba
ante la UNESCO

Excma.Sra. Soledad Cruz Guerra
Embajadora Extraordinaria y
Plenipotenciaria
Delegada Permanente de Cuba ante
la UNESCO

Sr. Hector Hernandez Gonzalez
Pardo
Ministro Consejero

Sra. Juana Esther Santana Acosta
Asistente-Secretaria

DANEMARK/DENMARK

Mr Torben Kornbech Rasmussen
Director
Ministry of Education
(Head of Delegation)

Ms Hanne Buch
Head of Division
Ministry of Education

Ms Gertie Lund
Chief Advisor
Ministry of Education

Ar Anders Berg-Sorensen
Head of Section
Ministry of Education

Mr Finn Ovesen
Deputy Secretary-General
Danish National Commission for
UNESCO

Mr Peder Kjogx
Chairman
Education Committee, Danish
National Commission for UNESCO

Mr Bo Lidegaard
Permanent Delegate of Denmark to
UNESCO

Professor Sven Caspersen
Rector
Aalborg University

Mr Christen Christensen
Rector
The School of Social Work, Arhus

Mr Henrik Hallinger
Chairman
Danish Teacher Training Students
Union

Ms Christine Hostbo
Deputy Permanent Delegate of Denmark to UNESCO

Ms Lisbeth Haenschke
Trainee
Permanent Delegation of Denmark to UNESCO

DJIBOUTI (REPUBLIQUE DE)/ REPUBLIC OF DJIBOUTI (THE)

S. Exc. m.a. Guireh Waberi
Ministre de l''education nationale
(Chef de la delegation)

S.Exc. M. Djama Omar Idleh
Ambassadeur extraordinaire et plenipotentiaire de Djibouti en France
Delegue permanent aupres de l'UNESCO

M. Mohamed Elmi Yabeh
Premier Conseiller a l'Ambassade

M. Aden Ali Mahamade
Deuxieme Conseiller a l'Ambassade

M. Saleban Omar Oudin
Directeur des affaires administratives
Education nationale

DOMINIQUE/DOMINICA

Honourable Ronald Green
Minister for Education, Sports, and Youth Affairs
(Head of Delegation)

H.E. Mr George Williams
Permanent Delegate of the Commonwealth of Dominica to UNESCO

Mrs Patsy Alexander
Secretary-General
Dominica National Commission for UNESCO

Mr Merrill Mathew
Director-Technical Division
Clifton Dupigny Community College

EGYPTE/EGYPT

Dr Gamal Abou El Makarem Al Azab Risk
President
Menia University
(Head of Delegation)

Dr Hassan Mohamed Hussein Hosni
President
Helwan University

H.E. Prof. Fathi Saleh
Ambassador Extraordinary and Plenipotentiary
Permanent Delegate to UNESCO

Dr Mageed Amin
President
Supreme Council of Univrsities

Prof. Hamed Taher Hassanein Fouad
Dean, Faculty of Dar El Oulm
Cairo University

Mrs Taysir Ramadan
Counsellor
Permanent Delegation to UNESCO

Mr Samy Rashed Gohar
Attaché
Permanent Delegation to UNESCO

EL SALVADOR

lcdo. Mario Fredy Hernandez
Presidente del Consejo de Educacion Superior
Ministerio de Educacion
(Jefe de la delegacion)

Dr Jose Benjamin Lopez Guillen
Rector
Universidad nacional de El Salvador

Ingeniero Roberto Argueta Quan
Rector
Universidad Poliecnica de El Salvador

Licda. Judith Virginia Mendoza de Diaz
Rectora
Universidad Modular Abierta de El Salvador

Arq. Juana Salazar Alvarenga de Pacheco
Rectora
Universidad Albert Einstein

Ing. Mario Ruiz
Rector
Universidad Francisco Gavidia

Dr Jose Dagoherto Gonzalex
Director de Asuntos Docentes y Administrativos
Universidad Jose Matias Delgado

Licda. Carmen Maria Gallardo de Hernandez
Universidad Technollgica de El Salvador

Sr. Mauricio Otmar Vasques Fuentes
Estudiante en Ciencias Agronomicas

Srta. Eileen Ismeny Rodriguez Garcia
Estudiante en Ciencias Economicas

Srta. Rosibel Perdomo Arias
Estudiante en Ciencias de la Educacion

Sr. Carlos Alberto Palma Zaldana
Estudiante en Relaciones Internacionales

Delegacion Permanente de El Salvador ante la UNESCO

Excmo. Sr. Ramiro Zepeda Roldan
Embajador Extraordinario y Plenipotenciario de El Salvador en Francia
Delegado Permanente ante la UNESCO

Sra. Rosa Ester Moreira de Lemoine
Ministro Consejero
Delegado Permanente adjunto

Sra. Nanette Viaud Desroches
Consejero

EMIRATS ARABES UNIS/UNITED ARAB EMIRATES

Dr Hadel Bin Jouan Al Dahiri
President
U.A.E. University
(Head of Delegation)

H.E. Mr Abdul Aziz Nasser Rahma Al Shamsi
Ambassador Extraordinary and Plenipotentiary of the United Arab Emirates in France
Permanent Delegate to UNESCO

H.E. Mr Saif Rashed Al Suweidi
Assistant Under-Secretary
Ministry of Higher Education & Scientific Research

Dr Sulaiman Al Jassem
Director, Depart. Social Affairs, Higher Technologies Faculties
U.A.E. University

Dr Khalifa Ali Al Suweidi
Vice-President of the Faculty of Culture
U.A.E. University

Dr Obeid Saif Al Hajiri
Secretary-General
United Arab Emirates National Commission for UNESCO

Mr Abdulla Tayeb Qassem
Deputy Permanent Delegate to UNESCO

Mme Safaa Bakdach
Assistant administratif

Mme Francoise Coste
Assistant administratif

EQUATEUR/ECUADOR

Excmo. Sr. Ab. Valadimiro alvarez
Ministro de Educacion y Cultura
(Jefe de la delegacion)

Dr Medardo Mora
Presidente
Consejo Nacional de Universidades y Escuelas politecnicas (CONUEP)

Excmo. Sr. Dr. Juan Cueva
Embajador Extraordinario y Plenipotenciario del Ecuador en Francia
Delegado Permanente ante la UNESCO

Dr Reinaldo Valarezo
Rector
Universidad Nacional de Loja

Ing. Victor Hugo Jaramillo
Rector
Universidad de Ambato

Ing. Gabriel Galarza
Rector
Universidad de Bolivar

Dr Alvaro Trueba
Rector
Universidad Tecnologica Equinoccial

Dr Homero Larrea
Director General de Relaciones Culturales
Ministerio de Relaciones Exteriores

Dr Hermuy Calle
Rector
Escuela Superior Politecnica de Chimborazo

Lcdo, Dario Moreira
Secretario General
Consejo Nacional de Universidades y Escuelas Politecnicas (CONUEP)

Soc. Julio Bustos
Representante de los Profesores Universitarios ante el CONUEP
(Miembro Substituto)

Sr. Santiago Diaz
Representante de los Estudiantes ante el CONUEP
(Miembro Substituto)

Dr Mauricio Montalvo
Delegado Permanente Adjunto del Eduador ante la UNESCO

Licda. Maria Eugenia Martinez de Rosado
Asesora de Educacion
Delegacion Permanente del Ecuador ante la UNESCO

ERYTHREE/ERITREA

H.E. Mr Osman Saleh
Minister of Education
(Head of Delegation)

Mr Petros Hailemariam
Director General
Ministry of Education

Dr Woldeab Yishak
President
University of Asmara (UoA)

Dr Wexenet Tewodros
Director of Academic Affairs
university of Asmara (UoA)

ESPAGNE/SPAIN

Excma. Sra. Da. Esperanza Aguirre y Gil de Biedma
Ministra de Educacion y Cultura
(Jete de la delegacion)

Excmo. Sr. D. Jesus Ezquerra Calvo
Embajador Extraordinario y Plenipotenciario
Delegado Permanente de Espana en la UNESCO

Excmo. Sr. D. Manuel Jesus Gonalez Gonzalez
Secretario de Estado
Secretario de Estado de Universidades, Investigacion y Desarollo

Ilmo. Sr, D. Ignacio Gonzalez Gonzalez
Subsecretario
Ministerio de Educacion y Cultura

Ilmo. Sr. D. Antonio Nufiez Garcia-Sauco
Director General de Relaciones Culturales y Cientificas Ministerio de Asuntos Exteriores

Ilmo. Sr. D. Javier Fernandez Lasquetty Blanc
Director
Gabinete de la Ministra de Educacion y Cultura

Ilmo. Sr. D. Tomas Garcia-Cuenca Ariati
Director General
Ensenanza Superior e Investigacion Cientifica

Ilmo. Sr. D. Pablo Benavides Orgaz
Delegado Permanente Adjunto de Espana en la UNESCO

Ilmo. Sr. D. Rafael Aries Alvarez
Secretario General
Consejo de Universidades

Ilma. Sar. Dona Isabel Mendoza Fernandez
Directora
Gabinete del Secretario de Estado de Universidades, Investigacion y Desarrolla

Ilma. Sar. Dona Clara Barreiro
Consejera de Educacion en la UNESCO

Excmo. y Mgfco. Sr. D. J. Jose Badiola Diez
Rector
Universidad de Zaragoza

Excmo. y. Mgfco. Sr. D. Jaume Pages i Fita
rector
Universidad Politecnica de Barcelona

Doctora Isabel Munoz-Cubells
Asesora del Gabinete de la Sra. Ministra

D. Jose Maria de Luxan Melendez
Vicesecretario de Estudios
Consejo de Universidades

D. Christian Ruiz Orfila
Asesor del Gabinete de la Ministra de Educacion y Cultura

D. Juan Arino Ortiz
Consejero Tecnico de Recursos e Informes
Consejo de Universidades

D. Luis Nunez Cubero
Comision Nacional Espanola de la UNESCO

D. Jose Antonio Gallego Gredilla
Vocal Asesor del Gabinete del Secretario de Estado de Universidades, Investigacion y Desarrollo

D. Francisco Feito Higueruela
Universidad Jaen

ESTONIE/ESTONIA

H.E. Mr Mait Klaassen
Minister of Education
(Head of Delegation)

Prof. Ain Heinaru
Head
Dept of Research and Higher Education, Ministry of Education

Prof. Olav Aarna
Rector
Tallinn Technical University

Dr Talvi Marja
Chairwoman
Culture Committee of Riigikogu, The Estonian Parliament

Mr Harri Annuka
Economic Counsellor
Embassy of the Republic of Estionia in France

ETATS-UNIS D'AMERIQUE/ UNITED STATES OF AMERICA

The Honourable David. A. Longanecker
Assistant Secretary for Postsecondary Education
Department of Education
(Head of Delegation)

Mr William McIlhenny
Permanent Observer of the United States of America to UNESCO

Ms Emily Vargas-Baron
Deputy Assistant Administrator, U.S. Agency for International Development
Director, Center for Human Capacity Development

Mr Keith Geiger
Director
Office of Academic Programs, United States Information Agency

Ms Maureen McLaughlin
Deputy Assistant Secretary for Postsecondary Education
U.S. Department of Education

Mr Raymond E. Wanner
Office of Technical Specialised Agencies - Bureau of International Organisation Affairs

Ms Lois B. Defleur
President
State University of New York at Binghamton

Ms Vera King Farris
President
Richard Stockton College of New Jersey

Ms Augustine Gallego
Channcellor
San Diego Community College District

Mr Stanley O. Ikenberry
President
American Council on Education

Mr David K. Scott
Channcellor
University of Massachusetts at Amherst (ACE)

ETHIOPIE/ETHIOPIA

H.M. Mrs. Gennet Zewide
Minister of Education
(Head of Delegation)

H.E. Dr Mulugeta Eteffa
Ambassador Extraordinary and Plenipotentiary of Ethiopia in France
Permanent Delegate to UNESCO

Dr Teshome Yizengaw
Head, Department of Higher Education
Ministry of Education

Mr Belette Demissie
Head, Science and Technology Panel of Higher Education
Ministry of Education

Mr Alemayehu Minas
Secretary General
Ethiopian National Agency for UNESCO

Mr Mulatu Keffelew
Deputy Permanent Delegate of Ethiopia to UNESCO

Dr Mogessie Ashenafi
President
Adis-Ababa University

Mr Tsehaye Debalkew
Director
Ethiopian Massmedia Training Center

FEDERATION DE RUSSIE/ RUSSIAN FEDERATION

M.A. Kondakov
Ministre-adjoint de l'education generale et professionnelle de la Federation de Russie
(Chef de la delegation)

S.Exc. Prof. Evgeny Sidorov
Ambassadeur extraordinaire et plenipotentiaire
Delegue permanent de la Federation de Russie aupres de l'UNESCO

Professeur I. Khaleeva
Recteur
Universite linguistique d'Etat de Moscou

Professeur A. Ivannikov
Directeur general du Centre de l'informatisation
Ministere de l'education generale et professionnelle de la Federation de Russie

M.V. Korotkov
Conseiller, Delegation permanente de la Federation de Russie aupres de l'UNESCO
(Expert de la delegation)

M.A. Prokopchuk
Assistant executif du Ministre, Ministere de l'education generale professionnelle
(Expert de la délégation)

M. N. Dmitryev
Chef adjoint, Division de la coopération internationale.
Ministére de l'éducation générale
(Expert de la délégation)

FIDJI/FIJI

Mrs Emi Rabukawaqa
Deputy Secretary for Education
Ministry of Education
(Head of Delegation)

FINLANDE/FINLAND

H.E. Mr Olli-Pekka Heinoner
Minister of Education
(Head of Delegation)

Ms Anita Lehikoinen
Counsellor for Education
University Division, Ministry of Education
(Deputy Head of Delegation)

Ms Sirkka-Leena Horkko
Senior Adviser
University Division, Ministry of Education

Mr Osmo Lampinen
Counsellor
Polytechnic Division, Ministry of Education

Mr Kauko Hamalainen
Secretary General, Higher Education Evaluation Council
Department for Education and Science Policy, Ministry of Education

Mr Tapio Markkanen
Secretary General, Finnish Council of University Rectors
Member of the Finnish national Commission for UNESCO

Ms Iris Schwanck
Deputy Director
Centre for International Mobility

Mr Henrik Moliis
First Secretary
Division for Africa and the Middle East, Ministry for Foreign Affairs

Ms Zabrina Holmstrom
Counsellor for Cultural Affairs
Secretary-General of the Finnish National Commission for UNESCO

Ms Taina Kiekko
Ambassador
Permanent Delegate of Finland to UNESCO

Mr Reijo Laukkanen
Counsellor
Permanent Delegation of Finland to the OECD

Ms Anne Lammila
Deputy permanent Delegate of Finland to UNESCO

FRANCE

S. Exc. M. Claude Allegre
Ministre de l'education nationale, de la recherche et de la technologie
(Chef de la delegation)

S. Exc. M. Jean Musitelli
Ambassadeur
Delegue permanent de la France aupres de l'UNESCO

Mme Francine Demichel
Directrice de l'enseignement superieur Ministere de l'education nationale, de la recherche et de la technologie

M. Francois Nicoullaud
Directeur general des relations culturelles, scientifiques et techniques
Ministere des affaires etrangeres

M. Emmanuel de Calan
Directeur de la mission multilaterale
(Suppleant)

M. Jean de Gliniasty
Directeur des Nations-Unies et des Organisations internationales
Ministere des affaires entrangeres

Mme Genevieve Galameau-Mack
Ministere des affaires etrangeres
(Suppleante)

M. Jean Favier
President
Commission de la Republique Francaise pour l'education, la science et la culture

M. Jean-Pierre Boyer
Secretaire general
Commission de la Republique francaise pur l'education, la science et la culture (Suppleant)

M. Jean Sirinelli
President d'Honneur
Commission de la Republique francaise pur l'education, la science et la culture

D. Daniel Nahon
Directeur de la recherche scientifique et technique
Ministere de l'education nationale, de la recherche et de la technologie

M. Albert Prévos
Délégué aux relations internationales et de la coopération
Ministére de l'éducation nationale, de la re cherche et de la technologie

Mme Suzy Halimi
Conseiller pour l'enseignement superieur (suppleante)

M. Bernard Saint-Girons
Premier Vice President
Conference des Presidents d'universite (CPU)

M. Guy Gautherin
Premier Vice President
Conference des directeurs d'ecoles et de formations d'ingenieurs

Pays Hote, Experts et Conseillers techniques:

Mme Nicole Becarud
Presidente de la Commission formation
Conseil national des ingenieurs et scientifiques francais

Mme Daniele Blondel
Professeur
Universite de Paris Dauphine

Mme Isabelle Deble
Chercheur
Universite Paris 1

M. Philippe Dechartre
Representant du Conseil economique et social

M. Andre Staropoli
Secretaire general
Comite national d'evaluation

M. Gerard Toulouse
Directeur de recherche au CNRS
Membre correspondant de l'Academie des sciences

Mme Anne-Marie Cocula
Presidente
Universite Bordeaux III

M. Michel Cobarnous
President
Universite Bordeaux 1

M. Yves Escouffier
President
Universite Montpellier II

Mme Helene Lamicq
Presidente
Universite Paris XII

M. Bernard Vareilles
President
Universite de Limoges

M. Jacques Lévy
Président
Conférence des grandes écoles

M. Jacques Gelas
Delegue aux affaires internationales
Conference des directeurs d'écoles de formation d'Ingenieurs

M. Michel Woronoff
President du Comite CAMPUS (Cooperation avec l'Afrique et Madagascar pur la promotion universitaire et scientifique)

M. Renaud Nattiez
Charge de la sous-direction des relations multilaterales
Ministere de l'education nationale, de la recherche et de la technologie

M. Jean-Francois Grunstein
Charge de mission a la Direction de la cooperation scientifique et technique
Ministere des affaires entrangeres

M. Michel Guyot
Charge de mission, Direction de l'enseignement superieur
Ministere de l'education nationale, de la recherche et de la technologie

Mme Calaudine Bourrel
Chargee de mission, Direction du developpement
Ministere delegue a la francophonie et a la cooperation

M. Jean-Pierre Regnier
secretaire general adjoint
Commission de la Republique francaise pur l'education, la science et la culture

mme Sylviane Legrand
Deuxieme Secretaire
Delegation permanente de la France aupres de l'UNESCO

GABON

S.Exc. M. Lazare Digombe
Ministre de l'enseignement superieur et de la recherche scientifique
(Chef de la delegation)

Prof. Dieudonne Ngaka Safu
Enseignant
Faculte de medecine et sciences de la sante
(Chef adjoint de la delegation)

Prof. Desire Benoni
Directeur de Cabinet politique adjoint a la Presidence de la Republique
Directeur de l'Ecole doctorale de Franceville

Prof. Celestin Nguemby Mbina
Recteur
Universite Omar Bongo

M. Mbatchi
Vice-Recteur
Universite des sciences et techniques de Masuku

M. Paul Bongue Boma
Depute a l'Assemblee nationale
President de la Commission des finances et de la comptabilite publique

M. Hilaire Adiaheno
Secretaire general
Ministere des finances, de l'economie, du budget et des participations, charge de la privatisation

M. Longho
Commissaire general au plan
Ministere de la planification, de l'environnement et du tourisme

Prof. Edouard Ngou-Milama
Conseiller a la recherche scientifique
Ministere de l'enseignement superieur et de la recherche scientifique

Mme Yolande Ozouaki
Directeur de l'enseignement superieur
Ministére de l'enseignement supérieur et de la recherche scientifique

Mme Maryvonne Kombia
Enseignante
Faculte de medecine et sciences de la sante

M. Minkoue
Conseiller en communication
Ministere de l'enseignement superieur et de la recherche scientifique

M. Gueboyi
Aide de camp du Ministre
Ministere de l'enseignement superieur et de la recherche scientifique

Delegation permanente du Gabon aupres de l'UNESCO

M. Eugene Philippe Djenno Okoumba
Delegue permanent du Gabon aupres de l'UNESCO

Mme Marie-Dominique Delafosse
Premier Conseiller

Mme Iréne Quentin-Ogwera
Premier Sécrétaire

M. Matos

GAMBIE/GAMBIA

Hon. Mrs Satang Jow
Secretary of State for Education
(Head of Delegation)

H.E. Mr N'jogou-Saer Bah
Ambassador Extraordinary and Plenipotentiary of The Gambia in France
Permanent Delegate to UNESCO

Mrs Anne Therese Ndong-Jatta
Director
Secondary and Tertiary Education

Mrs Juka Jabang
Director
Management Development Institute

Mr Jenung Manneh
Principal
Gambia College

Mr Makireh Njie
Principal
Gambia Technical Training Institute

Mrs Mam Sillah Cham
Secretary General
Gambia National Commission for UNESCO

MR Mawdo Juwara

Mr Moses Benjamin Jallow
First Secretary
The Embassy of the Republic of The Gambia

GEORGIE/GEORGIA

Mr Shota Dogonadze
Deputy Minister of Foreign Affairs
head of Delegation)

Mr Peter Metreveli
Secretary-General
Georgian National Commission for UNESCO

Mr George Matiashvili
Deputy Minister of Education

Mr Roin Metreveli
Rector
Tbilisi State University

Dr Ramaz Khetsuriani
Rector
Georgian Technical University

Mr Ramaz Khetsuriani
Rector
Tbilisi Medical University

Mr Napoleon Karkashidze
Rector
Georgian Agrarian University

Mr Vakhtang Sartania
Rector
Tbilisi Pedagogical University

Ms Maia Tevzadze
Vice-Rector
Tbilisi Pedagogical University

Mr Avtandil Nikoleishvili
Rector
Kutaissi State University
Permanent Delegation of Georgia to UNESCO

H.E. Mr Gotsha Tchogovadze
Ambassador Extraordinary and Plenipotentiary of Georgia in France
Permanent Delegate to UNESCO

Mme Nathela Laguidze
Deputy Permanent Delegate

GHANA

Hon. Dr Mohammed Ibn Chambas
Deputy Minister of Education
(Head of Delegation)

H.E. Mr. Harry O. Blavo
Ambassador Extraordinary and Plenipotentiary of Ghana in France
Permanent Delegate to UNESCO

H.E. Prof. Amonoo-Neizer
High Commissioner designated to Zimbabwe

Professor George Benneh
Chairman
National Council for Tertiary Education

Prof. Adrian Deheer-Amissah
Executive Secretary
National Council for Tertiary Education

Prof. Christopher Ameyaw-Akumfi
Policy Advisor
Ministory of Education

Mr Francis Anthony Ben-Eghan
Director
Finance & Administration
Ministry of Education

Mr John E. Aggrey
Director/IOCB
Ministry of Foreign Affairs

Mrs Esi Sutherland-Addy

Mr Joseph Adongo
President
Ministry of Education
(N.U.G.S.)

Mr Seth Ofori-Ohene
Deputy Secretary General
Ministry of Eduction (A.A.S.U.)

Mr Charles Nkansah
General Secretary
Ministry of Education (G.U.N.S.A.)

Mr Adolphus K. Arthur
Deputy Permanent Delegate of Ghana to UNESCO
Minister-Counsellor

GRECE/GREECE

Prof. Michalis Tsinisizelis
Conseiller du Ministre pour l'enseignement superieur
(Chef de la delegation)

M. Evangelos Livieratos
Professeur
Universite Aristote de Thessalonique

Mme Maria Eliou
Professeur a l'Université d'Athénes
Membre du Conseil d'administration de la Commission nationale grecque pour l'UNESCO

M. Georges Mavroidis
Conseiller pour l'education
Delegation permanente de la Grece aupres de l'UNESCO

GRENADE/GRENADA

Mr Martin Baptiste
Senior Education Officer
Planning and Development'(Head of Delegation)

GUATEMALA

Ing. Efrain Median Guerra
Rector
Universidad de San Carlos (USAC)
(Jefe de la delegacion)

Licda. Hada Alvarado Beteta
Decana de la Facultad de Ciencias Quimicas y Framacia
Universidad de San Carlos

Arq. Rodolfo Portillo Arriola
decano de la Facultad de Arquitectura
'Universidad de San Carlos

Dr. Luis Alfonso Leal Monterroso
Director General de Administracion
Universidad de San Carlos

Lcdo. Roberto Moreno Godoy
Viceministro de Educacion Superior, Ciencia y Tecnologia
(Subjefe de Delegacion)

Licda. Regina Caffaro
Asesora del Despacho Ministerial
(Suplente)

Dr Alvaro Rolando Torres Moss
Rector
Universidad Mariano Galvez

Lcdo. Leopoldo Colom Molina
Director General de Asuntos Estudiantiles
Universidad Mariano Galvez

Dr Alfredo Sanjose Gonzalez
Vice-Rector
Universidad Mariano Galvez

Dra. Ruby Melisanda Santizo Rosales de Hernandez
Secretario General, Universidad Mariano Galvez
(Suplente)

Dr Antonio Gallo Armosino, S.J.
Investigaciones Filosoficas
Universidad Rafael Landivar

Prof. Ruben Chaven Dufaul
Representante de Rectoria
Universidad Rural

Delegacion Permanente de Guatemala ante la UNESCO

Excma. Sra. Arq. Gloria Montenegro de Chirouze
Embajadora Extraordinaria y Plenipotenciaria de Guatemal en francia
Delegada Permanente ante la UNESCO

Sr. Juan Alberto Mendoza
Encargado de Negocios

Srta. Stephanie Hochstetter Skinner-Klee
Tercer Secretario

GUINEE/GUINEA

S.Exc. M. Ibrahima Sylla
Ambassadeur extraordinaire et plenipotentiaire de Guinee en France
(Chef de la delegation)

Dr Alioune Cherif Sylla
secretaire general
Ministere de l'enseignement superieur et de la recherche scientifique

Dr Mamadi Kourouma
Conseiller
Ministére de l'enseignement supérieur et de la recherche scientifique

Mr Fode Cisse
Conseiller
Ambassade de Guinee en France

Dr Ibrahima Morya Conte
Directeur national de l'enseignement superieur

Prof. Mohamed Lamnie Kaba
Recteur
Universite de Conakry

Dr Amadou Tidane Diallo
Directeur general
Institut superieur des sciences de l'education de Guinee (Maneah)

Dr Yazora Soropogui
Directeur general
Institute des sciences agrozootechniques de Faranah

Dr Seydouba Camara
Recteur
Universite de Kankan

M. Mody Kodougou Diallo
Vice-Recteur charge de la recherche scientifique
Universite de Conakry

M. Fancery Conde
Directeur general
Institut superieur de mine et geologie de Boke

Pr. Agr. Naby Daouda Camara
Doyen
Facykte de medecine-pharmacie (Universite Conakry)

Mme Hawa Fofana
Doyenne
Faculte de droit, des sciences economiques et de gestion (Universite Conakry)

Mme Aissatou Lamarana Diallo
Secretaire generale adjointe
Commission nationale guineenne pour l'UNESCO

GUINEE-BISSAU/GUINEABISSAU

S. Exc. Mme Maria Odete da Costa Semedo
Ministre de l'education nationale
(Chef de la delegation)

Dr Alexandrino Gomes
Directeur general enseignement superieur
Ministere de l'education nationale

Dr Julieta P.G, Mendes
Conseiller technique du Ministre de l'education nationale

M. Carlos Edmilons Marques Vieira
Attache
Ambasade de Guinee-Bissau a Paris

GUINEE EOUATORIALE/ EQUATORIAL GUINEA

Excmo. Sr. Don Federico Edjo Ovono
Rector Magnifico de la Universidad
Consejero Presidencial en los asuntos de la UNESCO
(Jefe de la delegacion)

GUYANA

Dr Horold Lutchman
Vice-Chancellor
University of Guyana
(Head of Delegation)

Mrs Carmen Jarvis
Secretary-General
Guyana National Commission for UNESCO

HAITI

S.Exc. M. Etzer Charles
Ambassadeur
Delegue permanent d'Haiti aupres de l'UNESCO
(Chef de la delegation)

M. Harry-Frantz Leo
Ministre Conseiller
Delegation permanente d'Haiti aupres de l'UNESCO

M. Creutzer Mathurin
Directeur de l'enseignement superieur et de la recherche scientifique
Ministere de l'education nationale

M. Michel Saint-Louis
Membre du Cabinent du Ministre de l'education nationale

M. Pierre Paquiot
Recteur
Universite d'Etat d 'Haiti

M. Jean-Renol Elie
Vice-Recteur a l'administration
Universite d Etat d'Haiti

M. Daniel Altine
Vice-Recteur a.i. aux affaires academiques
Universite Quisqueya

M. René Jean-Jumeau
Secrétaire général
Université Notre-Dame

M. Mario Alvarez
Doyen de la faculte de medecine
Universite d'Etat d'Haiti

M. Berard Cenatus
Doyen de l'Ecole normale superieure
Universite d'Etat d'Haiti

Mme Sylvive Bajeux
Secretaire permanente
Commission nationale haitienne de cooperation avec l'UNESCO

HONDURAS

Excmo. Sr. Abogado Ramon Calix Figueroa
Ministro de Educacion
Presidente de la Commision Hondurena de Cooperacion con la UNESCO
(Jefe de la delegacion)

Excma. Sra. Sonia Mendieta de Badaroux
embajadora Extraordinaria y Plenipotenciaria de Honduras en Francia
Delegada Permanente ante la UNESCO

Lic. Jorge Abraham Arita
Direccion de Planificacion Universitaria
Universidad Nacional Autonoma de Honduras

Ing. Carlos Rodriguez Pena
Direccion de Planificacion Universitaria
Universidad Nacional Autonoma de Honduras

Dr Pedro Saavedra
Rector
Universidad Pedagogica Nacional Framcosco Morazan

Dr Elio Alvarenga
Rector
Universidad Catolica

Lic. Jose Ferneli Pacheco Santos
Universidad Jose Cecilio del Valle

Lic. Gina Mendieta
Profesora
Sector Educacion Privada

HONGRIE/HUNGARY

S. Exc. M. Zoltan Pokomi
Ministre de l'education nationale
(Chef de la delegation)

Prof. Jozsef Palinkas
Secretaire d'Etat
Ministere de l'education nationale

Prof. Adam Kiss
Secretaire d'Etat adjoint
Ministere de l'education nationale

Prof. Norbert Kroo
Academicien Secretaire d'Etat adjoint
Ministere de l''education nationale

M. Péter Soltész
Directeur général
Ministére de l'éducation nationale

M. Tibor Gyula Nagy
Directeur general
Ministere de l'education nationale

Prof. Jozsef Reffy
Directeur
Ministere de l'education nationale

Mr Zooltan Vermes
directeur du serice de presse
Ministere de l'education nationale

M. Mihaly Rozsa
Secretaire general
Commission nationale hongroise pour l'UNESCO

M. Tamas Skultety
President
Conference des etudiants hongrois

Delegation permanente de la Republique de Hongrie aupres de l'UNESCO

S. Exc. M. Pal Pataki
Ambassadeur extraordinaire et plenipotentiaire
Delegue permanent aupres de l'UNESCO

M. Peter Karikas
Delegue permanent adjoint

ILES SOLOMON/SOLOMON ISLANDS (THE)

Dr Kabini Sanga
Deputy Director
Solomon Islands College of Higher Education
(Head of Delegation)

ILES VIERGES BRITANNIQUES/BRITISH VIRGIN ISLANDS

Dr Charles Wheately
President
H. Lavity Stoutt Community College
(Head of Delegation)

Mrs Jennie Wheatley

Ms Medita Wheately
Secretary General
National Commission for UNESCO

INDE/INDIA

H.E. Dr Murli Manohar Joshi
Minister of Human Resource Development and Science & Technology
(Head of Delegation)

Mr Mahmood-Ur-Rahman
vice Chancellor
Aligarh Mulim University

Shri Om Nagpal
Eminent Educationist

Shri M.M. Jha
Joint Secretary
U &He- Department of Education

Mr Kireet Joshi
Eminent Educationist

Mr Ravi Capoor
PS to Human Resource Minister

Permanent Delegation of India to UNESCO

H.E. Mr Chiranjiv Singh
Ambassador
Permanent Delegate of India to UNESCO

Mr Gauri Shankar Gupta
counsellor
Permanent Delegation of India to UNESCO

Mr Ram Dutt
Second Secretary
Permanent Delegation of India to UNESCO

INDONESIE/INDONESIA

H.E. Mr Soedarso Djojonegoro
Ambassador
Permanent Delegate of Indonesia to UNESCO
(Head of Delegation)

Prof. Dr Cecep Syarifuddin
Member of the Indonesian Parliament

Mr Entang Sastraatmadja
Member of the Indonesian Parliament

Mr Avip Syaefullah
Member of the Indonesian Parliament

Prof. Dr Bambang Soehendro
Director General of Higher Education
Ministry of Education and Culture

Dr Satryo Soemantri Brojonegoro
Director
Directorate of Development of Academic Facilities, Ministry of Education and Culture

Dr Yanto Santoso
Educational and Cultural Attache
Indonesian Embassy, Paris, France

Dr Gatot Hari Priowirjanto
Educational and Cultural Attache
Indonesian Embassy, Bonn, Germany

Mr Aam Hamdani
Head
The Economics Science College Foundation, Garut, Indonesia

Mr Imam Santoso
Deputy Permanent Delegate
Permanent Delegation of Indonesia to UNESCO

IRAK/IRAQ

S. Exc. M. Abdul-Jabbar Tawfeeq
Ministre de l'enseignement superieur, de la recherche et de la technologie
(Head of Delegation)

S. Exc. M. Abdul-Amir Al-Anbari
Ambassadeur extraordinaire et plenipotentiaire
Delegue permanent de 'Irak aupres de l'UNESCO

Dr Abdul-Ilah Alk-Khashab
President
Universite de Bagdad

Mr Sa'd Mohamad Salih
Ministere de l'enseignement superieur

Dr Haitham Jassam Al-Ani

Dr Hassan Hattab

Dr Tahir Tawfeeq Salam

Dr Hassan Khatab Omar

Dr Ahmad Al-Azawi

Mr Iyad Aflak

IRAN (REPUBLIQUE ISLAMIQUE D') ISLAMIC REPUBLIC OF IRAN (THE)

S.Exc. Dr. Mostafa Moin
Ministre de la culture et de l'enseignement superieur
President de la Commission nationale iranienne pur l'UNESCO
(Chef de la delegation)

S. Exc. M. Ali-Reza Moaiyeri
Ambassadeur extraordinaire et plenipotentiaire en France

S.Exc Dr. Ahmad Jalali
Ambassadeur
Delegue permanent de la Republique islamique d'Iran aupres de l'UNESCO

Dr Ahmad Shariatmadari
President
Academie de la science de la Republique islamique d'Iran

Dr Jafar Tofighi
Vice-Ministre pour l'education
Ministere de la culture et enseignement superieur

Dr Abdolali Sharghi
Directeur general du Bureau de cooperations scientifiques et internationales
Ministere de la culture et enseignement superieur

Dr Mohammad Ali Tavokol Kossari
President
Institut de recherche et planification de l'enseignement superieur

Dr Jalil Shahi
Secretaire general
Commission nationale iranienne pour l'UNESCO

M. Davoud Saidipur
Membre du Cabinet du Ministre

IRLANDE/IRELAND

H.E. Mr Tom Kitt TD
Minister of State at the Department of Enterprise, Trade and Employment
(Head of Delegation)

H.E. Mr Patrick O'Connor
Ambassador Extraordinary and Plenipotentiary of Ireland in France
Permanent Delegate to UNESCO

Mr David Cooney
Deputy Permanent Delegate to UNESCO

Ms Eleanor O'Brien
Principal Officer
Higher Education Division, Department of Education and Science

Ms Anne-Marie Moore
Assistant Principal Officer
Higher Education Division. Department of Education and Science

Ms Coliona Manahan Leslie
First Secretary
Permanent Delegation

Mr Se Goulding
Assist Principal Officer
International Division, Department of Education and Science

Mr John Hughes
Private Secretary
Department of Enterprise, Trade and Employment

Ms Marie Fitzpatrick
Secretary

ISLANDE/ICELAND

H.E. Mr Bjorn Bjarnason
Minister of Education, Science and Culture
(Head of Delegation)

Dr Pall Skulason
rector
University of Iceland

Mr Thordar Kristinsson
Director of Academic Affairs
University of Iceland

Dr Thorsteinn Gunnarsson
Rector
University of Akureyri

Mr Stefan Stefansson
Head of Division
Ministry of Education, Science and Culture

Permanent Delegation of Iceland to UNESCO

H.E. Mr Sverrir Haukur Gunnlaugsson
Ambassador Extraordinary and Plenipotentiary of Iceland in France
Permanent Delegate to UNESCO

Mr Gudmundur B. Helgason
Counsellor
Delegation of Iceland to UNESCO

ISRAEL

Prof. Nehemia Levtzion
Chairperson, Planning and Budgeting Committee
Council for Higher Education
(Head of Delegation)

Mr Emanuel Zismann
Chairman
Knesset Education and Culture Committee

Mr Nissan Limor
Director General
Council for Higher Education

Mr Yair Levin
Deputy Director-General
Ministry of Education, Culture and Sport

Prof. Gad Gilbar
Rector
University of Haifa

Prof. Aliza Shenhar
President
Emek Yezrael College

Dr zvi Artzi
Rector
Zinman College of Physical Education and Sport Sciences

Ass. Prof. Majid Al-Haj
Council for Higher Education

Mr Naftali Weitman
Secretary
Council for Higher Education

Mr Eran Weintraub'
Chairman
National Union of Israeli Students

Delegation permanente d'Israel aupres de l'UNESCO

S. Exc. M. Avi Shoket
Ambassadeur
Delegue permanent d'Israel aupres de l'UNESCO

Mme Elisabeth Cohen-Tannoudji
Assistante

Mr Roi Amit
Assistant

ITALIE/ITALY

S.Exc. M. le Professeur Luigi berlinguer
ministre de 'education, l'universite et la recherche scientifique et technologique
Professeur en droit
(Chef de la delegation)

M. le Conseiller Michelangelo Pipan
Conseiller diplomatique du Ministre

Mme Lolanda Cei Semplici
Directeur general du Departement pour l'autonmie universitaire et les etudiants
Ministere de l'universite et la recherche scientifique et technologique

M. le Professeur Paolo Blasi
President
Conference permanente des recteurs des universites italiennes

M. Giorgio Bruno Civello
Chef adjoint
Cabinet du Ministre

M. Giunio Luzzatto
Professeur de mathematiques
Universite de Genes

Prof. Luigi Capogrossi
Professeur de droit romain
Universite de Rome

Mme Antonella Cammisa
Departement pur l'autonomie universitaire et les etudiants
Ministere de l'universite et la recherche scientifique et technologique

Mme Francesca Morelli
Direction generale de la cooperation au development du Ministere des affaires etrangeres

Mme Lisa Zaffi
Direction generale des relations culturelles du Ministere des affaires etrangeres

Mme Serena Fabrizi
Representant de I'Association des etudiants U.D.U.

Commission nationale italienne pour I'UNESCO

Mme le Senateur Tullia Carettoni
Presidente

M. le Ministre plenipotentiaire Carlo Calia
Secretaire general

Prof. Giovanni Puglisi
President du Comite "Education"

Prof. Sira Miori

Delegation permanente de I'Italie aupres de I'UNESCO

S. Exc. L'Ambassadeur Gabriele Sardo
Delegue permanent de I'Italie aupres de I'UNESCO

M. le Conseiller Pietro Sebastiani
Delegue permanent adjoint

JAMAHIRIYA ARABE LIBYENNE POPULAIRE ET SOCIALIST PEOPLE'S LIBYAN ARAB JAMAHIRIYA

S. Exc. Dr. Ali Treki
Ambassadeur de la Jamahiriya arabe libyenne en France
(Chef de la delegation)

M. Mohamed Ahmad Elaswad
Ambassadeur
Delegue permanent de la Jamahiriya arabe libyenne aupres de 'I'UNESCO

Dr Abdullah A. El-Hammali
Directeur general des relations scientifiques et cooperation technique

Dr Sheib Y. El-Mansuri
President du Conseil de planification de 'education

Dr Abdalla M. Zarrugh
Secretaire general
Commission nationale de la Jamahiriya arabe libyenne pour I'education, la science et la culture

Dr Abdalla A. El-Mansori
Directeur general
Centre national pour I'education

Dr Najaah El-Ghabsi
Secretaire adjoint secteur des sciences
Universite El-Fateh

Ar Ali H. El-Hawat
Professeur
Universite El-Fateh

Dr Ibrahim Elghaly
Delegue permanent adjoint de la Jamahiriyaarabe libyenne aupres de I'UNESCO

Dr Mahmoud Saeid Abdalla
President
Universite de Garyounes

Dr Abdalla Z. Zaied
President
Universite Omar El-Mokhtar

M. Farag Alsherif
Delegue de I'Union generale des etudiants

JAMAIQUE/JAMAICA

Senator the Honourable Burchell Whiteman
Minister of Education &Culture
Chairman, Jamaica National Commission for UNESCO
(Head of Delegation)

Professor the Honourable Rex Nettleford, O.M.
Vice-Chancellor
University of the West Indies
(Deputy Head of Delegation)

Prof. Hilary Beckles
University of the West Indies

H.E. Ms Sybil Campbell
Ambassador
Permanent Delegation of Jamaica to UNESCO

Dr Ethley London
Executive Director
University Council of Jamaica

Prof. Lawrence Carrington
Director
School of Continuing Stuides
University of the West Indies

Dr Simon Clarke
Special Adviser to the Minister of Education & Culture

Ms Sylvia V. Thomas
Secretary-General
Jamaica National Commission for UNESCO

JAPON/JAPAN

H.E. Dr Teiichi Sato
Vice Minister
Ministry of Education, Science, Sports and Culture
(Head of Delegation)

H.E. Mr Koichiro Matsuura
Ambassador Extraordinary and Plenipotentiary of Japan to France

H.E. Mr Azuza Hayashi
Ambassador
Permanent Delegate of Japan to UNESCO

Mr Yasuharu Suematsu
Vice-Chairperson, Japanese National Commission for UNESCO
President, Kochi University of Technology

Ms Naoko Shimura
Japanese National Commission for UNESCO
President, Tsuda College

Mr Kan-ichi Miyaji
President, The Association for Promotion of Satellite Education
Immediate Past President, International Association of University Presidents (IAUP)

Mr Yukiyasu Harano
Executive Director
Association of the Private Universities of Japan

Mr Masayuki Inoue
Director, International Affairs Planning Division
Science and International Affairs Bureau, Ministry of Education, Science, Sports and Culture

Mr Wataru Iwamoto
Director, Technical Education Division
Higher Education Bureau, Ministry of Education, Science, Sports and Culture

Mr Hiroyuki Uchiyama
Senior Specialist, Cooperation with International Organization
International Affairs Planning Division, Ministry of Education, Science, Sports and Culture

Mr Daisuke Machida
First Secretary
Permanent Delegation of Japan to UNESCO

Mr Akira Takeda
Second Secretary
Permanent Delegation of Japan to UNESCO

Mr Tomoyuki Ono
Attache
Permanent Delegation of Japan to UNESCO

JORDANIE/JORDAN

H.E. Dr Fawzi Gharaibeh
Minister of Education
Chairman of the Jordanian National Commission
(Head of Delegation)

Dr Mohammad Hamdan
Secretary-General
Higher Council for Science and Technology

Dr Sa'ad Hijazi
President
Jordan University of Science and Technology

Miss Janette Bermamet
Cultural Attache
Jordanian Embassy in Paris

KAZAKHSTAN

H.E. Mr Krymbek Kusherbaev
Minister of Education, Culture and Public Health of the Republic of Kazakhstan
Chairman of the National Commission for UNESCO
(Head of Delegation)

H.E. Mr Nurlan Danenov
Ambassador Extraordinary and Plenipotentiary of the Republic of Kazakhstan to France
Permanent Delegate to UNESCO
(Chef Adjoint de la delegation)

Prof. Kupzhasar Naribaev
Rector
Al-Farabi Kazakh State national University

Mr Bazar Damitov
Vice-Chairman, Committe for Education
Head, Department of Higher and Secondary Education

Mr Rustam Muzafarov
First Secretary
Permanent Delegation of Kazakhstan to UNESCO

KENYA

H.E. Mr Steven Andrew Loyatum
Ambassador Extraordinary and Plenipotentiary of Kenya in France
Permanent Delegate to UNESCO
(Head of Delegation)

Mr Joseph S. Obonyo
Senior Deputy Director of Education
Ministry of Education and Human Resource Development

Prof. George Eshiwani
Vice-Chancellor
Kenyatta University

Prof. Justin Irina
Secretary
Commission for Higher Education

Prof. Chacha Nyaigotti-Chacha
Secretary
Higher Education Loans Board

Prof. Geoffrey Nguru
Deputy Vice Chancellor
Daystar University

Dr Margaret J. Kamar
Principal
Chepkoilel Campurs - Moi University

Mr Peter Oloo Okaka
Director of Technical Training
Ministry of Technical Training and Applied Tecnology

Mr Erastus Muthuuri Kiugu
Secretary-General
Kenya National Commission for UNESCO

Mr Jones A.M. Nzeki
Education Attache
Kenya Embassy in Paris

Ms Ruth Cheruiyot
Assistant Secretary General
Kenya National Commission for UNESCO

KIRGHIZISTAN/KYRGYZSTAN

H.E. Professor Dr Sovetbek Toktomyshev
Minister of Education, Science and Culture of the Kyrgyz Republic
(Head of Delegation)

Mrs Ainura Abdyldaeva
Deputy National Director
The European Union's Tacis Programme Tempus Information Point in Kyrgyzstan

Mr T.B. Bekbolotov
Rector
Djalal-Abad State University

KIRIBATI

Mr Meita Beiabure
Permanent Secretary
Ministry of Education, Training and Technology
(Head of Delegation)

Mr Nauto Tekaiara
Senior Education Officer
Ministry of Education, Training and Technology
(Deputy Head of Delegation)

KOWEIT/KUWAIT

H.E. Dr Abdul Aziz Al-Ghanem
Minister of Education and Higher Education
(Head of Delegation)

Prof. Dr Faizah Al-Kharafi
President/Rector
Kuwait University
(Deputy Head of Delegation)

H.E. Dr Musaed R. Al-Haroun
Ambassador
Permanent Delegate of Kuwait to UNESCO

Dr. Humoud Al-Mudhaf
Director General
The Public Authority for Applied Education & Training

Mr Sulaiman Al Onaizi
Secretary-General
Kuwait National Commission for UNESCO

Dr Asad Ismaeel
Vice President for Research
Kuwait University

Mr Fahed Al-Ajmi
Director
Office of H.E. The Minister of
Higher Education

M Taleb Al-Baghli
Delegue permanent adjoint de
l'Etat du Koweit aupres de l'UNESCO

Melle Hanaa Hussain
delegation permanente de l'Etat du
Koweit aupres de l'UNESCO

L'EX-REPUBLIQUE YOUGOSLAVE DE MACEDOINE/FORMER YOUGOSLAV REPUBLIC OF MACEDONIA (THE)

S. Exc. Mme Sofija Todorova
Ministre de l''education et de
l''education physique
(Chef de la delegation)

S. Exc. M. Luan Starova
Ambassadeur extraordinaire et
plenipotentiaire
Delegue permanent de la
Republique de macedoine aupres
de l'UNESCO

M Dimitrija Popovski
President de la Commission de
l''education et de la science aupres
de l'Assemblee nationale
Professeur a la faculte de
l''education physique

Dr Tito Belicanec
Professor
Faculty of Law

Prof. Vladimir Dukovski
Head of Department
University "Sts Civil and
Methodius" Faculty of
Mechnical Engineering

Mrs Divna Sipovik
Chief of Cabinet
Ministry of Education and Physical
Culture

LESOTHO

Honourable Lesao Lehohla
Minister of Education and
Manpower Development
(Head of Delegation)

Mr. B.M. Paneng
Principal Secretary
Ministry of Education and
Manpower Development

Dr. T. Jonathan
Pro-Vice Chancellor
National University of Lesotho

Mr. O.M. Makara
Chief Education Officer
Tertiary

Mrs M. Makakole
Director Education Planning

Miss J. Pulane Lefoka
Director
Institute of Education, National
University of Lesotho

Mr. Karabo T. Marite
Counsellor
Embassy of the Kingdom of Lesotho

LETTONIE/LATIVA

Dr Baiba Rivza
Chairperson
Council of Higher Education
(Head of Delegation)

Prof. Voldemars Strikis
Rector
Latvian Agricultural University

H.E. Ms Aina Nagobads-Abols
Ambassador
Permanent Delegate of the
Republic of Latvia to UNESCO

Dr Janis Sikstulis
Secretary General, Latvian
National Commission for UNESCO
Associate Professor of the
University of Lativia

Mr Dainis Ozolins
Deputy Head of the Department of
Educational Strategy
Member of the Latvian National
Commission for UNESCO

LIBAN/LEBANON

S.Exc. M. Fawzi Hobeiche
Ministre de la culture et de
l''enseignement superieur
(Chef de la delegation)

Dr Assaad Diab
President
Universite libanaise

S. Exc. M. Sami Kronfol
Ambassadeur
Delegue permanent du Liban
aupres de l'UNESCO

Professeur Georges Tohme
President du conseil
d'administration
Conseil national de la recherche
scientifique

Dr Mtanios Al-Halabi
Directeur general'
Ministere de la culture et de
l'enseignement superieur

Mme Salwa Baassiri
Secretaire generale
Commission nationale libanaise
pour l'UNESCO

Mme Bahia Hariri
Deputee, Presidente
Commission parlementaire de
l''education nationale, de la culture,
de la jeunesse et des sports

Prof. Assaad El-Naderi
Doyen de la faculte d''information
et de documentation de l''information
et de documentation de l'Universite
libanaise
Titulaire de la Chaire UNESCO
des sciences de l'information et de
la documentation

Prof. Joseph Abou-Nohra
Doyen de la faculte de pedagogie
de l'Universite libanaise
Titulaire de la chaire UNESCO
des scicences de l''education de
l'Universite libanaise

Dr. Abdel Hassan El-Husseini
Comité des équivalences de
l'Université libanaise

Prof. Hachem El-Husseini
Titulaire de la chaire UNESCO
des sciences de l'information et de
la documentation

M. Noel Fattal
Conseiller
Delegue permanent adjoint du
Liban aupres de l'UNESCO

Experts:

Dr Henri Awit
Universite Saint-Joseph

Dr Nabil Haidar
Universite americaine de Beyrouth

Dr Georges Nahas
Universite du Balamand

Dr Hassan Al-Halabi
Universite islamique du Liban

Dr Fathi Abou-Ayana
Universite arabe de Beyrouth

Dr Jean Khanjian
Universite Haikazian

Pere Antoine Khalife
Recteur
Universite Saint-Esprit de Kaslik

Dr Nabil Khalife
Responsable des affaires estudiantines
Université Saint-Esprit de Kaslik

Mme Angele Khawand Zeenni
Presidente
Association des libanaises universitaires (ADLU)

Mr Nadim Jabbour
Commissaire de la Commission des equivalences
Ministere de la culture et de l'enseignement superieur

M. Joseph El-Metni
Attache de Presse
Ministere de la culture et de l''enseignement superieur

LIBERIA

Hon. Thomas B. Collins
Deputy Minister of Education
(Head of Delegation)

H.E. Mr James Molly Scott
Ambassador Extraordinary and Plenipotentiary of Liberia in France
Permanent Delegate to UNESCO

Dr Lawrence S. Bestman
Executive Director
National Commission of Higher Education

Dr Frederic Gbegbe
President
University of Liberia

Dr Louise York
President
African Methodist Episcopal University (A.M.E.U.)

Dr William Saa-Salifu
Vice-President for Academic Affairs
A.M.E. University

Dr Habib M. Sesay
Acting President A.M.E. Zion University

Dr Melvin J. Mason
President
Cuttington University College

Mrs Hawah Goll-Kotchi
Secretary General
Liberia National Commission for UNESCO

Mr Jeff Gongoer Dowana, Sr.
Delegate

Mrs Lily Behna
Delegate

LITUANIE/LITHUANIA

H.E. Mr Kornelijus Platelis
Minister of Education and Science
(Head of Delegation)

Mr Juozas Antanavicius
President of Rector's Conference

Mr. Kestutis Krisciunas
Rector
Kaunas Technological University

Mr Rolandas Povilionis
Rector
Vilnius University

Ms Sandra Civinskaite
Member of Student's Council

Ms Romualda Hofertiene
Member of Lithuanian Parliament

Mr Rimantas Slizys
Director of Department of Higher Education and Science
Ministry of Education and Science

Mr Albertas Zalys
Advisor of the Government

Mr Gintautas Braziunas
President
Association of College Directors

H.E. Ms Ugne Karvelis
Ambassador Extraordinary and Plenipotentiary
Permanent Delegate of Lithuania to UNESCO

LUXEMBOURG

S. Exc. Mme Erna Hennicot Schoepges
Ministre de l''education nationale
(Chef de la delegation)

S. Exc. M. Jean-Marc Hoscheit
Ambassadeur extraordinaire et plenipotentiaire de Luxembourg en France
Delegue permanent aupres de l'UNESCO

M. Patrick Engelberg
Delegue permanent adjoint

M. Jean Tagliaferri
Professeur-Attache
Ministre de l'education nationale

M. Albert Retter
Directeur de l'Institut superieur de technologie

Mme Julie-Suzanne Bausch
Docteur en philosophie

MACAO/MACAU

Dr Jorge Alberto Rangel
Secretary for Public Administration, Education and Youth
(Head of Delegation)

Prof. Zhou Ligao
Rector (president)
University of Macau

Mr Luis Maria de Oliveira Dias
President
Macau Polytechnic Institute

Mr Antonio Rodrigues Junior
President
Macau Foundation

MADAGASCAR

S. Exc. M. Joseph Sydson
Ministre de l'eneignement superieur
(Chef de la delegation)

S. Exc. M. Boniface Levelo
Ministre de l'enseignement technique et de la formation professionnelle

S. Exc. M. Jacquit Simon
Ministre de l'enseignement secondaire et de l'education de base

S. Exc. M. Jose Vianey
Ambassadeur
Delegue permanent de Madagascar aupres de l'UNESCO

M. Alisoana Raharinirivonirina
Directeur de l'enseignement superieur
Ministere de i'enseignement superieur

M. Ralaisoa Emile Rakotomahanina
Recteur
Universite Antananarivo

M Georges Remy
Recteur
Universite nord de Madagascar

M. Marie Dieudonne Michel Razafindrandriatsimaniry
Recteur
Universite de Fianarantsoa

M. Claude Hortense Solofonniaina
Recteur
Universite de Mahanjanga

M. Eugene Mangalaza
Recteur
Université de Toamasina

M. Marcel Napetoka
Recteur
Universite de Toliara

Mme Violette Ramanankasina
Directeur general de la Maison de la communication des universites

Prof. Raoelina Andriambololona
Directeur general
Institut national des sciences et techniques nucleaires (I.N.S.T.N)

Mme Farasoa Ravalitera
Directeur du Department tertiaire
Institut superieur de technologie

Mme Ravaomalala Rasoanaivo
delegue permanent adjoint de Madagascar aupres de l'UNESCO

M. Benjamin Claude Babany
Conseiller Culturel
Delegation permanente de Madagascar aupres de l'UNESCO

Melle Hantanirinarisoa Simon
Conseiller scientifique
Delegation permanente de Madagascar aupres de l'UNESCO

MALAISIE/ MALAYSIA

Dr Johari Mat
Secretary-General
Ministry of Education
(Head of Delegation)

Dr Abdullah Abdul Shukor
Director General of Education

H.E. Mr Ahmad Hussein
Ambassador
Permanent Delegate of Malaysia to UNESCO

Dr Anuwar Ali
Vice Chancellor
National University of Malaysia

Mr Mukhtar Boerhannoeddin
Deputy Permanent Delegate of Malaysia to UNESCO

Mr Abdul Aziz Abdul Halim
Lecturer
University of East London

MALAWI

Hon. Brown J. Mpinganjira, M.P.
Minister of Education
(Head of Delegation)

Dr Sam D.D, Safuli
Secretary for Education

Dr Dan Chimwenje
Director of Studies
Mzuzu University

Prof. Leonard A. Kamwanja
Acting Principal
Bunda College

Dr. S. Hau
Principal
Domasi College of Education

Mr. F.R. Mkandawire
Deputy Executive Secretary General
Malawi National Commission for UNESCO

Prof. Terence Davis, OBE
Vice Chancellor
Mzuzu University
Permanent Delegation of Malawi to UNESCO

H.E. Mr Zililo P.Y. Chibambo
Ambassador Extraordinary and Plenipotentiary of Malawi in France
Permanent Delegate to UNESCO

Dr. Gadi G.Y. Mgomezulu
Deputy Ambassador and Deputy Permanent Delegate to UNESCO

Mrs Esther Kamlongera
First Secretary

MALDIVES

H.E. Mr Mohamed Latheef
Minister of Education
(Head of Delegation)

Mr Midhath Hilmy
Director General
Ministry of Education

MALI

S. Exc. Professeur Younouss Hameye Dicko
Ministre des enseignements secondaire, superieur et de la recherche scientifique
(Chef de la delegation)

M. Abdoulaye Salim Cisse
Conseiller technique
Charge de l''enseignement superieur

M. Sahaloum Ould Youbba
Conseiller technique
Charge de la cooperation

M. Mamadou Bani Diallo
Charge de mission
Charge du development de l'universite

M. Abdoulaye Drame
Directeur national de l'enseignement superieur

M. Boubacar Sidiki Cisse
Recteur
Universite du Mali

Mme Aminata Sall
Secretaire Generale
Commission nationale malienne pour l'UNESCO

Mme Djeneba Traore
Secretariat de la Commission nationale des equivalences
Direction nationale de l'enseignement superieur

Mr Abdramane Megninta
Syndicat national de''
l''enseignement superieur

M. Baba Moussoudou Toure
Syndicat national de l''education et de la culture

Mr Keoule Boundy
Professor at University
Official in charge of mission at the Presidency of the Republic
Delegation permanente du Mali aupres de l'UNESCO

S. Exc. Mme Madina Ly-Tall
Ambassadeur extraordinaire et plenipotentiaire du Mali en France
Deleguee permanente aupres de l'UNESCO

M. Amidou Doucoure
Conseiller culturel
delegue permanent adjoint

MALTE/MALTA

H.E. Mr Vincent Camilleri
Ambassador Extraordinary and Plenipotentiary
Permanent Delegate of Malta to UNESCO
(Head of Delegation)

Prof. Roger Ellul Micallef
Rector
University of Malta

Mr Pierre Clive Agius
First Secretary
Deputy Permanent Delegate of Malta to UNESCO

Mr Hubert Dalli
Education Coordinator
University Students Council

MAROC/MOROCCO

S. Exc. M. Najib Zerouali
Ministre de l'enseignement superieur, de la formation des cadres et de la recherche scientifique
(Chef de la delegation)

Délégation permanente du Royaume du Maroc aupres de l'UNESCO

M. Aniss Birrou
Directeur
Cabinet du Ministre de l'enseignement supérieur

M. Mokhtar Anaki
Directeur de l'enseignement supérieur
Ministére de l'enseignement supérieur

M. Abdelhamid Ahmady
Recteur
Université Abou chouaib Doukkali

Mme Rahma Bourqia
Doye
Facultédes lettres et des scieces huamines de Mohamédia

Mme Naïma Hbabi
Professeur
Faculté de médecine de Rabat

M. Abdelkader Mokhlisse
Doyen
Faculté des sciences Semlalia de Marrakech

Mme Naïma Tabet
Secrétaire général
Commission nationale marocaine pour l'UNESCO

Mme Anas Leyt
Membre du Cabinet du Ministre de l' enseignement supérieur

S. Exc. M. Mohamad Berrada
Ambassadeur extraordinaire et plénipotentiaire du Royaume du Maroc en France
Délégué permanent auprés de l'UNESCO

Mme Fatima M'hamedi-Bounafaâ
Ministre plenipotentiaire aupres de l'Ambassade du Maroc a Paris

M. Adil Ghallab
Conseiller

MAURICE/MAURITIUS

Hon. Ramsamy Chedumbarum Pilly
Minister of Education & Human Ressource Development
(Head of Delegation)

Mr Siva Subramanien
Permanent Secretary
Ministry of Education and Human Resource Development

Miss Medha Devi Moti
Director
Ministry of Education and Human] Resource Development - Ag. Technical Officer

Prof. Goolam Mohamedbhai
Vice Chancellor
Univrsity of Mauritius

Dr Raj Lutchmeah
Director
Tertiary Education Commission

Mr R. Dubois
Director
Indisutrial and Vocational Training Board

Permanent Delegation of the Republic of Mauritius to UNESCO

H.E. Mrs Marie France Roussety
Ambassador Extraordinary and Plenipotentiary of the Republic of Mauritius in France
Permanent Delegate to UNESCO

Mr Dooladren Pillay Tirvengadum
Minister Counsellor
Deputy Permanent Delegate

Mr Nadrajen Chedumbarum
First Secretary

MAURITANIE/MAURITANIA

S. Exc. M. Ahmedou Ould Moustapha Ould Senhoury
Ministre de l''education nationale
(Chef de la delegation)

S. Exc. M. Abou Demba Sow
Ambassadeur extraordinaire et plenipotentiaire
Delegue permanent de Mauritanie aupres de l'UNESCO
(Chef adjoint de la delegation)

M. Salah Ould Moulaye Ahemd
Conseiller technique du Ministre Charge de l'enseignement superieur

M. Ely Ould Boubout
Secretaire general
Commission nationale pour l''education, la science et la culture

M. Mohamed Ould Bagga
Directeur, planification et cooperation
Ministere de l''education nationale

M. Izidbih Ould Mohamed
Directeur de l'enseignement supérieur

M. Mohamed Ould Sidya Ould Khabaz
Recteur
Université de Nouakchott

M. Mohamed Ould Sidiya
Directeur
Ecole normale superieure

M. El Moktar Ould Mohamed Yahya
Directeur des ressources humaines
Ministere des affaires economiques et du developpment

M. Lemrabott Ould Benahi
conseiller
Delegation permanente de
Mauritanie aupres de
l'UNESCO

MEXIQUE/MEXICO

Dr Daniel Resendiz Nunez
Subsecretario de Educacion
Superior
Secretaria de Educacion Publica
(Jefe de la delegacion)

Dip. Fed. Sr Armando Chavarria
Barrera
Presidente
Comision de Educacion de la
Camara de Diputados

Dr. Francisco Barnés de Castro
Rector
Universidad Nacional Autónoma
de México (UNAM)

Ing. Diodoro Guerra Rodriguez
Director General
Instituto Politecnio Nacional
(IPN)

Dr Julio Rubio Oca
Secretario General Ejecutivo
Aspciacion Nacional de
Universidades e Instituciones de
Educacion Superior (ANUIES)

Lic. Carlos Bazdresch Parada
Director General
Consejo Nacional de Ciencia y
Technologia (CONACYT)

Dip. Fed. Cupertino Alejo
Dominguez
Secretario de la Comision de
Educacion de la Camara de
Diputados

Dip. Fed Jose Ricardo Fernandez
Candia
Secretario de la Comision de
Educacion de la Camara de
diputados

Dip. Fed. Maria del Carmen
Escobedo Perez
Secretaria de la Comision de
Educacion de la Camara de
Diputados

Ing. Armando Baez Pedrajo
Coordinador de Asesores de la
subsecretaria de Planeacion y
Coordinacion
comision Nacional de los estados
Unidos Mexicanos para la
UNESCO (CONALMEX)

Observadores:

Mtra. Joan M.W. de Landeros
Representante
Federacion de Instituciones
Mexicanas Particulares de
Educacion Superior

Arq. Xavier Cortes Rocha
Secretario General de la
Universidad Nacional Autonoma
de mexico (UNAM)

Delegacion Permanente de Mexico
ante la UNESCO

Excmo. Sr. Mario Ojeda
Embajador, Representante
Permanente de Mexico ante la UNESCO

Ministro Zadalinda Gonzalez y
reynero
Representante alterno de Mexico
ante la UNESCO

Sra. Adriana Valades de Moulines
Segundo Secretario Diplomatico
Delegacion Permanente de Mexico
ante la UNESCO

MONGOLIE/MONGOLIA

Dr. D. Bardach
President
Consortium of Universities
(Head of Delegation)

Mr. M.L. Baasanjav
Vice Director, Department of Policy Implementation and Coordination
Ministry of Science, Technology, Education and Culture

Mr Radnaabazaryn altangerel
Third Secretary
Permanent Delegation to UNESCO

Mr Tsend Batbuyan
Permanent Delegation to UNESCO

MOZAMBIQUE

H.E. Mr Arnalod Valdo Valente Nhavoto
Minister of Education
(Head of Delegation)

Mr Brazao Mazula
Rector
Eduaro Mondlane University

Prof. Carlos Machili
Rector
Pedagogical University

Mr Taimo U. Jamisse
Rector
Hihger Institute for International Relations (ISRI)

Mr Paulo Ivo Garrido
Rector
Higher Institute for Science and Technology (ISCTEM)

Mr Cremildo Momade Chitara
Legal Advisor of the Minister of Education

Mr Arlindo Chilundo
Director of Planning
University Eduardo Mondlane

Mr Januario Mutaquiha
Secretary General
National Commission for UNESCO

Lic. Rosita Alberto
Representative
Women Academic Nucleus
NUMAC

Mr Boaventura Chi Chicuele
Students' Association
Representative
Universidade Eduardo Mondlane

Delegation permanente de la Republique de Mozambique aupres de l'UNESCO

S. Exc. M. Jose Rui Mota do Amaral
Ambassadeur extraordinaire et plenipotentiaire de la Republique du Mozambique en France
Delegue permanent aupres de l'UNESCO

M. Filimone Julio Tasmbe
Conseiller

MYANMAR

Dr. Thein Myint
Director General
Department of Higher Education
(Head of Delegation)

H.E.U. Nyunt Tin
Ambasador Extraordinary and Plenipotentiary of the Union of Myanmar to France
Permanent Delegate to UNESCO

Mr U. Than Tun
Counsellor
Embassy of the Union of Myanmar

Mr U Aung Latt
Second Seretary
Embassy of the Union of
Myanmar, Paris

Mr U Aung Myint
Second Secretary
Embassy of the Union of Myanmar

Mr U Khin Maung Oo
Attaché
Embassy of the Union of Myanmar,
Paris

Mr U Tun Aung Bo
Attache
Embassy of the Union of Myanmar,
Paris

NAMIBIE/NAMIBIA

H.E. Mr Nahas Angula
Minister of Higher Education
(Head of Delegation)

H.E. Mr Leonard Nangolo lipumbu
Ambassador Extraordinary and
Plenipotentiary of Namibia to
France
Permanent Delegate to UNESCO

Prof. Peter H. Katjavivi
Vice-Chancellor
University of Namibia

Dr Tjama Tjivikua
Rector
Polytechnic of Namibia

Ms Pushukeni J. Shoombe
Chairperson
Committe of Human Resoruces of
the National Assembly

Mr Colin Komehozu
Secretary-General
Nambia National Students Organization

Mrs Ailly Ernesta Kustaa
National Treasurer
Namibia National Teachers Union

Mrs Trudie Amulungu
Secretary-General
Namibia National Commission for
UNESCO

Miss Etambuyu Mbuye
Director of Higher Education

Dr Itah Kandji-Murangi
Director of International Relations
University of Namibia

Mr Zach J. N. Kazapua
Registrar
University of Namibia

NEPAL

H.E. Mr Indra Bahadur Singh
Ambassador Extraordinary and
Plenipotentiary of Nepal to France
Permanent Delegate to UNESCO
(Head of Delegation)

Mr Khem Raj Regmi
Secretary-General, Nepal National
Commission for UNESCO
Secretary, Ministry of Education

Dr Suresh Raj Sharma
Vice-Chancellor
Kathmandu University

Dr Hom Nath Bhattarai
Member Secretary
University Grant Commission

Mrs Radha Sharma
Associate Professor
Faculty of Education, Tribhuwan
Univerisity

M. Tej Prasad Koirala
Delegue permanent adjoint

NICARAGUA

Licenciada Milena Lucia Lanzas Monge
Ministro Consejero de la Embajada de Nicaragua en Francia
(Jefe de la delegacion)

Lic. Francisco Guzman Pasos
Presidente del Consejo Nacional de Universidades
Rector de la Universidad Nacional Autonoma de Nicaragua-Managua

Ing. Telemaco Talavera
Rector
Universidad Nacional Agraria

Dr Eduardo Valdes
Rector
Universidad Centroamericana

Dr Ernesto Medina Sandino
Rector
Universidad Nacional Autonoma de Nicaragua-Leon

Lic. Mariano Vargas
Secretario Tecnico del Consejo Nacional de Universidades

Ing. Mario Caldera
Rector
Universidad nacional de Ingenieria

Dr Owyn Hodgson
Rector
Bluefield Indian a. Caribe University (BI-CU)

Br. Francisco Porras Aleman
Dirigente Estudiantil Nacional

Ms Marta Caldera
Attachee
Delegacion Permanente de Nicaragua ante la UNESCO

NIGER

Prof. Issoufou Kouada
Secretaire general du Ministere de l'enseignement superieur, de la recherche et de la technologie
(Chef de la delegation)

Prof. Daouda Hamani
Vice-Recteur
Universite Abdou Moumouni de Niamey

M. Mahamane Saadou
Doyen
Faculte des sciences, UAM

M. Karimou Ambouta
Doyen
Faculte d' agronmie, UAM

M. Hassane Abdo
Doyen
Faculte des sciences economiques et juridiques, UAM

M. Ousseini Iisa
Doyen
Faculte des lettres et sciences humaines, UAM

M. Abdoulaye Marichetou Mahamane
Directeur
Ecole normale superieure, UAM

Prof. Pierre Foulani
Coordonnateur du projet Banque Mondiale sur les strategies de l'enseignement superieur
Direction des projects education

M. Amadou Tcheko
Delegue permanent adjoint du Niger aupres de l'UNESCO

M. Traore Abou
directeur de l'enseignement superieur, de la recherche et de la technologie

M. Boukary Mahamane Sani
Conseiller technique du Recteur
UAM

Mme Hadiza Hama
Attache academique
Ambassade du Niger a Paris

NIGERIA

Alhaji Mahmud Yayale Ahmed
Permanent Secretary
Federal Ministry of Education
(Head of Delegation)

Dr Peter Shehu Abdu
Director
Educational Support Services
Federal Ministry of Education

Dr Usman Bokani Ahemd
Director
Department of Formal Education
Federal Ministry of Education

Mrs Joyce Aluko
Chairperson
Nigerian National Commission for UNESCO

Mrs M. Olubanke A. Alorunfunmi
Deputy Director
Federal Ministry of Education

Mrs M.Y. Katagum
Secretary
Social & Human Sciences Sector,
NATCOM UNESCO

Professor Munzali Jibril
Executive Secretary
National Universities Commission

Mr Chubado Mahammed Jada
Principal Administrator
Federal Ministry of Education

Dr A.T. Abdullahi
Executive Secretary, National Board for Technical Education
(Alternate Delegate)

Prof. Bello/Ahmad Salim
Registrar
Joint Admissions & Matriculation Board

Dr Kabiru Isyaku
Executive Secretary, National Commission for Colleges of Education (Alternate Delegate)

Prof. Wale Omole
Vice-Chancellor
Obafemi Awolowo Univeristy, Ilelfe

Mr Y.M.O. Nwafor
Secretary-General, Nigerian National Commission for UNESCO
(Alternate Delegate)

Permanent Delegation of Nigeria to UNESCO

H.E. Dr E.O. Akinluyi
Ambassador, Permanent Delegate

Mr Umar M. Ahmed
Deputy Permanent Delegate

Mrs Bridget Zidon
Senior Counsellor

Mr Y. Lijadu
Counsellor

NORVEGE/NORWAY

Mr Jan Schreiner Levy
Director General
Royal Norwegian Ministry of Education, Research and Church Affairs
(Head of Delegation)

Ms Kari Blom
Rector
Bergen College

Miss Cecilie P. Oyen
Immediat Past President
Norwegian Association of Students

Mr Ole Danbolt Mjos
Professor
University of Tromso

Mr Sverre Rustad
Deputy Director General
Network Norway Council

Ms Elizabeth Jacobsen
Head, Section for Development Cooperation
Department for Bilateral Affairs
Ministry of Foreign Affairs

Ms Birgitta Naess
president
Norwegian National Commission for UNESCO

Ms Anne Rygg
Immediate Past President
National Union of Students in Norway

Ms Norunn Grande
Senior Executive Officer
The Norwegian National Commission for UNESCO

Mr Per Wright
Rector
The Norwegian University of Sport and Physical Education

Permanent Delegation of Norway to UNESCO

H.E. Mr Rolf Trolle Andersen
Extraordinary and Plenipotentiary Ambassador of Norway in France
Permanent Delegate to UNESCO

Mrs Lizzie R. Dahm
Deputy Permanent Delegate to UNESCO

NOUVELLE-ZELANDE/NEW ZEALAND

Mr Vince Catherwood
Senior Manager
Tertiary Charters and Funding, Minsitry of Education
(Head of Delegation)

Hon. Russell Marshall
Chairperson
New Zealand National Commission for UNESCO

Prof. Sylvia Rumball
Assistant to the Vice-Chancellor (EEO), Massey University
Member of the New Zealand National Commission for UNESCO

Mr Turoa Royal
Executive Chairperson
Tauihu o Nga Wananga, National Association of Wananga

Mr Rob Crozier
Executive Director
Association of University Staff

Ms Mary Oliver
First Secretary
Deputy Permanent Delegate of New Zealand to UNESCO

OMAN

H.E. Shaikh Salim Bin Mustahil Bin Ahmed Al-Maashani
Undersecretary, Ministry of Higher Education
(Head of Delegation)

H.E. Dr Musa bin Jaffar bin Hassan
Ambassador
Permanent Delegate of Oman to UNESCO
(Deputy Head of Delegation)

Shaikh Khalid bin Mohammed bin Zahir Al - Hanai
Director General, General Directorate of Educational Information and Relations
General Secretary, National Commission for Education, Culture and Science

Dr Abdallah Bin guma Bahwan
Consultant, The Office of H.E. the Undersecretary

Dr Talib bin Issa Al-Salimi
Director
Higher Studies Directorate

Mr Kamal bin Hassan Macki
Deputy Permanent Delegate of Oman to UNESCO

Mr Ali Bin Naser Al-Awaisi
Director, Undersecretary Office

Dr Abdelrahaman El-Rufaai

OUGANDA/UGANDA

Hon. Dr Abel J.J. Rwendeire
Minister of State for Education
(Head of Delegation)

Mr Francis Lubanga
Permanent Secretary
(Alternate Head of Delegation)

Prof. Peter Kanyandago
Deputy Vice-Chancellor
Uganda Martyrs University Nkozi

Rev. Canon Dustau Bukenya
Vice-Chancellor
Uganda Christian University Mukono

Dr Justine Epelu-Opio
Deputy Vice-Chancellor
Makerere University

Prof. J.P. Ocitti
Head, Department of Higher Education
School of Education, Makerere University

Prof. A. Lutalo-Bbosa
Principal
Institute of Teacher Education, Kyambogo

Ms Anastansia Nakkazi
Uganda National Commission for UNESCO
(Technical Staff)

H.E. Dr David K. Kazungu
Ambassador Extraordinary and Plenipotentiary of Uganda in France
Permanent Delegate to UNESCO

Mr Godfrey Kwoba
Deputy Permanent Delegate

Ms Irene Ellen Ssemakula
Commission Secretary

Mr Patrick Ezaga Onen
Chairperson, Uganda Students Association

Ms Avitas Tibarimbasa
University Secretary- Makerere University

M. Eriabu Lugujjo

OUZBEKISTAN/UZBEKISTAN

Dr Takhir Agzamov
Leading Expert on Education
Cabinet of Ministers
(Head of Delegation)

Dr Alisher Akhmedov
Head of Education Department
National Commission of Uzbekistan for UNESCO

Dr Shavkat Kurbanov
Senior Consultant on Education
Administration of President

Dr Khikmatualla Lutfullaev
Vice-Rector
Tashkent State Economic
University

S.Exc. M. Takhirjon Mamajonov
Ambassadeur extraordinaire et
plenipotentiaire de la Republique
d''Ouzbekistan en France
Delegue permanent aupres de
l'UNESCO

PAKISTAN

Dr Safdar Mahmood
Federal Secretary Education
Ministry of Education
(Head of Delegation)

Miss Asma Anisa
Permanent Delegate of Pakistan to
UNESCO
(Deputy Head of Delegation)

Mrs Riffat Masood
Deputy Permanent Delegate of
Pakistan to UNESCO
(Deputy Head of Delegation)

PALESTINE

H.E. Dr Munthir Salah
Minister of Higher Education
(Head of Delegation)

S. Exc. M. Awad Yakhlef
Ambassadeur
Observateur permanent de
Palestine aupres de l'UNESCO

Dr Lily Feidy
Director General for International
and Cultural Relations

Dr Ribhi Abu Sneineh
Director General for University
Education

Dr Ziad Jweiles
Director General for Colleges and
Technical Education

Dr Rami Al-Hamdallah
President
An-Najah National University

Dr Muhammad Shubeir
President
Islamic University

Dr Daoud Zatari
Acting President of the Polytechnic

Dr Thssan Al-Agha
Professor
Islamic University

Mr Tamer Thabet
Student Representative
Al-Azhar University

Ms Suha abu-Arkoub
Student Representative
Polytechnic

Mr Jihad Qurashuli
Secretary General
Palestinian National Commission
for Education, Culture, and Science

Mr Ahmad Dari
Deputy Permanent Observer to
UNESCO

Mr Anwar abu Eisheh

PANAMA

Prof. Jorge Delgado Castellano
Director General del Instituto
Nacional de Cultura
(Jefe de la delegacion)

Sr. Hermann Castro
Rector
Universidad Latinoamericana de Ciencias y Tecnologia

Sr. Julio Vallarino
Vicerrector de Investigacion y Postgrado
Universidad Naicional de Panama

Ing. Hector Montemayor
Rector de la Universidad Tecnologica de Panama

Prof. Jorge Arosemena
Director Ejecutivo
Fundacion Ciudad del Saber

Dra. Berta Torrijos de Arosemena
Rectora
Universidad Especializada de las Americas

Prof. William Salom
Rector
Universidad Intermamericana de Panama

Prof. Virgilio Olmos
Rector
Universidad Autonoma de Chiriqui

Dra. Noemi Castillo Jaen
Rectora
Nova Southeastern University

Prof. Lucrecia Herrera Cozzarelli
Rectora
Universidad de la Paz

Sr. Aristides Isaac Gomez de Leon
Director de Cooperacion Internacional y Asistencia tecnica
Universidad de Panama

Sr. Jose Felix liopis Lamela
Delegado Permanente ante la UNESCO

Srta. Maria Elena de Aguilar
Delegado Permanente Adjunto

Sr. Jorge Patino
Tercer Secretario

PAPOUASIE NOUVELLE GUINEE/PAPUA NEW GUINEA

H.E. Dr John Waiko
Vice Minister for Higher Education
(Head of Delegation)

Mr Jerry Kuhena
Deputy Secretary for Higher Education

Dr Mark Solon
Vice Chancellor of the University of Goroka

Permanent Delegation of Papua New Guinea to UNESCO

Mr Kappa Yarka
Permanent Delegate of Papua New Guinea to UNESCO

Mr David Anere
Deputy Permanent Delegate of Papua New Guinea to UNESCO

PARAGUAY

Excma. Sra. Maria Celsa Bareiro de Soto
Ministra de Educacion y Cultura
(Jefe de la delegacion)

Excmo. Sr. Dr. Ruben Bareiro Saguier
Embajador Extraordinario y Plenipotenciario de la Republica del paraguay en Francia
Delegado Permanente ante la UNESCO

Dr Luis H. Berganza
Rector
Universidad nacional de Asuncion

Sr. Carlos Andres Couchonnal Zeiser
Director del Gabinete del Ministerio de Educacion y Cultura

Licda. Elvia Zayas de Von Bargen
Catedratica de la Universidad Catolica de Encarnacion

Don Sila Estigarribia
Delegado Permanente Adjunto
Delegacion Permanente del Paraguay ante la UNESCO

PAYS-BAS/NETHERLANDS

Prof. P.W.M. de Meijer
President
Commission nationale pour l'UNESCO
(Chef de la delegation)

Mme J.A. Offermans
Ministere de l'enseignement, de la culture et des sciences

Mme M.E. Leegwater
Ministere de l'enseignement, de la culture et des sciences

M. L.M.E. Wolfs
Ministere des affaires etrangeres

Mme S. Pantelic
Ministere des affaires etrangeres

M.F.J.M. van Kalmthout
Conseil pur l'enseignement professionnel superieur

M.G.W. Noomen
Federation des universities neerlandaises

Prof. L.F.M. Dubbeldam
Commission nationale pur l'UNESCO

Mme M. Rietbergen
Syndicat national des etudiants

M.W.A. van Helden
Delegue permanent adjoint aupres de l'UNESCO

M.D. Lageweg
Commission nationale pour l'UNESCO
(Suppleant)

Mme M. Engelkes
Ministere de l'enseignement, de la culture et des sciences
(Suppleante)

PEROU/PERU

Dr Cesar Paredes Canto
Rector de la Universidad Nacional de Cajamarca
Presidente de la Asamblea Nacional de Rectores
(Jefe de la delegacion)

Ing. Esau Caro Meza
Rector
Universidad nacional del Centro

Dr jorge Benitez Robles
Rector
Universidad Privada San Pedro

Representacion Permanente del Peru ante la UNESCO

Excma. Sra. Maria Luisa Federici
Embajadora
Delegada Permanente del Peru ante la UNESCO

Ministro J. Alberto Carrion T.
Delegado Permanente Adjunto del Peru ante la UNESCO

Sr. Carlos Vasquez Corrales
Primer Secretario

PHILIPPINES

Hon. Angel C. Clcala
Chairman
Commission on Higher Education
(Head of Delegation)

Hon. Hector K. Villarroel
Ambassador Extraordinary and Plenipotentiary of the Philippines to France and Portugal
Permanent Delegate to UNESCO
(Deputy Head of Delegation)

Hon. Andrew Gonzalez
Secretary
Department of Education, Culture and Sports

Hon. Rosario G. Manalo
Undersecretary of Foreign Affairs
Acting Secretary-General, UNESCO National Commission of the Philippines

Hon. Isagani R. Cruz
Commissioner
National Commission on Culture and Arts

Hon. Milagros Hernandez
Deputy Director-General
Technical Education and Skills Development Authority

Dr Arturo P. Casuga
Vice-President, Philippines Association of the State Universitites and Colleges
President, Eulogio Amang Rodriguez Institute of Science and Technology, Manila

Fr. Roderick Salazar, SVD
President
Catholic Education Association of the Philippines

Dr Alicia Bustos
President
Federation of Accrediting Agencies of the Philippines

Dr Adriano Arcelo
President
Fund for Assistance to Private Education

Hon. Dante Liban
Representative, House of Representatives
(Adviser)

Hon. Mona D. Valisno
Commissioner, Commission on Higher Education
(Adviser)

Hon. Teresa Aqiomp-Oreta
Senator, Senate of the Philippines
(Adviser)

Ms Deanna O. Recto
First Secretary and Senior Foreign Affairs for UNESCO
Permanent Delegation of the Philippines to UNESCO

Ms Jeannette D. Tuason
Deputy Executive Director II
UNESCO National Commission of the Philippines

Ms Kristine G. Floria
Development Management Officer III
UNESCO National Commission of the Philippines

Mr Earl Victor L. Rosero
Executive Assistant to Dr. Mona Valisno

POLOGNE/POLAND

S.Exc. M. Miroslaw Handke
Ministre de l'education nationale
(chef de la delegation)

M. Aleksander Luczak
Representant du Parlement de la Republique de Pologne
Depute, Vice-President de la Commission de l'education, de la science et de la jeunesse

M. Tadeusz Skoskiewicz
academie polonaise des sciences
(Vice -President de la delegation)

M. Wojciech Falkowski
Secretaire general, Commission nationale polonaise pour l'UNESCO
(Vice-President de la delegation)

M. Jerzy Woznicki
Rect. de l'Universite technologique de Varsovie
Vicepresident de la Conference des recteurs des ecoles academiques en Pologne

Mme Magdalena Mazinska
Directeur du Departement de l'integration europeenne et de la cooperation internationale
Ministere de l'education nationale

S. Exc. Mme Alicja Ciezkowska
Ministre plenipotentiaire
Delegue permanent de la Pologne aupres de l'UNESCO

M. Henryk Ratajczak
Ancien Recteur de l'UNIVERSITE DE Wroclaw
Directeur de Centre de l'Academie polonaise des sciences a Paris

M. Janusz Reykowski
Directeur de l'Institut de psychologie
academie polonaise des sciences

M. Ryszard Mosakowski
universite technologique de Gdansk

PORTUGAL

Prof. Alfredo Jorge Silva
Secretaire d'Etat pour l'enseignement superieur
(chef de la delegation)

S. Exc. M. Jarge Ritto
Ambassadeur
Delegue permananet du Portugal aupres de l'UNESCO

Prof. Sergio Machado dos Santos
professeur universitaire

Prof. Luis Sousa Lobo
Recteur de l'Université nouvelle
Vice-President du Consil des recteurs des universités portugaises

Prof. Luis Soares
President du Conseil coordinateur des instituts superieurs polytechniques

M. Antonio Jorge G. Rodrigues
Membre de la Direction
Association protugaise de l'enseignement superieur prive

Mme Maria Eduarda Boal
Directuer du Cabinent des affaires europeennes et relations internationales

M. Lopes Serrado
Secretaire executif et President par interim
Commission nationale portugaise pour l'UNESCO

Prof. Martin Lusi Pinto
Sous Directeur
Department de l'enseignement superieur

Mme Maria de Lurdes Paixao
Membre du conseil coordinateur pour l'education
Commission nationale portugaise pour l'UNESCO

Mme Maria Manuel Durao
Delegue permanent adjoint du Portugal aupres de l'UNESCO

M.Fernando Medina
Representant des associations d'etudiants

M. Luiz de albuquerque Veloso
Secretaire d'Ambassade
Delegation permanente du Portugal aupres de l'UNESCO

QATAR

H.E. Dr Mohammed Abdul-Rahim Kafoud
Minister of Education and Higher Education
Chairman of Qatar National Commission
(Head of Delegation)

Dr Ibrahim El-Nouami
Rector
University of Qatar

Dr Darwish El-Emadi
Dean
Faculty of Humanities Studies, University of Qatar

Dr Abdurahmane Abdulla Al-Mulawi
Directeur des relations culturelles
Ministere de l'Education

M. Abdul Aziz Al-Ansari
Secretaire general
Commission nationale du Qatar pour l'UNESCO

Mr Ahmmed Yousef Asheer
Director
Minister's Office for Higher Education

Permanent Delegation of the State of Qatar to UNESCO

Mr Ibrahim Bubshit
Permanent Delegate of the State of Qatar to UNESCO

Mr Mohamed Fathi Awad

Mr Youssef Ahmed

REPUBLIQUE ARABE SYRIENNE/SYRIAN ARAB REPUBLIC

S. Exc. Mme Dr. Salha Sounkor
Ministre de l'enseignement superieur
(Chef de la delegation)

Mme Nabila Chaalan
Ministre plenipotentiaire
Delegue permanent de la Republique arabe syrienne aupres de l'UNESCO

Dr Abdul Gani Maa El Bared
Recteur
Universite de Damas

Dr Mohammed Ali Houriya
Recteur
Universitie d'Alep

Dr Mohi Eddine Issa
Vice Ministre pour l'enseignement superieur

Dr Mohammed Elissa
Sous Secretaire de l'Universite Al Baath pur les affaires scientifiques

Ing. Moukram Nabil El Rifai
Ministere de l'enseignement superieur

Dr Guazi Mansour
Secretaire des bureaux regionaux de l'enseignement superieur et des etudiants

Dr Omar Blache
Membre du bureau executif du syndicat des enseignants

Dr Mahmoud Elsayed
Membre du corps enseignant de l'Universite de Damas

Dr Abdul Latif Youssef
Membre du corps enseignant de l'Universite de Tichrine

Mme Dr. Amal Kabous
Membre du crops enseignant de l'Universite d'Alep

REPUBLIQUE CENTRAFRICAINE/CENTRAL AFRICAN REPUBLIC

S. Exc. M. Theophile Touba
Ministre de l'enseignement superieur, de la recherche scientifigue et technologique
(Chef de la delegation)

S. Exc. M. Jean Poloko
Ambassadeur extraordinaire et plenipotentiaire de la Republique centrafricaine en France
Delegue permanent aupres de l'UNESCO et de la Francophonie

Mme Georgine Gresenguet
Chargee de missions
Ministere de l'enseignement superieur, de la recherche scientifique et technologique

M. Loth Kitodjim
Premier Conseiller
Ambassade centrafricaine en France

M. Gilbert-Gil Nandiguinn
Conseiller culturel
Ambassade centrafricaine en France

M. Dominique Malot
Vice Doyen
facul. de droit et sciences economiques

REPUBLIQUE DE COREE/ REPUBLIC OF KOREA

H.E. Mr Dong Chil Yang
Ambassador Extraordinary and Plenipotentiary
Permanent Delegate of the Republic of Korea to UNESCO
(Head of Delegation)

Mr Gul-woo Lee
Education Attache
Permanent Delegation of the Republic of Korea to UNESCO

Dr Mu-keun Lee
President
Korean Research Institute for Vocational Education and Training

Dr Hyun-chung Lee
Director-General
Korean Council for University Education

Dr Young-chul Kim
Senior Fellow
Center for Education Policy Research-Korean Education Development Institute

Dr Jae Woong Kim
Vice-Dean, Academic Affairs
Korean National Open University

Ms Myung-suk Woo
Assistant Director of Academic
Research Support Bureau
Ministry of Education

**REPUBLIQUE DE MOLDOVA
REPUBLIC OF MOLDOVA**

S. Exc. M. Anatol Gremalschi
Ministre de l''education et de la science de la Republique de Moldova
(Chef de la delegation)

S. Exc. M. Mihai Popov
ambassadeur extraordinaire et plenipotentiaire de la Republique de Moldova en France
Delegue permanent aupres de l'UNESCO

M. Andrei Gallben
Recteur
Universitie libre internationale de Moldova

M. Petru Tolocenco
Recteur
Universite d'Etat de Tiraspole

M. Stefan Tiron
Conseiller
Ministere l''education et de la science de la Republique de Moldova

M. Marcel Botnaru
Premier Secretaire
Anbassade de la Republique de Moldova en France

REPUBLIQUE DEMOCRATIQUE DU CONGO/DEMOCRATIC REPUBLIC OF THE CONGO

M. Ngobasu Akwesi
Delegue permanent de la Republique democratique du Congo
(Chef de la delegation)

Melle Nkanga Mpasi
Conseillere
Delegation permanente de la Republique democratique du Congo aupres de l'UNESCO

Melle Aming Akwesi
Consultant

M. Shongo Mutambwe
Professeur

M. Mpele Nimba
Consultant

M. Lokoho Rene Okitaudiji
Professeur

REPUBLIQUE DEMOCRATIQUE POPULAIRE LAO/LAO PEOPLES'S DEMOCRATIC REPUBLIC

S. Exc. M. Khamtanh Chanthala
Vice Ministre de l'education
(Chef de la delegation)

S. Exc. M. Khamphan Simmalavong
Ambassadeur extraordinaire et plenipotentiaire de la Republique democratique populaire lao en France
Delegue permanent aupres de l'UNESCO

M. Khamliene Nhouyvanisvong
Delegue permanent suppleant de la Republique democratique populaire lao aupres de l'UNESCO

M. Bosengkham Vongdara
Recteur
Ministere de l''education

M. Sikhamtath Mitaray
Directeur
Ministere de l'education, Dept enseignement superieur, technique et professionnel

M. Thammarath Nakhavith
Directeur adjoint
Ministere de l''education, Dept. enseignement superieur, technique et professionnel

M. Khouanta Phalivong
Conseiller
Delegue permanent adjoint de la Republique democratique populaire lao aupres de l'UNESCO

REPUBLIQUE DOMINICAINE/ DOMINICAN REPUBLIC

Lic. Alejandrina German
Secretaria de Estado
Presidenta del Consejo Nacional de Eduacion Superior, CONES
(Jefe de la delegacion)

Lic. Pedro Antonio Eduardo
Director Ejecutivo
Consejo nacional de Educacion Superior, CONES

Dr Edylberto Cabral Ramirez
Rector
Universidad Autonoma de Santo Domingo, UASD

Mons. Agripino Nunez Collado
Rector
Pontifica Universidad Catolica Madre y Maestra, PUCMM

Lic. Rafael D. Toribio
Rector
Instituto Technologico de Santo Domingo, INTEC

Mons. Romon Benito Angeles Fernandez
Rector
Universidad Technologica del Cibao, UTECI

Dr Frankyn Holguin Hache
Rector
Universidad Apec

Dr Angel Hernandez
Rector
Universidad Abierta para Adultos, UAPA

Dr Luis Ivan Brugal
Vucerector Academico
Universidad Autonoma de Santo Domingo

Dr Gustavo Batista
Vicerector Academico
Universidad Iberoamericana. UNIBE

Lic. Rosa Escoto de Matos
Vicerectora Administrativa
Universidad Iberoamericana

Delegacion Permanente de la Republica Dominicana ante la UNESCO

S. Exc. Mme Laura Faxas
Ambassadeur
Deleguee permanente aupres de l'UNESCO

Mme Laura Calventi
Premiere Secretaire

REPUBLIQUE POPULAIRE DEMOCRATIQUE DE COREE/ DEMOCRATIC PEOPLE'S REPUBLIC OF KOREA

H.E. Mr Tae Gyun Ri
Ambassador Extraordinary and Plenipotentiary
Permanent Delegate to UNESCO
(Head of Delegation)

Mr Jae Hon Kim
Deputy Permanent Delegate to UNESCO

Mr Chang Min Kim
Senior Secretary
National Commission for UNESCO, Pyongyang

Mr Sok Chol Han
first Secretary
Permanent Delegation

Mr Dae Song Choi
Official
Ministry of Higher Education, Education Commission, Pyongyang

REPUBLIQUE TCHEQUE/ CZECH REPUBLIC

H.E. Dr Eduard Zeman
Minister of Education, Youth and Sports
(Head of Delegation)

Dr Vladimir Brabec
Director of Cabinet of Minister
Ministry of Education, Youth and Sports

Dr Josef Benes
Director of Higher Education Department
Ministry of Education, Youth and Sports

Dr Pavel Cink
Director of Department of International Relations and European Integration
Ministry of Education, Youth and Sports

Dr Petr Kratochvil
Member
Presidium of the Academy of Sciences of the Czech Republic

Dr Helena Sebkova
Director
Centre for Higher Education Studies

Dr Jan Hron
President of the Czech Rectors Conference
Czech University of Agriculture

Mr Ivan Wilhelm
President of the Czech Universities Council

Mr Jan Moravek
President of the Czech University Council
Student Chamber

Dr Ladislav Cerych
The Centre of Educational Strategy
Pedagogical Faculty, Charles University

Permanent Delegation of the Czech Republic to UNESCO

H.E. Mr Petr Lom
Ambassador Extraordinary and Plenipotentiary of the Czech Republic in France
Permanent Delegate to UNESCO

Mr David Masek
Deputy Permanent Delegate

REPUBLIQUE-UNIE DE TANZANIE/UNITED REPUBLIC OF TANZANIA

Hon. Dr Pius N'gwandu (MP)
Minister for Science, Technology and Higher Education
(Head of Delegation)

Mr Abdulhamid Yahya Mzee
Principal Secretary
Ministry of Education, Zanzibar

Prof. Geoffrey Mmari
Vice Chancellor
Open University of Tanzania

Prof. Peter Msolla
Deputy Vice Chancellor
Sokoine University of Agriculture

Prof. Leticia K. Rutashobya
Dean, Faculty of Commerce
University of Dar es Salaam

Dr Ram R. Ntuah
Acting Director Higher Education
Ministry of Science, Technology and Higher Education

Permanent Delegation of The United Republic of Tanzania to UNESCO

H.E. Mr Kassim M.J. Mwawado
Ambassador Extraordinary and Plenipotentiary of the United Republic of Tanzania in France Permanent Delegate to UNESCO

Prof. Mohammed Shaaban Sheya
Deputy Permanent Delegate to UNESCO

ROUMANIE/ROMANIA

S. Exc. M. Andrei Marga
Ministre de I'education nationale
(Chef de la delegation)

Professeur Mihai Korka
Secretaire d'Etat
Ministere de I'education nationale
Departement de I'enseignement superieur

Professeur Liviu Marghitas
Directeur du Corps du controle du Ministre de I'education nationale

Prof. Dr Cezar Barzea
Directeur de I'Institut des sciences pour I'education
President du Conseil BIE

Professeur Horia-Catalin Gavrila
Secretaire general
Ministere de I'education nationale

M. Mircea Muresan
Directeur
Direction des relations avec le public- Ministere de I'education nationale

Delegation permanente de la Roumanie aupres de I'UNESCO

S. Exc. M. Dan Haulica
Ambassadeur
Delegue permanent de Roumanie Upres de I'UNESCO

Mme Elisa Diaconescu
Deleguee permanente adjointe

M. Viorica Nicolae

M. Ion Novac

ROYAUME-UNI DE GRANDE BRETAGNE ET D'IRLANDE DU NORD/UNITED KINGDOM OF GREAT BRITAIN AND NORTHERN IRELAND

Baroness Tessa Blackstone
Minister of State for Education and Employment
(Head of Delegation)

Mr George Foulkes, M.P.
Parliamentary Under Secretary of State for International Development
(Alternate Head of Delegation)

Mr Tony Clark
Director, Higher Education
Department for Education and Employment
(Deputy Head of Delegation)

Mr Clive Tucker
Director International, Department for Education and Employment
(Alternate Deputy Head of Delegation)

Mr Graeme Dickson
Head of Higher Education Division
Scottish Office

Mr Kevin McLean
Head of International Students Team, DFEE
(Alternate Delegate)

Ms Myra Harrison
Chief Education Advisor, DFID

Mr Stephen Packer
Senior Education Adviser, Department for International Development
(Alternate Delegate)

Mr Barnaby Shaw
Head of International Relations Division, DfEE
(Alternate Delegate)

Mr Michael Francis
Senior Education Adviser, DFID
(Alternate Delegate)

Ms Diana Warwick
Chief Exec.
Cite of Vice Chancellors & Principals

Mr Tony Bruce
CVCP
(Alternate Delegate)

Mr Tim Cox
Executive Secretary,
Standing Conference of Principals (SCOP)

Mr Brian Fender
Chief Executive
Hiher Education Funding Council for England (HEFC)

Professor Clive Booth
Chairperson
Teacher Training Agency (TTA)

Ms Lona Wakely
National Union of Students

Mr Robert Mace
DfEE

United Kingdom Permanent Delegation to UNESCO

H.E. Mr David Leslie Stanton
Ambassador

Mr Geoffrey Haley
Deputy Permanent Delegate

RWANDA

S. Exc. Col Dr. Joseph Karemera
Ministre de l'education
(Chef de la delegation)

Dr Emile Rwamasirabo
Recteur
Universite nationale du Rwanda
(U.N.R.)
(Chef adjoint de la delegation)

Dr Stanislas Rwakabamba
Rector
Kigali Institute of Science,
Technology and Management

Dr Ephrem Kanyarukiga
Directeur de l'enseignement
superieur et technique
Ministere de l'education

Mme Anne Gahongahire
Coordinatrice de FAWE Rwanda

M. Augustin Musonera
Directeur ISAE

M. Eliphaz Bahizi
Secretaire permanent
commission nationale rwandaise
pour l'UNESCO

M. Emmanuel Ryamuhenga
charge de la cooperation en
education
Ministere de l'education

M. Modeste Rutabayiru
Delegue permanent a.i. du Rwanda
aupres de l'UNESCO

Mme Made Haguma
Secretaire administrative
Ambassade du Rwanda, Paris

SAINT-CHRISTOPHE-ET-NEVIS/SAINT CHRISTOPHER AND NEVIS

Hon. Rupert e. Herbert
Minister of Education, Labour and
Social Security
(Head of Delegation)

Dr Hermia Morton-Anthony
Registrar
Clarence Fitzroy Bryant College
(Deputy Head of Delegation)

Ms Dauna Manchester
Secretary-General
St. Kitts and Neivs National
Commission for UNESCO

SAINT-MARIN/SAN MARINO

S.E. Sante Canducci
Secretaire d'etat a l'education
nationale, aux affaires scoiales, aux
institutions culturelles
(Chef de la delegation)

M. Alexandre Reza
Ministre plenipotentiaire
Delegue permanent adjoint de
Saint-Marin aupres de l'UNESCO

M. Guido Ceccoli
Conseiller juridique
Delegation permanente de Saint
Marin aupres de l'UNESCO

Mme Elisabetta Lonfemini
Secretaire particulier
Secretariat d'Etat a l'education
natioale, aux affaires sociales, aux
institutions culturelles

SAINT-SIEGE/HOLY SEE

Monseigneur Lorenzo Frana
Observateur permanent du Saint
Siege aupres de l'UNESCO
(Chef de la delegation)

Monseigneur Patrick Valdrini
Recteur
Institut catholique de Paris

Monseigneur Jean Passicos
Consulteur de la Delegation du Saint-Siege

Soeur Enrica Rosanna
recteur
Faculte pontificale des sciences de l'education (Rome)

Mme Beatrix Forcade
Expert

Frere Daniel Boulier
Expert

SAINT-VINCENT-ET-GRENADINS/ SAINT VINCENT AND THE GRENADINES

Honourable Alpian Allen
Minister of Education
(Head of Delegation)

Mr Macaulay Peters
Chief Education Officer
Ministry of Education

Ms Marcia Kirby
Secretary General
UNESCO National Commission

Permanent Delegation of Saint Vincent and the Grenadines to UNESCO

H. E. Mr Wafic Said
Ambassador
Permanent Delegate of Saint Vincent and the Grenadines to UNESCO

Ms Angela Wilins
Deputy Permanent Delegate

Mrs Carole Arsan
Attache

SAINTE-LUCIE/SAINT LUCIA

H.E. Mr Gilbert R. Chagoury
Ambassador
Permanent Delegate of Saint Lucia to UNESCO
(Head of Delegation)

Dr George forde
Principal
Sir Arthur Lewis Community College
(Deputy Head of Delegation)

Dr Joseph Arsan
Deputy Head of Delegation of Saint Lucia to UNESCO

Mrs Vera Lacoeuilhe
First Secretary
permanent Delegation of saint Lucia to UNESCO

Mrs Shery Alexander Heinis
Secretary-General
Saint Lucia National Commission for UNESCO

SAMOA

Mr Magele Mauiliu Magele
Vice-Chancellor
National University of Samona
(Head of Delegation)

SAO TOME ET PRINCIPE/SAO TOME AND PRINCIPE

Mme Natalia Umbelina Neto
Secretaire generale
commission nationale pour l'UNESCO
(Chef de la delegation)

SENEGAL

S. Exc. M. Andre Sonko
Ministre de l'education nationale
(Chef de la delegation)

S. Exc. M. Balla Moussa Daffe
Ministre de la recherche scientifique et de la technologie

S. Exc. M. Keba Birane Cisse
Ambassadeur extraordinaire et plenipotentiaire du Senegal en france
Delegue permanent aupres de l'UNESCO

M. Ousmane Blondin-Diop
Delegue permanent adjoint du Senegal aupres de l'UNESCO

M. Souleymane Bachir Diagne
Conseiller technique a la Presidence de la Republique

M. Tamsir Mbaye
Conseiller technique a la Primature

M. Assane Hane
Secretaire general
Commission nationale du Senegal pour l'UNESCO

M. Ouseynou Dia
Directuer de l'enseignement superieur

M. Thiam Khadidiatan
Adjoint du Directeur de l'enseignement superieur
Ministere de l'education nationale

M. Souleymane Niang
Recteur
Université Cheikh Anta Diop de Dakar

M. Ahmadou Lamine Ndiaye
Recteur
Université Gaston Berger de Saint-Louis

M. Ndiawar Sart
Professeur
Universite Gaston Berger

Prof. Falilou Ndiaye
Professeur, Universite Cheikh Anta Diop de Dakar
Representant les syndicats des enseignants de i'enseignement superieur

M. Cheikhna Sankhar
Conseiller
Delegation permanente du Senegal aupres de l'UNESCO

M. Honore Georges Ndiaye
Administrateur
Projet d'amelioration de l'enseignement superieur

SEYCHELIES

H.E. Mr Danny Faure
Minister of Education
(Head of Delegation)

S. Exc. M. Callixte d'Offay
Ambassadeur extraordinaire et plenipotentiaire des Seychelles en France
Delegue permanent aupres de l'UNESCO

Mrs MacSuzy Helena Mondon
Director General of Education Management

Mr. Vincent Meriton
Director General of Employment
Ministry of Social Affiars & Manpower Development

Melle Renette Nicette
Troisieme Secretaire

SIERRA LEONE

Prof. Ernest H. Wright
Vice Chancellor
University of Sierra Leone
(Head of Delegation)

Mr Alfred Bobson Sesay
Director General
Ministry of Education, Youth and Sports

Alhaji Usman Nurudin Sahid Jah
Sierra Leone's Representative on ISESCO Executive Board

SLOVAQUIE/SLOVAKIA

Assoc. Prof. Marian Tolnay
Director General
Ministry of Education-Section for Higher Education Institutions
(Head of Delegation)

Prof. Ludovit Molnar
President
Slovak National Commission for UNESCO

Dr Peter Magdolen
Director
Ministry of Education- Dept of the Higher Education Institutions and PhD Studies

Assoc. Prof. Miroslav Zima
Rector
Slovak Agriculture University, Nitra

Prof. Marian Dzimko
Vice-Rector
University of Zilina

Prof. Jan Slezak
First Vice-President
Slovak Academy of Sciences, Bratislava

Prof. Peter Liba
Rector
Constantine the Philosopher University, Nitra

Prof. Jozef Polak
Director, Institut of Technologie and Education IRIE
Constantine the Philosopher University, Nitra

Assoc. Prof. Ivan J. Szabo
Dean, Pedagogical Faculty
Constantine the Philosopher University, Nitra

S. Exc. M. Valadimir Valach
Ambassadeur extraordinaire et plenipotentiaire de la Slovaquie en France
Delegue permanent aupres de l'UNESCO

M. Igor Navrátil
Delegue permanent adjoint

SLOVENIE/SLOVENIA

Dr Pavle Zgaga
State Secretary
Ministry of of Education and Sport
(Head of Delegation)

Ms Zofija Klemen Krek
Director of the Office
Secretary General of the Slovene National Commission for UNESCO

Ms Majda Sirok
State Secretary
Ministry of Education and Sport

Dr Dane Melavc
Representative of the Council for Hihger Education of the Republic of Slovenia

Dr Katja Breskvar
Vice Chancellor
Uniersity of Ljublijana

Dr Ludvik Toplak
Chancellor
University of Maribor

Mr Uros Vajgl
Representative
Student Organisation of the Republic of Slovenia

Dr Andrej Predin
Representative of the Trade Union for Education and Science of the Republic of Slovenia

Permanent Delegation of the Republic of Slovenia to UNESCO

H.E. Mr Jozef Kunic
Ambassador Extraordinary and Plenipotentiary of Slovenia in France
Permanent Delegate to UNESCO

Ms Ana Vilfan
Deputy Permanent Delegate

SOMALIE/SOMALIA

H.E. Mr Said Hagi Mohamud Farah
Ambassador Extraordinary and Plenipotentiary of Somalia in France
Permanent Delegate to UNESCO
(Head of Delegation)

Mr Ahmed Haji Ali

Mr Asha Shekh Ali

Mr Bashir Kenadid

SOUDAN/SUDAN

H.E. Prof. Ibrahim Ahmed Omer
Minister of Higher Education and Scientific Research
(Head of Delegation)

Prof. Hassan Mohamed Salih
Secretary-General
Ministry of Higher Education and Scientific Research

Prof. Abdelmalik Mohamed Abdel-Rahman
Deputy Vice Chancellor
"University of Khartoum"

Prof. Moses Machar
Vice Chancellor
"Upper Nile University"

Prof. Ali Mohamed Abdelrahman Bari
Vice Chancellor
"Shendi University"

Dr Gassim Yousif Badri
Vice Chancellor
"Ahfad University"

Mr Ibrahim Abdel Basit
Director general
Higher Education Grants Committee

Mr Salah Mohammed Ahmed Saeed
Executive Manager
Secretary General' Office

Mr Younis Ahmed Younis
Director-General
Higher Education Coordination Dept.

Dr Mohamed Abdulla El Nagrabi
Director-General Planning

Mr Mubarak Yahia Abbas
Secretary-General
Sudanese National Commission

Permanent Delegation of Sudan to UNESCO

H.E. Dr Eltigani Salih Fidail
Ambassador Extraordinary and Plenipotentiary of Sudan in France
Permanent Delegate to UNESCO

Mr Mohamed Ibrahim Mohamed
Assistant Permanent Delegate

SRI LANKA

Hon. Watareke Aratchchillage Visva Warnapala
Depute Minister
Ministry of Education and Higher Education
(Head of Delegation)

Mr Ambalangodage Andrew De Silva
Ministry of Education and Higher Education
(Deputy Head of Delegation)

Prof. Sirisena Tilakaratna
Chairperson
University Grants Commission

Prof. Senake Bandaranayake
Vice Chancellor
University of Kelaniya

SUEDE/SWEDEN

H.E. Mr Ingemar Lindahl
Ambassador
Permanent Delegate of Sweden to UNESCO
(Head of Delegation)

Mr Ulf Melin
Member of Parliament
Standing Committee on Education

Ms Christina Ullenius
President
University of Karlstad

Ms Margareta Norell
professor
University of Lund

Mr Torsten Husen
Professor emeritus
University of Stockholm

Mr Gustaf Lindencrona
President
Stockholm University

Mr Bert Fredriksson
SULF (The Swedish Assosciation of University Teachers)

Ms Sara Winnfors
SFS (The Swedish National Union of Students)

Mr Nils Eklund
Special Adviser
Ministry of Education and Science

Ms Eva Hermanson
Deputy Secretary General
Swedish National Commission for UNESCO

Mrs Berit Olsson
Chief of Unit for Universities and Bilateral Cooperation
Swedish International Development Cooperation Agency

SUISSE/SWITZERLAND

M. Charles Kleiber
Secretaire d'Etat a la science et a la recherche
Departement federal de l'interieur
(chef de la delegation)

M. Christian Scharer
Directeur suppleant
Office federal de la formation professionnelee et de la technologie, Dept federal de l'economie

Dr Nivardo Ischi
Secretaire general
Conference universitaire suisse

Prof. Luc. Weber
Delegue
Conference des recteurs des universities suisses

Dr Andrea Schenker-Wicki
cheffe de section "Affaires universites
Office federal de l'education et de la science, Department federal de l'interieur

Mme Gabriela Amarella
Secretaire politique
Union Nationale des etudiants de Suisse

Dr Marino Ostini
Chef de Section suppleant,
Cooperation Internationale en education
Office federal de l'education et de la science (Secretaire de la delegation)

Delegation permanente de la Suisse aupres de l'UNESCO

S. Exc. M. Benedict de Tscharner
Ambassadeur extraordinaire et plenipotentiaire de la Suisse en France
Delegue permanent de la Suisse aupres de l'UNESCO

S. Exc. Mme Sylvie Matteucci
Ambassadeur
Delegue permanent adjoint de la Suisse aupres de l'UNESCO

SURINAME

Prof. Dr Wilfried Roseval
Rector
Anton de Kom University of Suriname
(Head of Delegation)

Mr Drs Archie Marshall
Principal
Advanced Teacher Training College

Ms Drs Renate Teuwsen
Educational Technologist
Department of Higher Education
Ministry of Education and Community Development

SWAZILAND

Hon. Solomon M. Dlamini
Minister of Education
(Head of Delegation)

Mr Sibusiso S. Mkhonta
Director of Education

Mr Cisco Magagula
Director
University of Swaziland, Institute Distance Education

Mr Sipho S. Vilakati
Registrar
University of Swaziland

Mrs Dorothy Littler
secretary-General
Swaziland National Commission for UNESCO

Mr Clement T. Mabuza
Swaziland Higher Commission in London

TADJIKISTAN/TAJIKISTAN

H.E. Mr Rahmatullaev Erkin
Minister of Foreign Affairs
(Head of Delegation)

M.N. Abdoulaieva
Recteur
Institut tadjik d'Etat des langues etrangeres

M.K. Abdoulaieva
Pro-Recteur
Universite pedagogique d'Etat de Douchanbe

Mme A.D. Akhrorova
Pro-Recteur
Universite technique tadjike

TCHAD/CHAD

S. Exc. M. Adoum Goudja
Ministre de l'enseignement superieur et de la recherche scientifique
(Chef de la delegation)

S. Exc. M. Omar Zeidan
Ambassadeur extraordinaire et plenipotentiaire
Delegue permanent de la Republique du tchad aupres de l'UNESCO

M. Mahamat Ali Mustapha
Directeur general enseignement superieur et recherche

M. Abderamane Koko
Secretaire Executif
Comite national pour i'education et la formation en liaison avec l'emploi (CONEFE)

M. Khalil Alio
Recteur
Universite de N'Djamena

M. Moadjidibaye Titingar
Directeur
Institut superieur des sciences de i'education

M. Bendiman Sadj Asso
Directeur de la recherche scientifique et technique

M. Samouh Bayan
Delegue permanent adjoint

M. Ndjaha Ngabo
President
Union des etudiants du Tchad

THAILANDE/THAILAND

Assoc. Prof. Dr Tong-In Wongsothorn
Deputy Permanent Secretary for University Affairs
(Head of Delegation)
Prof. Dr Prawase Wasi
Senator
Laureat of the Comenius II Medal

Mrs Savitri Suwansathit
Deputy Permanent Secretary for Education
Secretary-General of the Thai National Commission for UNESCO

Dr Tongyoo Kaewsaiha
Director-General
Department of Non-formal Education, Ministry of Education

Assoc. Prof. Dr Sumonta Promboon
Representative of the Council of University Presidents of Thailand
President, Srinakarinwot University

Dr Pornchai Mongkonvanit
President, Siam University
President of the Association of Private Higher Education Institutions of Thailand

Asst. Prof. Numyoot Songthanapitak
Vice-President for Academic Affairs
Rajamangala Institute of Technology

Ms Porntip Kanjananlyot
Director, International Cooperation Division
Office of the Permanent Secretary, Ministry of University Affairs

Ms Chadarat Singhadechakul
Chief. International Cooperation Development Section, International Cooperation Division
Office of the Permanent Secretary, Ministry of University Affairs

TOGO

S. Exc. M. Edo Kodjo Maurille Agbodli
Ministre de l'education nationale et de la recherche scientifique
(Chef de la delegation)

M. Adji Oteth Ayassor
Secretaire general
Ministere de l'education nationale et de la recherche

Prof. Emmanuel Mawulikplimi K.A. Edee
Directeur general de l'enseignement superieur

Prof. Osseini Tidjani
Vice-Recteur
Universite du Benin

M. Sambiani Sankardja Lare
Secretaire general
Commission nationale togolaise pour l'UNESCO

S. Exc. M. le Professeur Kondi Charles Agba
Ambassadeur extraordinaire et plenipotentiaire du Togo en France
Delegue permanent aupres de l'UNESCO

M. Senamu Noglo
Delegue permanent adjoint

Professeur Ampah Johnson
Representant du Tog au Conseil executif de l'UNESCO

TONGA

Mr Mana Latu
Deputy Director of Education, Culture and Sport
Ministry of Education
(Head of Delegation)

TRINITE-ET-TOBAGO/ TRINIDAD AND TOBAGO

Prof. Compton Boune
Principal
St. Augustine Campus, University of the West Indies (UWI)
(Head of Delegation)

Dr Alvin Ashton
Vice-President of Higher Education
National Institute of Higher Education, Research, Science and Technology (NIHERST)

Mr Deake Cateau
President
Guild of Students, University of the West Indies

TUNISIE/TUNISIA

S. Exc. M. Dali Jazi
Ministre de l'enseignement superieur
(Chef de la delegation)

Prof. Houcine El Oued
Secretaire general
Commission nationale tunisienne pour l'education, la science et al culture

Prof. Abderrazak Zouari
Conseiller aupres du Ministre de l'enseignement superieur

Prof. Hammadi Ben Jaballah
conseiller aupres du Ministre de l'enseignement superieur

Prof. Zeineb Ben Ahmed
Directeur general de la renovation universitaire
Ministere de l'enseignement superieur

Prof. Hedi Ktari
Directeur general de l'enseignement superieur

Prof. Moncef El Guaied
Directeur general de la recherche scientifique et technique

Prof. Zakia Bouaziz
Directeur general
Centre de recherche d'etudes, de documentation et d'information sur la femme (CREDIF)

Prof. Noomane Ghodbane
Directeur de la cooperation internationale et des relations exterieures
Ministere de l'enseignement superieur

Prof. Mohamed El Mahdi Abdeljaouad
Directeur de la mission universitaire a Paris

Prof. Samir Marzouki
Directeur
Ecole normale supérieure de Tunis

Prof. Amel Gaaied
Directeur
Ministére de l'enseignement supérieur

Delegation permanente de Tunisie aupres de l'UNESCO

S. Exc. M. Mongi Bousniana
Ambassadeur extraordinaire et plenipotentiaire de Tunisie en France
delegue permanent aupres de l'UNESCO

Mme Dhouha Boukhris

Mme Saida Charfeddine

TURQUIE/TURKEY

H.E. Mr Turhan Firat
Ambassador Extraordinary and Plenipotentiary
Permanent Delegate of Turkey to UNESCO
(Head of Delegation)

Professor Dr Kemal Guruz
President
Higher Education Council of Turkey

H.E. Mr Metin Goker
Ambassador
Director General for Cultural Affairs, Ministry of Foreign Affairs

Prof. Dr Ismail Tosun
Deputy President
Council of Higher Education

Ass. Prof. Aydogan Ataunal
Director General for Higher Education

Prof. Dr Arsin Aydinuraz
President
Turkish National Commission for UNESCO

M. Daver Darende
Minister Counsellor
Deputy Permanent Delegate to UNESCO

Prof. Dr Sait Yazicioglu
Coordinator for the educational Expertise Committee
Turkish National Commission for UNESCO

Mr Gengiz Sanay
Head of Department for Cultural Affairs
Ministry of Foreign Affairs

Ass. Prof. Gulten herguner
Lecturer
University of Kadir Has

Ms Gulseren Celik
First Secretary
Permanent Delegation to UNESCO

Mr Turan Kebelioglu
Deputy Counsellor for Education
Turkish Embassy in Paris

M. Ozgur Uluduz
Third Secretary
Permanent Delegation to UNESCO

TUVALU

Mr Sotago Paape
Senior Education Officer
(Head of Delegation)

UKRAINE

H.E. Mr Mykhailo Zgurovsky
Minister of Education of Ukraine
(Head of Delegation)

H.E. Mr Anatoliy Zlenko
Extraordinary and Plenipotentiary
Ambassador of Ukraine to
France Permanent Delegate to
UNESCO
(Deputy Head of Delegation)

Prof. Volodymyr Golub
Deputy Head of the Department on
Humanitarian Development
Administration of President of
Ukraine

Prof. Andriy Gurzhiy
Deputy Head of the Department on
Education
Cabinet of Ministers of Ukraine

Dr Mykhaylo Stepko
Head of the Department of Higher
Education
Ministry of Education of Ukraine

Prof. Leonid Hubersky
Director of the Institute of
International Relations Taras
Schevchenko Kyiv State University
Member of the Ukrainian National
Commission for UNESCO

Mr Vyacheslav Sotnykov
Counsellor
Permanent Delegation of Ukraine
to UNESCO

Mrs Teyana Sayenko
First Secretary
Ukrainian National Commission
for UNESCO

URUGUAY

Excmo. Sr. Prof. Yamandu Fau
Ministro de Educacion y Cultura
(Jefe de la delegacion)

Doctor Rafael Guarga
Rector
Universidad de la Republica

Dr Jose Luis Mendizabal S.J.
Rector
Universidad Catolica (privada)

Ing. Julio C. Fernandez
Decano de Desarrollo Academico
Universidad ORT

Lic. Ernesto Puiggros
Director de Educacion
Ministerio de Education y Cultura

Ing. Jorge Servian
Delegado
Ministerio de Educacion

Prof. Jorge Emilio Landinelli
Decano
Facultad de Ciencias Sociales,
Universidad de la Republica

Ing. Agr. Nestor Eulacio
Representante Docente
Universidad de la Republica

Sr. Javier Royer
Representante estudiantil
Universidad de la Republica

Ing. Raul Boado
Delegado por los egresados
Universidad de la Republica

Esc. Graziella de la Rosa
Facultad de Derecho, Universidad
de la Republica
(Observador)
Delegacion Permanente de
Uruguay ante la UNESCO

Excom. Sr. Embajador Miguel Angel Semino
Delegado Permanente

Sr. Ministro Pedro Mo Amaro
Delegado Permanente Adjunto

Sra. Mariella Crosta Rodriguez
Consejero
Delegation Permanente de Uruguay ante la UNESCO

Mr Edgar Flores

Sra. Maria Guerrini
Secretaria

VANUATU

H.E. Mr Joe Natuman
Minister of Education, Youth and Sports
(Head of Delegation)

Mr Raymond Malapa
Political Advisor for the Minister of Education
Ministry of Education, Youth and Sports

Mr George Andrews
Director General
Ministry of Education, Youth and Sports

Mr Jesse Dick
Acting Director
Planning, Statistics and Project Management

VENEZUELA

Excomo. Sr. Antonio Luis Cardenas Colmenter
Ministro de Educacion
(Jefe de la delegacion)

Excmo. Sr. Francisco Kerdel-Vegas
Embajador Extraordinario y Plenipotenciario de Venezuela en Francia
Delegado permanente ante la UNESCO

Sr. Jose Domingo Mujica
Presidente
Fundacion Gran mariscal de Ayacucho (FUNDAYACUCHO)

Sr. Gabriel Zambrano Chaparro
Director General Sectorial de Educación Superior
Ministerio de Educación

Sr. José Antonioa Pimentel
Director
Oficina de Planificacion del Sector Universitario

Sr. Trino Alcides Diaz
Rector
Universidad Central de Venezuela

Sr. Felipe Pachano
Rector
Universidad de Los Andes

Mg. Neuro Villalobos
Rector
Universidad del Zulia

Prof. Asdrubal Antonio Romero
Rector
Universidad de Carabobo

Sr. Freddy Malpica
Rector
Universidad Simon Bolivar

Sra. Mercedes Di Vora
Presidente
Fundacion International para el Desarrollo de la Creatividad
(Fundacreatividad)

Srta. Cristiane Engelbrecht
Segundo Secretario

Srta. Clarelena Agostini
Tercer Secretario

VIET-NAM (REPUBLIQUE SOCIALISTE DU)/ SOCIALIST REPUBLIC OF VIETNAM

S. Exc. M. Trinh Duc Du
Ambassadeur, Delegue permanent de la Republique socialiste du Viet nam aupres de l'UNESCO
Representant personnel du Chef de l'Etat pour la francophonie
(Chef de la delegation)

M. Do Van Chung
Directeur du Department de l'enseignement superieur
ministere de l'education et de la formation

M. Nguyen Van Hanh
Vice-Recteur
Universite de Ho Chi Minh Ville

M. Le Cao Thang
Vice-Recteur
Universite de Thai Nguyen

M. Nguyen Van Loi
Directeur
Ecole de langues etrangeres, Universite de Ha Noi

Dr Nguyen Khanh Quac
Directeur adjoint de l'universite de Thai Nguyen
Recteur de l'universite de l'agriculture et de la foret de Thai Nguyen

Mme Nguyen Thi Hoi
Secretaire general
Commission nationale vietnamienne pour l'UNESCO

Mme Nguyen Pham Kim Chi
Specialiste de l'education
Commission nationale vietnamienne pour l'UNESCO

YEMEN

S. Exc. Dr. Yahiya Al-Shoaiby
Ministre de l'education
President de la Commission nationale
(chef de la delegation)

Dr Abubaker Abdullah Al Qirbi
Professeur
Universite de Sana'a

Dr Nasser Al-Aulaqui
President
IBB University

Dr Wahiba Faaregh
President
Queen Arwa University

Dr Salah Basurrah
President
Universite de Aden

Dr Abdullah Al Moujahid
President
Dhamar University

Dr Ali Hood Ba-Abbad
President
Hadhramout University of Science & Technology

Dr Yassin Shaibany
Directeur du Departement du developpment academique

M. Mohamed Al Duayse
Commission nationale

M. Adel Ahmed Muthanaa
C.A.B. Ministere

Delegation manente du Yemen aupres de l'UNESCO

S. Exc. M. Abdallah El-Zine
Ambassadeur extraordinaire et plenipotentiaire
Delegue permanent aupres de l'UNESCO

Dr Ali Zaid
delegue permanent adjoint

ZAMBIE/ZAMBIA

Mr Newton Isaiah Nguni
Deputy Minister
Ministry of Science,
Technology and Vocational Training
(Head of Delegation)

Mr Mwamaka Lweya Mulaga
Director, Planning Unit
Ministry of Science,
Technology and Vocational Training

Dr Geoffrey Lungwangwa
Director, Higher Education
School of Education,
University of Zambia

Mr Sandford Abraham Mupanga
Director, Department of
Technical Education and
Vocational Training Ministry of Science,
Technology and Vocational Training

Mr Lawrence Amos Chibutu
Acting Director
Zambia National Commission for
UNESCO

ZIMBABWE

Hon. Ignatius Morgan Chiminya
Chombo, MP
Minister of Higher Education and
Technology (Head of Delegation)

Dr M.N. Mambo
Secretary for Higher Education and
Technology (Deputy Head of Delegation)

H.E. Mr J.M. Bimha
Ambassador Extraordinary and
Plenipotentiary to France

Mr J.J. Mhlanga
Minister Counsellor
Education, Scientific and Cultural Affairs

Dr Phinias m. Makhurane
Vice-Chancellor
National University of Science &
Technology

Mr Mennas S. Machawira
Deputy Director and Acting
Secretary-General
Zimbabwe National Commission
for UNESCO

Ms Miriam D Patsanza
Vice President of Joy T.V.
Managing Director of Talent Consortium

GROUP II

OTHER ORANISATIONS

ORGANIZATIONS OF THE UNITED NATIONS SYSTEM

ORGANIZATIONS DU SYSTEME DES NATIONS UNIES

ORGANIZACIONES DEL SISTEMA DE LAS NACIONES UNIDAS

Economic Commisssion for Africa
Mrs Lalla Ben Barka

International Labour Organization
Mr. Michel Henriques
Mr. Frans Lenglet
Mr. Bill Ratteree

International Maritime Organization
Dr. Karl Laubstein
(World Maritime University)

United Nations
Prof. Dr. H. Van Ginkel
(Representative of Mr Kofi Annan)

United Nations Children's Fund
Mr. Sheldon Shaeffer

United Nations Development Programme
Mr. John Lawrence

United Nations Division for Social Policy and Development
Ms Louise Frechette
Mr Maxwell Heward

United Nations Food and Agriculture Organization
Dr. Willaim Handley

United Nationas Industrial Development Organization
Mr. Sarwar Hobohm

Universal Postal Union
Mr. Christian Gheorghiev

United Nations Relief and Works Agency for Palestine Refugees in the Near East
Dr. Muhyieddeen Touq
Dr. Tafeeda Jarabwi

United Nations University
Prof. Dr. H. Van Ginkel
(WCHE Advisory Group)
Prof. Ingrid Moses
Dr. T. Della Senta
Prof. Jose Joaquin Brunner Ried
Mr. Peidor Konz
Ms Caterina Casullo

Other Delegates:
Dr. Brendan Barret
Dr. German Velasquez
Father Lucien Michaud
Mr. Ng Chong
Mr. Ted Tschang
Prof. Marisa Luisa Martin
Dr. Magdallen N. Juma
Mr. Shirabe Ogino
Mr. Kiyoshi Nakabayashi
Mr. Kazumasa Noda

World Bank

Dr. Maris O'Rourke
Dr. Bruce Johnstone
Dr. Jamil Salmi
Mr. William Experton
Mr. Lauritz Holmm-Neilsen
Mr. William Saint
Mae Chu Chang

World Food Programme

Ms Ute Meier

World Health Organization

Dr. Charles Boelen

World Meteorological Organization

Dr. Ion Draghici

INTER-GOVERNMENTAL ORGANIZATIONS

ORGANISATIONS INTER-GOUVERNEMENTALES

ORGANIZACIONES INTER-GUBERNAMENTALES

ACP Group

Dr. Bern Hans

African Development Bank (AfDB)

Mrs Zeinab El-Bakri

Arab Bureau of Education for the Gulf States (ABEGS)

Dr. Alil M. Al-Towagry
Dr. Saeed M. Al-Mullais
Mr. Shafi Al-Jahdari

Arab Education, Cultural and Scientific Organization (ALESCO)

Mr. Mahmoud El Milli
Mr. Youssef Rahmania

Arab Organization for Agricultural Development (AOAD)

Dr. Abdel Latief Walid

Asian Development Bank (AsDB)

Dr. S.A. Chowdhury

Caribbean Community Secretariat (CARICOM)

Dr. Carole Maison- Bishop

Caribbean Development Bank (CDB)

Dr. Jeffrey Dellimore

Commonwealth of Learning (C.O.L.)

Mr Patrick Guiton

Commonwealth Secretariat

Prof. Stephen Matlin
Dr. Cream Wright
Dr. Jasbir Singh
Ms Alison girdwood
Dr. Magdallen Juma

Council of Europe

Mr. Jaroslav Kalous
Mr. Janmes Wimberley

Economic and Monetary Union of Western Africa

Dr. Soungalo Ouedraogo

European Bank for Reconstruction and Development (BERD)
Mr. Nicolas Stern

European Commission
Mr. Domenico Lenarduzzi
Mrs Angelique Verli
Mrs Ginette Nabavi
Mr. Piergiorgio Mazzochi
Mr. Renaud-Grancois Moulinier

European Space Agency (ESA)
Mr. Rene Oosterlinck

Gulf Arab States Educational Research Center (GASERC)
Dr. Rasheed Al Hamad
Inter- American Development Bank (IDB)
Mr. Enriqe V. Iglesias
Mr. Andres Bajuk
Mr. Leo Harari
Mr. Rod Chapman
Mr. Ziga Vodusek

Islamic Development Bank (ISDB)
Mr. Ousmane Seck
Mr. Syed Shahid Hussain
Dr. M. Ali Hibshi
Mr. Mansour Sy

Islamic Educational, Scientific and Cultural Organization (ISESCO)
Dr. Abdulaziz Othman Altwaijri
Mr. Mohamed Ghemari
Dr. Mohamed Chtatou
Dr. Mekki Al Mrouni
Mr. Mohamed Riffi

League of Arab States
Mr. Mohamed Trabelsi
Mr. Mohamed Tahar Adouani
Mr. Abdelmajid Klai

Maghreb Arab Union
Mrs Saida Mendili

Organization of African Unity (OAU)
Prof. Couaovi A. Leonce Johnson

Organization of American States (OAS)
Dr. Benno Sander

Organization for Economic Co-operation and Development (OECD)
Mr. Thomas Alexander
Dr. Abrar Hasan
Dr. Alan Wagner
Mr. Richard Yelland
Mr. Jan Karlson

Organisation internationale de la Francophonie (OIF)
Recteur Michel Guillou

SEAMO Regional Centre for Higher Education and Development (SEAMO RIHED)
Dr. Tong- In Wongsothorn
Dr. Padoongchart Suwanawongse

Southern African Development Community (SADC)
Mr. S.S. Mkhonta
Mr. Jabulani G. Kunene

Technical Assistance Office Socrates & Youth
Mrs Sarah Lamigeon

Union Latine
Mr. Ernesto Bertolaja
Mrs Lil Despradel
Mrs Cristina Bonini

NON-GOVERNMENTAL ORGANIZATIONS OF THE COLLECTIVE CONSULTATION

ORGANISATIONS NON-GOVERNMENTALES DE LA CONSULTATION COLLECTIVE

ORGANIZACIONES NO GUBERNAMENTALES DE LA CONSULTACION COLECTIVA

Association of African Universities (AAU)

Prof. Narciso Matos
Prof. Akilagpa Sawyerr
Mr. Zoumana Bamba
Prof. Chris Nwamuo
Prof. Godwin Ekhaguere

Association of Arab Universities (AArU)

Dr. Marwan Kamal

Association of Commonwealth Universities (ACU)

Prof. Michael Gibbons
Mrs Dorothy Galand
Mrs Sue Kirkland
Mr. Ezri Carlebach
Ms Svava Bjarnason
Mr. Richard Mawditt

Association des Etats Generaux des Etudiants de l'Europe (AEGEE)

Mlle Helene Berard
Mlle Carmen Hilario
Mlle Orsolya Peter
Mlle Alessia Pastorutti
Mlle Isabella Casartelli
M. Erik Krier
M. Rok Mejak
M. Stevan Vukovic
M. Refet Saban
Mlle Alessandra Siniscalco
M. Ali Alper Akyuz

International Association of Students in Economics and Management (AIESEC)

Mr. Nzima Sany Joseph
Mr. Morgan Abu
Ms Claire Bowers
Mr. Gosia Kania
Mr. Shantini Balasubramaniam
Mr. Dedomey Leonard
Mr. Jallouli Khalil
Ms Karolina Daszynska
Ms Erika Tauraite
Mr. Fulvio Bartolucci
Ms Christel Scholten

Association Internationale de la Pedagogie Universitaire (AIPU)

Prof. Daniele Cros
Prof. Ahmed Chabchoub
Prof. Hamidou Sall Nacuzon
Prof. Amparo Fernandex- March
Prof. Jacques Taskin

Association Internationale des Universities (AIU)

Dr. Wataru Mori
Dr. Flavio Fava de Moraes
Dr. Michel Falise
Dr. Franz Eberhard
Mme Eva Egron-Polak
Prof.Guy Neave
Mme Claudine Langlosis

Association of Southeast Asian Institutions of Higher Learning (ASAIHL)

Dr. Ninnat Olanvoravuth

Association of Universities of Asia and the Pacific (AUAP)

Prof. Dr. Ruben C. Umaly
Prof. Zhou Li-Gao
Dr. Emmanuel Y. Angeles
Prof. Dr. Wichit Srisa- an
Prof. Toshio Nakamura
Prof. Dr. Don McNicol

Agence Universitaire de la Francophonie (AUPELF-UREF)
Prof. Michel Guillou
Mme Leila Rezk
M. Philippe Ducray
M. Didier Oillo
M. Joel Jallais
M. Jean- Pierre Denis

Council on International Educational Exchange (CIEE)
Dr. Guy Haug
Dr. Gisela Baumgratz
Dr. Mustapha Belhareth
Dr. Peter Luigi Fedon

Association of European Universities (CRE)
Prof. Joseph Bricall
Dr. Andris Barblan
Prof. Kenneth Edwards
Prof. Lucy Smith
Ms Mary O'Mahony
Mr. Eric Lauzon

Confederation Syndicale Mondiale de l'Enseignement (CSME)
M. Louis Van Beneden
M. Gaston de la Haye
M. Razvan Constantin Bobulescu
M. Herman Brinkhoff
M. Rudy Van Renterghem

Communiaute des Universities Mediterraneennes (CUM)
Prof. Luigi Ambrosi
Prof. Carlo Di Benedetta
Mlle Giovanna Diana
Porf. Leonardo Plantamura
Ing. Carlo des Dorides

European Association for International Education (EAIE)
Mrs Hilary Callan
Mrs Marianne Hildebrand
Dr. Romuald Rudzki
Ms Beatrice Merrick
Ms Sirje Uprus

European Democrat Students (EDS)
Mr. Michalis Peglis
Mr. Holger Thuss
Ms Juliet Frendo
Mr. Andreas von Gehlen
Mr. Ukko Metsola
Ms Victoria Cristobal
Ms Riina-Rikka Kupparinen
Mr. Emilian Djindic
Mr. Helge Skinnes
Mr. Cristian Popescu

Education International (EI)
Mme Mary HatwoodFutrell
Mme Monique Fouihoux
Mme Denise Angers
M. Elago R.T. Elago
Mme Virginia Ann shadwick

European Lifelong Learning Initiative (ELLI)
Prof. Norman Longworth
Dr. Michael Kelleher
Prof. Michael Thorne
Mr. Jean Charlent
Mr. Marku Markkala

European Law Students Association (ELSA)
Ms Burke Serbetci
Mr. Angelo Santi
Mr. Philipp Von Trotha
Ms Eleaor Daly
Mr. Daniele Barini
Mr. Malgorzata Nesterowiez
Ms Andra Avotina
Mr. Roy Hans
Mr. Wojciech Wiewiorowski
Mr. Taco Hovius
Ms Agnieszka Stobiecka

The National Unions of Students in Europe (ESIB)

Mr. Peter Sondergaard
Ms Judith Sargentini
Ms Kathrine Vangen
Ms Hilde W. Wibe
Mr. Tom van Thienen
Mr. Zoltan Feher
Mr. Andreas Wagner
Mr. Regimantas Buozius
Mr. John Skottun
Mr. Christoph Horhan
Mr. Mads Engholm

Federation Internationale des Femmes des Carrieres Juridiques (FIFCJ)

Maitre Claire Jourdan

Federation Internationale des Femmes Diplomees des Universities (FIFDU)

Mme Linda Souter
Mme Marianne Bernheim
Dr. Daphne C. Elliott
Mme Clara Osinulu
Mme Anne Holden Ronning
Dr. Elizabeth Poskitt
Mme Madeleine Deves Senghor
Mme Francoise Sauvage
Mme Murielle Joye

Federation Internationale Syndicale des Enseignants (FISE)

Prof. Abdou Salam Sall
Prof. Bachir Benjilali
Prof. Mrinmoy Bhattacharyia
Prof. Issam Khalife
Prof. Carlos Poblete Avila
Prof. Daniel Monteux

Federation Internatioanle des Universities Catholiques (FIUC)

Prof. Andrew Gonzalez
Prof. Bartholomew J. Mc Gettrick
M. Paul Gallagher
Prof. Guy-Real Thivierge
Prof. Vincent Hanssens

Global Alliance for Transnational Education (GATE)

Dr. Marjorie Peace Lenn
Mr. David Zonker
Dr. Tom Clawson
Mr. Kari Hypponen
Mrs Jennifer Reason Moll

International Association of Agricultural Students (IAAS)

Ms Barbara Sterk
Ms Tanja Buzeti
Mr. Frederik Oberthur
Ms Polona Kolarek
Ms Elena Panichi
Ms An Saye
Ms Anne Rosling
Ms Dorota Dzik
Mr. Cord Kroeschell
Mr. David Mc Donald
Mr. Yawson Felix Abeeku

International Association of Dental Students (IADS)

Mr. Christpher Orr
Ms Valentina Sterjova
Mr. Eric Normand

International Association for Educational Assessment (IAEA)

Dr. Michal Beller
Dr. Thomas Kellaghan
Dr. Christina Stage
Dr. Bryan Dockrell

International Association for Educational and Vocational Guidance (IAEVG)

Prof. Jose Ferreira Marques
Mr. Jean-Luc Brun
Prof. Dr. Raoul Van Esbroeck
Mr. Stuart Conger
Mr. A. Jean Long

International Association of University Presidents (IAUP)

Dr. Donald R. Gerth
Dr. Maurice Harari
Prof. Robert Jones
Prof. Graeme Fogelberg
Dr. James Roach
Dr. Jozef Van Der Perre
Prof. George Benneh
Mr. Fujia Yang

International Association of Univerisity Professors and Lecturers (IAUPL)

Prof. Carlo Alberto Mastrelli
Prof. Denis Levy
Prof. Louis-Philippe Laprevote
Prof. Claude Javeau
Prof. Predrag B. Djordjevic

International Council for Distance Education (ICDE)

Prof. Armando Rocha Trindade
Prof. Jim Taylor
Dr. Molly Corbett Broad
Mr. Bernard Loing
Prof. Anne Auban

International Council for Engineering and Technology (ICET)

Mr. Pierre Pecoux
Dr. Vivian Saminaden
Mr. Pierre-Edouard de Boigne

International Council of Jewish Women (ICJW)

Mrs Norma Anav

International Council of Nurses (ICN)

Ms Fadwa Affara
Mrs Adele Bakhache
Ms Nicole Lake

International Council of Scientific Unions (ICSU)

Prof. Daniel A. Akyeampong
Prof. Albert E. Fischli

International Federation of Business and Professional Women (IFBPW)

Mrs Sylvia G. Perry
Mrs Sharon Selkirk
Mrs Ellen Bartsch- Saouli
Ms Claire K. Niala
Dr. Monique Siegel
Dr. Antoinette Ruegg

International Federation of Medical Students Association (IFMSA)

Mr. Thiago Monaco
Mr. Tibar Hlavaty
Ms Paola Erba
Mr. Mohammed El Bata
Ms Tine Nymark
Mr. Aleksandar Bodiroza
Mr. Sanjeeb Sapkota
Mr. Carel Schaars
Mr. Ahmed Shokry
Mr. Acharya Arunkumar
Ms Bjorg Thorsteinsdottir

International Forestry Students Association (IFSA)

Mr. Emmanuel Marfo
Mr. Agus Salim
Mr. Peter Sprang
Ms Joanna Schoenenberger
Mr. Thies Eggers
Ms Nicole Mirza
Mr. Giorgio Andrian

International Pharmaceutical Students Federation (IPSF)

Ms Alison Sutherland
Mr Goncalo Sousa Pinto
Ms Adriana Ivama
Mr. Mitja Kos
Ms Danielle Zammit
Mr. Oriol Lacorte

International Round Table for the Advancement of Counselling (IRTAC)

Prof. Courtland Lee
Dr. Jean Guichard
Dr. Sandra I. Lopez-Baez
Prof. Ronald Barnett
Ms Wendy Sim
Dr. Hans E. Hoxter

International Union of Students (IUS)

Mr. Ingo Jager
Mr. Samwin Banienuba
Ms Jennifer Story
Mr. Abdourahamane Zakaria
Mr. Frage Sherif
Mr. Bernd Schneider
Mr. James Parker
Mr. Nicholas Ajayi

Junior Association for Development in Europe (JADE)

Ms Cynthia Wolsdorff
Ms Poliana Caio Junqueira
Mr. Flavio Nijs
Mr. Philop Scherenberg
Mr. Cristiano Zaroni
Mr. Christoph Obholzer
Ms Katharina Scholetke
Mr. Alessio Loreti
Ms Saskia Nimz
Ms Bettina Klingebiel
Ms Paloma Nieto

Jeunesse Etudiante Catholique Internationale (JECI)

Mlle Anita Wenger
M. Julio Casas Calderon
Mle Rima Sleiman
M. Tarsoo Linus Ade
M. Miguel Angel Garcia Lopez
M. Kondi Napo Sonhaye
M. Aleemi William Kenyi
M. Andreas Greis
Pere Xavier Maurin
Mlle Angela Schmitz
Mlle Anne-Claire Foutel

Mouvement International des Etudiants Catholiques (MIEC)

M. Walter Prysthon Junior
M. Roland Ranaivoarison
Mlle Parinya Boonridrerthaikul
Mlle Florence Nsumbu
M. Thierry Bonaventura
Mlle Suzana Pacheco
Mlle Yvette Moussavou
M. Alcivam Paulo de Oliveira
M. Antoine-Michel Rodriguez
Mlle Alison Gilhespie
Mlle Natalia Mendez Andres
Mlle Katalin Gelenscsir

Organisation Universitaire Interamericaine (OUI)

Prof. Juan Carlos Romero Hicks
Prof. Lauro Ribas Zimmer
Prof. Luis Garita Bonilla
Prof. Pierre Cazalis
Dr. Pierre Van Der Donckt

Programme de Recherche et de Liaison Universitaires pur le Developpement (PRELUDE)

Prof. Georges Thill
Prof. Guy Berger
Prof. Francoise Coupe
Prof. Maria Kaila
Prof. Fatou Sarr

Soroptimist Internatioal
Mme Hilary Page
Mme Suzanne Loko
Mme Yseult Kaplan
Mme Monique Pinthon
Mme Margaret Alderson
Mme Jeannine Jacquemin

Society for Research into Higher Education (SRHE)

Prof. Healther Eggins
Prof. Diana Green
Prof. Jennifer Bone
Prof. Elane El Khawas
Prof. Oliver Fulton

Union des Universites de I' Amerique Latine (UDUAL)
Ing. Luis Pinto Faverio
Dr. Abelardo Villegas Maldonado
Dr. Salomon Lerner Febres
Lic. Magdalena Sosa Ortega

Union Internationale des Architectes (UIA)
M. Fernando Juan Ramos Galino
M. Alexandur Sandu
Dr. Enrico Vivanco Riofrio
Mme Paula Liberato

World Federation of Engineering Organisations (WFEO)
Prof. Miguel Angel Yadarola
Dr. Nicole Becarud
Prof. Dr- Ing Vollvath Hopp
Mr. Janos Ginsztler
Ing. Conrado Bauer

World Federation for Medical Education (WFME)
Dr. Hans Karle

World Student Christian Federation (WSCF)
Mr. Kangwa Mabuluki
Ms Agnes Pangyansky
Mr. Lawrence Nana Brew
Mr. Modeste Mfashwanayo
Ms Edwina Hunter
Mr. Moses Paul Peter
Mr. Soeren Asmus
Mr. Waguih Alef Khalil
Mr. Horacio Mesones
Ms Nicole Lake

World University Service (WUS)
Mrs Wieke Wagenaar
Mr Koe Saunders
Mrs Ximena Erazo
Mrs Irene Kisule
Mr. Devender Kakar
Mrs Manquel Tejeda
Ms Silvia Villagra
Mr. Hernan Rosekranz
Mrs Corinne Salinas-Meoni

Zonta International
Mme Helene Gachet
Mme Aline Demars Diot
Mme Janine Ndiaye
Mme Yvonne Pernet
Mme Maria Francisca Mourier Martinez

OTHER NGOs

AUTRES ONG

OTRAS ONG

Academic Cooperation Association (ACA)
Dr. Pieter van Dijk
Prof. Dr Konstantinos Kerameus

Americans for the Universality of UNESCO
Mr. Richard K. Nobbe

Associations of Christian Colleges and Universities. International Ecumenical Forum (ACU- IEF)
Dr. Duncan S. Ferguson
Dr. Robert Sorensen
Dr. Mani Jacob
Dr. Jusuf Udaya
Dr. Rudolf Ficker

Association pour le Developpment de I'Education en Afrique (ADEA)
M. Richard Sack

Association pour le Developpment des Methodes de Formation dans I'Enseignement superieur (ADMES)
Mme Marie-Francoise Fave-Bonnet
Mme Annie Bireaud

Association Europeenne des Enseignants (AEE)
Prof. Maurice-Paul Gautier

Association de Universidades Amazonicas (UNAMAZ)
Prof. Cristovam Wanderley Picanco Diniz
Prof. Alberto Valencia Granada

Associacion de Universidades Group Montevideo (AUGM)
Prof. Wrana Panizzi
Prof. Dr. Jose Rubens Rebelatto
Prof. Dr. Rodolfo Joaquim Pinto da Luz
Ing. Luis Julian Lima
Dr. Cesar Gottfried

Associacion de Universidades e Institutos de Investigacion del Caribe (UNICA)
Dr. Orville Kean
Sr. Gerard Latortue
Sra. Mabel Maduro

Asociacion Universitaria Iberoamericana de Postgrado (AUIP)
Dr. Ignacio Berdugo Gomez de la Torre
Dr. Angel Espina Barrio
Dr. Vïctor Cruz Cardona

Conseil Africain et Malgache pour l'Enseignement Superieur (CAMES)
M. Rambre Moumouni Ouiminga

Centre Catholique International pour l'UNESCO (CCIC)
M. Gilles Deliance
Mme Claire Herrmann

Center for Higher Education (CHE)
Dr. Tilman Kuechler

Center for Higher Education Policy Studies (CHEPS)
Dr. Peter Maassen

Centre Panafricain d'Etudes et de Recherches en Relations Internationales et en Education pour le Developpement (CEPARRED)
Prof. Remi Clignet

Centre for Research and Development of Higher Education (CRDHE)
Prof. Montohisa Kaneko

Collectif Interuniversitaire pour la Cooperation avec les Universites Palestiniennes (CICUP)
Prof. Mohamed Jouini
M. Fouad Badran

Collective Consulation on Literacy
Mme Odile Moreau
Mme Karine Brun

Confederation Interionale des Fonctionnaires (CIF)
M. Claude Roche
Mme Evelyne Huguet

Conseil Interuniversitaire de la Communaute francaise (CICF)
M. Etienne Loeckx

Consell International de la Philosophie et des Sciences Humanies (CIPSH)
M. Luca Maria Scarantino

European Association of Distance Teaching Universities (EADTU)
Mr. Piet Henderikx

European Association for Research and Development in Higher Education (EARDHE)
Dr. Brigitte Berendt

Expertise Centrum Hoger Onderwijs (ECHO)
Dr. Marloes De Bie

European University Continuing Education Network (EUCEN)
Prof. Victor de Kosinsky

European Association of Institutions in Higher Education (EURASHE)
Dr. Edward Dhondt
Mr. Soren Norgaard

Federation mondiale des Associations, Centres et Clubs UNESCO (FMACU)]
M. Patrick Gallaud

Forum for African Women Educationalists (FAWE)
Dr. Eddah Gachukia
Dr. Dorothy Njeuma
Dr. Elenore Nerine
Mme Florence K. Nyamu
Hon. Esi Sutherland-Addy

Federation africaine des associations des parents d'eleves et d'etudiants
M. Martin Itoua

Federation Mondiale des Travailleurs Scientifques (FMTS)
M. Andre Jaegle

GRETAF
Prof. Raymond Lallez

Corporation INCORVUZ
M. Guennadi Kalioujuyi
Prof. Dr Michail Fedorov
Prof. Teodor Shanin

Institute for Policy, Practice and Research in the Education of Adult
Prof. Eric Bockstael

International Baccalaureate Organisation (IBO)
Mme Antuna -Baragano

International Congress of University Adult Education (ICUAE)
Dr. John F. Morris

International Council of Adult Education (ICAE)
Mrs Lalita Ramdas

International Council of Women (ICW)
Prof. Judith Parris
Mme Monique Leveque

International Social Science Council (ICSS)
Mr Leszek Kosinski
Mrs Maria Pilar Magannon
Mrs Lihua Zhang

International Union of Biological Sciences (IUBS)
Prof. Jean -Claude Mounolou

International Network for Quality Assurance Agencies in Higher Education (INQAAHE)
Dr. David Woodhouse
Mr. Richard Lewis

Institut de Recherche sur l'Economic de l'Education (IREDU)
M. Serge Cuenin

La Voix de l'Enfant
Mme Claire Honigman

Lobby Europeen des Femmes
Mme Jacqueline de Groote

Liftia Rabbani Foundation (Euro-Arab Dialog Forum)
M. Mahmoud Rabbani

Office Internatonal de l'Enseignement Catholique (OIEC)
M. Guy Pican

Office National d'Information Sur les Enseignements et les Professions (ONISEP)
M. Michel Valdiguie

Organization of Open Education (OOE)
H.E. Bashir Bakri

Rotary International
M. Marc Levin

Societe Internationale pour le Developpement (SID)
M. Jacques Godchot

Union Mathematique Africaine
Prof. Ahmed Kerkour

World Council of Associations for Technology Education (WOCATE)
Dr. Kati Langer
Dr. Detlef Wahl

World Council for Vocational Education (WCVE)
Prof. Prithvi Kaula

RECTORS' CONFERENCES/ NATIONAL HIGHER EDUCATION BODIES

CONFERENCE DES RECTEURS/ INSTITUTIONS NATIONALES D'ENSEIGENEMENT SUPERIEUR

CONFERENCIAS DE RECTORES/ INSTITUCIONES NACIONALES DE ENSENANZA SUPERIOR

AFRICA

<u>COTE D'IVOIRE</u>

Conference des Recteurs des Universities Francophones d'Afrique Occidentale Centrale et de 'Ocean Indien (CRUFAOCI)
Prof. Hauhouot Asseypo
Prof. Dago gerard Lezou

<u>NIGERIA</u>

Committee of Vice-Chancellors of Nigerian Federal Universities
Prof. C.O.G. Obah
Prof. A.S. Sambo
Prof. F.O. Aboaba

National Universities Commission
Prof. Munzali Jibril
Prof. Salihu Mustafa
Dr. Kabiru Isyaky
Prof. J.F. Ade Ajayi

<u>SENEGAL</u>

Centre de Recherches pour le Developpment International (CRDI)
M. Alioune Camara

SOUTH AFRICA
Center for Higher Education Transformations (CHET)
Mr. Tembile Kulati

Committeee of University Principals of South Africa (SAUVCA)
Prof. Jan Kirsten
Prof. Stef Coetzee
Prof. C. Abrahams

UGANDA
Inter-University Council for East Africa
Mr. Eric K. Kigozi

ARAB STATES

BAHRAIN
University of Bahrain
Dr. Mohammed Alghatam
Dr. Khalid Bugahoos
Dr. Nakhle Wehbe
Mr. Ali Engineer

PALESTININ AUTHORITY
Al-Quds Open University
Dr. Nader Abu-Khalaf

ASIA AND PACIFIC

FIJI
Uuniversity of the South Pacific
Mr. Pio Manoa

INDIA
National Institute of Educational Planning and Administration
Prof. Jandhyala Tilak

Association of Indian Universities
Prof. K.B. Powar

JAPAN
Association of Private Universities of Japan
Dr. Duniko Tanioka
Dr. Ichiro Tanioka

TAJIKISTAN
Technological University of Tajikistan
Prof. Poulat Poulatov

THAILAND
Private Univrsities Association of Thailand
Dr. Prathip Komolmas

EUROPE AND NORTH AMERICA

AUSTRIA
Osterreichische Rekotrenkonferenz
Dr. Peter Skalicky

BELARUS
Belarussian State Polytechnical Academy
Prof. Mikhail Dxiamchuk

BELGIUM
Conseil des Recteurs
M. Marcel Crochet

Conferation des Conferences des Recteurs de I'Union Europeenne
Prof. Dr. Hans-Uwe Erichsen

CANADA
Association des Universities et Colleges du Canada (AUCC)
Mrs. Sally Brown

Conference des Recteurs et des Principaux des Universities du Quebec (CREPUQ)

Mr. Jacques Bordeleau
Mr. Pierre Lucier
Mr. Francois Tavenas

Conseil Superieur de l'Education

Dr. Celine Saint-Pierre

CZECH REPUBLIC

Czech Rectors Conference

Prof. Lubomir Dvorak
Prof. Petr Zuna

DENMARK

Rektorkollegiet

Prof. Henrik Toft Jensen
Mr. Henrik Tvarno

FINALND

Finnish Council of University Rectors

Prof. Paavo Uronen
Prof. Lauri Lajunen
Prof. Yrjo Sotamaa

Rectors Conference of Finnish Polytechnics (ARENE)

Mr. Veijo Hintsanen

FRANCE

Conference des Presidents d'Universites (CPU)

M. Jean-Pierre Finance
M. Bernard Raoult
M. Alain Gaudemer

GERMANY

German Rectors Conference

Prof. Dr. Michael Daxner
Prof. Dr. Erich Hodl
Mr. Christian Tauch

HUNGARY

Hungarian Rectors' Conference

Prof. Laszlo Frenyo
Dr. Andras Rona-Tas
Prof. Jozsef Tihanyi

ITALIA

Conferenza Permanente dei Rettori

Prof. Luciano Modica
Dr. Emanuela Stefani
Prof. Enrico Rizzarelli

NORWAY

Norwegian Council of Universities/ Association of Nordic University Rectors' Conferences

Prof. Lucy Smith
Prof. Hans Peter Jensen
Dr. Per Nyborg

PORTUGAL

Associao das Universidades de Lingua Portuguesa (AULP)

Prof. Ruy Pauletti
Prof. A, Simoes Lopes
prof. Jorge Souza Brito

Associacao Portuguesa de Ensino Superior Privado (APESP)

Sr. Antonio Jorge Goncalves Rodrigues

Portuguese National Conference of Rectors (CRUP)

Sr. Julio Pedrosa de Jesus
Sr. Luis Sousa Lobo

ROMANIA

National Rector's Council

Prog. Gheorghe Zgura

SPAIN

Conferencia de Rectores de las Universidades Espanolas (CRUE)

Sr. Felix Garcia Lausin
Sr. Saturnino de la Plaza Perez
Sr. Carles Sola Ferrando

UNITED KINGDOM OF GREAT BRITAIN AND NORTHERN IRELAND

Committee of Vice-Chancellors and Principals of the Universitieis of the United Kingdom (CVCP)

Prof. Robert Boucher
Ms Dianna Warwick
Dr. Tony Bruce

UNITED STATES OF AMERICA

American Association for Higher Education (AAHE)

Dr. Margaret A. Miller
Dr. Dolores E. Cross

American Association of State Colleges and Universities (AASCU)

Dr. James B. Appleberry
Dr. Ed Elliott
Dr. Emita Hill

Association of American Universities (AAU)

Dr. Nils Hasselmo
Mr. Myles Brand
Dr. Cornelius Pings

American Council on Education (ACE)

Dr. Madeleine Green
Dr. Robert Scott
Mrs Michele Myers

Hispanic Assocation of Colleges and Universities (HACU)

Dr. Antonio Flores Rios
Dr. Tomas A. Arciniega
Dr. Ricardo R. Fernandez

Institute of International Education/ Council for International Exchange of Scholars (IIE/CIES)

Mr. David D. Arnold
Dr. Patti McGill Peterson
Dr. Piedad Robertson

Institute for Higher Education Policy (IHEP)

Dr. Jamie Merisotis

National Association of Independent Colleges and Universities (NAICU)

Mr. David L. Warren
Mrs Patricia Ewers

National Association of State Universities and Land-Grant Colleges (NASULGC)

Dr. C. Peter Magrath
Dr. Michael Malone
Dr. Martin Jischke

National Council of Educational Opportunity Associations (NCEOA)

Mr. Arnold Mitchem

LATIN AMERICA AND THE CARIBBEAN

ARGENTINA

Consejo Interuniversitario Nacional (CIN)

Ing. Agr. Alberto Cantero
Sr. Carlos Omar Dominguez
Dr. Humberto Antonio Herrera

Consejo de Rectores de Universidades Privadas (CRUP)

Dr. Mario Armando Mena

BRAZIL

Associacao Nacional dos Dirigentes das Instituicoes Federais de Ensino Superior (ANDIFES)

Dr. Odilon Marcuzzo Do Canto
Dr. Dader Nunes De Oliverira
M. Sc. Fernando Lima

Conselho de Reitores das Universidades Brasileiras (CRUB)

Sr. Mario Veiga de Almedia
Prof. Julio Fernando Pessoa Correia
Sr. Almor De Souza Maia
Prof. Luciane de Paula Chermann

CHIEF

Consejo de Rectores de las Universidades Chilenas (CRUC)

Sr. Jaime Godoy Jorquera
Sr. Jesus Gonzalex Lopez
Sr. Ubaldo Zuniga Quintanialla

Centro Interuniversitario de Desarollo (CINDA)

Sr. Luis Eduardo Gonzalez

Corporacion de Universidades Privadas

Dr. Hector Zuniga Salinas
Sr. Jose Luis Zabala

COLOMBIA

Asociacion Colombiana de Universidades (ASCUN)

Dr. Galo Armando Burbano Lopez
Dr. Luis Alfonso Ramfrez Pena
Dr. Gustavo Antonio Tellez Iregui

Instituto Colombiano para el Fomento de la Educacion Superior (ICFES)

Dr. Jesus Maria Ferro Bayona
Dr. Ilse Moraima Bechara Castilla

COSTA RICA

Consejo Nacional de Rectores (CONARE)

M.Sc. Jose Andres Masis
Dra. Yamileth Gonzalez
Dr. Jorge Vargas

Consejo Superior Universitario Centroamericano (CSUCA)

Dr. Ricardo Sol Arriaza
Msc. Francisco Alarcon Alba
Dra. Maria Perez Yglesias
Br. Antonio Vicente Berrios Ordonez
Br. Roberto Antonio Melgar Monterrosa

HONDURAS

Asociacion de Universidades Privadas de Centroamerica (AUPRICA)

Ing. Ricardo Jaar

MEXICO

Asociacion de Universidades e Instituciones de Educacion Superior (ANUIES)

Mtra. Dolores Sanchez Soler
Mtro. Antonio Gago Huguet
Dr. enrique Doger Guerrero

NICARAGUA

Consejo Nacional de Universidades

Lic. Francisco Guzman Pasos
Ing. Francisco Telemaco Talavera Siles
Dr. Eduardo Valdes Barria
Lic. Mariano Vargas

PERU

Asambela Nacional de Rectores

Dr. Jose Javier Perez Rodriguez

PUERTO RICO

Consejo de Educacion Superior de Puerto Rico

Prof. Eduardo Aponte-Hernandez
Lic. Sandra Espada Santos
Dr. Ethel Rios Orlandi
Dr. Juan Fernandez-Velazquez

VEMEZUELA

Consejo Academico Latinoamericano (CALA)

Dr. Sulbey Naranjo de Adarmes

Consejo Nacional de Universidades

Prof. Jesus Maria Rivero Lopez
Dra. Migdalia Concepcion Perozo Bracho

Grupo Universitario Latinoamericano de Estudios para la Reforma y el Perfeccionamiento de la Educacion (GULERPE)

Dra. Elyzabeth Y. de Caldera

ASSOCIATIONS/UNIONS OF PROFESSORS

ASSOCIATIONS/SYNDICATS DE PROFESSEURS

ASOCIACIONES/SINDICATOS DE PROFESORES

AFRICA

BURKINA FASO

Syndicat National des Enseignants du Superieur et du Secondaire (SNESS)

Prof. Longin Some
Prof. Domedassov Jean-Francois Somda

CAMEROON

Syndicat National des Enseignants du Superieur (SYNES)

Prof. Pierre Kamtchouing

CHAD

Syndicat National des Enseignants et Chercheurs du Superieur (SYNECS)

Mr. Danna Abba
Mr. Soultan Malloum

COTE D'IVOIRE

Syndicat National de la Recherche et de l'Enseignement Superieur (SYNARES)

Prof. Kessie Raymond Koudou
M. Messou Nguessan Nyamien

MADAGASCAR

Syndicat des Enseignants Chercheurs de l'Enseignement Superieur (SECES)

M. Gibert Ramonjy Rabedaoro
M. Lala Andriamampianina

MALI

Syndicat National de l'education et de la Culture

Dr. Toure Baba Moussoudou
Mme Doumbia Mama Koite

NIGER

Syndicat National des Enseignants et Chercheurs du Superieur (SNECS)

M. Mmadou Seidou Hassane Maiga
M. Boureima Diadie

SENEGAL

Syndicat Autonome de l'Enseignement Superieur

M. Mamadou Samba Kah
M. Abdoul Wahib Kane

SOUTH AFRICA

South African Democratic Teachers' Union (SADTU)

Mr. Bobby Mthombeni
Mr. Dan More

ZAMBIA

Zambia National Union of Teachers

Mr. Kenneth Kasehela

ARAB STATES

IRAQ

Federation of Arab Teachers

Mr. Hishan Nimir Mustafa Mukahhal

KUWAIT

Kuwait Teachers' Society

Dr. Ahmed Al Houly
Mr. Ahmed Al Munaify

MOROCCO

Syndicat National de l'Enseignement Superieur (SNE sup)

Prof. El Kebir Bazzaoui
Prof. Abdenbi Rajouani

PALESTINIAN AUTHORITY

General Union of Palestinian Teachers (GUPT)

Mr. Mohammed Sowan
Mr. Hazem Qumsieh

ASIA AND PACIFIC

AUSTRALIA

National Tertiary Education Union (NTEU)

Dr. Carolyn Alport

BANGLADESH

Bangladesh College-University Teachers' Association (BCUTA)

Prof. Dr. Mohammed Akhtaruzzaman
Prof. M.A. Bari
M.B. Jahanara Zaman

INDIA

All India Federation of University and College Teachers' Organisations

Mr. Mrinmoy Bhattacharyya

All India Federation of Educational Associations

Mr. Biswanandan Dash
Prof. Dahiya Dalel Singh

EUROPE AND NORTH AMERICA

ALBANIA

Trade Union Federation of Education and Science (FSASH)

Mr. Xhafer Dobrushi
Mrs Valentina Ikonomi

CANADA

Federation Quebecoise des Professeures et Professeurs d'Universite (FQPPU)

Dr. Roch Denis

Centrale de l'enseignement du quebee

Mme Monique Richard

Canadian Association of University Teachers (CAUT)

Prof. Claude Dionne
Prof. William Graham

CROATIA

Independent Union of Research and Higher Education Employees of Croatia

Mr. Kresimir Rozman
Mrs Visnja Besendorfer

DENMARK

Fra Dansk Magisterforening (Danish Association of Masters and Ph.D.s.)

Mr. Jens Vraa-Jensen
Mr. Nils-Georg Lundberg

FINLAND

Finnish Union of University Researchers and Teachers (FUURT)

Dr. Kari Pitkanen

FRANCE

Federation des syndicats generaux de l'Education nationale et de la Recherche publique (SGEN CFDT)
M. Michel Deyme

Federation de l'Education Nationale (FEN UNSA)
M. Guy Lachenaud

Federation Syndicale Unitaire (FSU)
M. Michel Deschamps

GERMANY

International Confederation of free Teachers Unions (GEW)
Dr. Gerd Kohler
Mr. Romin Reich

IRELAND

Irish Federation of University Teachers (IFUT/CEMO)
Mr. Daltun O Ceallaigh
Ms Maureen Killeavy

LATVIA

Education and Scientific Workers' Trade Union of Latvia
Astrida Harbacevica
Solveiga Skotele

FORMER YUGOSLAV REPUBLIC OF MACEDONIA

Trade Union of Education, Science and Culture (SONK)
Mr. Done Gersanovski
Mr. Stojan Nikolovski

The NETHERLANDS

General Education Trade Union (AOB)
Mr. Martin Knoop

NORWAY

Forsker Forbundet
Kari Kjenndalen
Sigrid Lem

POLAND

National Science Section NSZZ "Solidarnose"
Dr. Hanna Witkowska

PORTUGAL

Federacao Nacional dos PROFESORES (FENPROF)
Prof. Joao Cunha Serra
Prof. Mario Carvalho

RUSSIAN FEDERATION

Education and Science Employees' Union of Russia
Mr. Vladimir Yakovlev
Mr. Nikolay Kolobashkin

SPAIN

CC.OO. Sindicato de Ensenanza
Sr. Pedro Gonzalez

Federacion de Trabajadores de la Ensenanza de la UGT (FETE-UGT)
Sra. Teresa Munoz Rodriguez

SWEDEN

Swedish Association of University Teachers (SULF)
Mrs Gorel Stromqvist

UNITED kINGDOM OF GREAT BRITAIN AND NORTHERN IRELAND

Association of University Teachers (AUT)
Mr. David Triesman

UNITED STATES OF AMERICA

National Education Association (NEA)
Mr. Roger Knutsen

American Association of University Professors (AAUP)
Mrs. Mary Burgan
Mr. James Richardson

American Federation of Teachers (AFT)
Prof. Norman Swenson
Prof. William Scheuerman

LATIN AMERICAN AND THE CARIBBEAN

BRAZIL

Sindicato dos Estabelecimentos de Ensino no Estado de Sao Paulo (SIEEESP)
Sr. Jose Aurelio Camargo

Sinidicato Nacional dos Docentes das Instituicoes de Ensino Superior (ANDES-SN)
Prof. Anibal Sanchez Moura
Prof. Francisco Jaime Bezerra Mendonca

CUBA

Sindicato Nacional de los Trabajadores de la Educacion la Ciencia y el Deporte (SNTECD)
Prof. Luis Abreu Mejias

DOMINICAN REPUBLIC

Associacion de Empleados Universitarios (ASODEMU)
Sr. Fausto Herrera Catalino

MEXICO

Federacion Nacional de Sindicatos Universitarios (FNSU)
Dr. Jesus Hernandez Torres
Ing. Agustin Rodriguez Fuentes

PUERTO RICO

Asociacion Puertorriquena de Profesores Universitarios
Prof. Waldemiro Velez Cardona

ACADEMIES OF SCIENCES

ACADEMIES DES SCIENCES

ACADEMIAS DE CIENCIAS

AFRICA

KENYA

The African Academy of Sciences
Prof. Gideon Okelo

COTE D'IVOIRE

Federation de Associations Scientifiques de la Cote d'Ivoire
Prof. Ignace Yace

ARAB STATES

MAROC

Centre National de Coordination et de Planification de la Recherche Scientifique et Technique
M. Said Belcadi

EUROPE AND NORTH AMERICA

FRANCE

L'Aacademie des Sciences
Mr. Yvan Assenmacher

POLAND

Polish Academy of Sciences Center in Paris
Mr. Henryk Ratajczak

ROMANIA

Academia Romana
Mrs Gabriela Tarabega

SLOVAKIA

Slovak Academy of Sciences
Prof. Stefan Luby

UZBEKISTAN

Academy of Sciences of Uzbekistan
Mr. Turabekh Dalimov
Mr. Ilkham Ikramov

LATIN AMERICA AND THE CARIBBEAN

BOLIVIA

Academia Nacional de Ciencias de Bolivia

Mr. Carlos Aguirre B.

BRAZIL

Academia Brasilera de Ciencias

Mr. Eduardo Krieger

STUDENTS' ASSOCIATIONS

ASSOCIATIONS D'ETUDIANTS

ASOCIACIONES DE ESTUDIANTES

AFRICA

AASU - All African Students Union
Ms Ester Adjoa Adams, Ghana
Mr. Haruna Iddrisu, Ghana
Mr. Samuel Pimpong, Ghana
Mr. Sountoucoung Drame, Senegal
Mr. Benson Obua Ogwal, Uganda
Mr. Mamabolo Jacob Sasco

BENIN

Federation Nationale des Etudiants du Benin (FNEB)

M. Marcellin Laourou

Union Nationale des Scolaires et Etudiants du Benin (UNSEB)

Mlle Mathurine Sossoukpe

BOTSWANA

Botswana Students' Union

Mr. Gregory Keleyboney

GAMBIA

Gambia Students Union

Mr. Momodou Sillah

GHANA

Ghana United Nations Students and Youth Association (UNSA)

Mr. Malcolm Ebernezer

MAURITIUS

Mauritius Union of Students Councils (MUSC)

Mr. Savoondary Mootoosamy

Mauritius Students Union

Mr. Siamal Jadoo

SIERRA LEONE

Beginners Club

Ms Isatu Kamara

SOUTH AFRICA

South African Students Congress (SASCO)

Mr. Jacob Mamabulu

ZAMBIA

University of Zambia Students Union (UNZASU)

Mr. Oliver Sepiso Shalala

OTHER DELEGATES

CAMEROON/IVORY COAST

Students' Parliament of Cameroon

Mr. Tene Kwetche Sop Guillaume

ARAB STATES

GUAS - General Union of Arab Students
Mr. Adel Daw. Egypt
Mr. Kaled Masharka, Jordan
Ms Randala Hilal, Lebanon
Mr. Touriya Lahrech, Morocco
Mr. Mohammed Abu Daggo, Palestine
Mr. Abdallah Al-Najjar, Palestine
Mr. Ibrahim Khrisha, Palestine
Mr. Saied Mohammed, Tunisia
Mr. Tayseer Mashareqa

ALGERIA

La Ligue Nationale des Etudiants Algeriens

M. Mahdi Kehlifa
M. Smail Inezarene

EGYPT

Union of Progressive Youth

Ms Raguia ElHusseiny

JORDAN

Yarmouk University Students Union

Mr. Monked Al - Roussan

MOROCCO

Union Generale des Etudiants du Maroc

Mr Taha Mohamed
Mr Hicha Al Abdelaoui

SUDAN

General Union of Sudanese Students

Mr. Hamdi Sulaiman

ASIA AND THE PACIFIC

ASA-Asian Students Association

Ms Sarah Helm, New Zealand
Mr. Arun Nepal, Nepal
Mr. Renato Jr. Reyes, Philippines
Mr. Norman Uy Carnay, Philippines
Mr. Ahmed Rajbally, Mauritius
Mr. Sadeck Futloo, Mauritius
Mr. Tsui Wai-Hang, Hong Kong
Mr. Anand Chang, Fiji

AUSTRALIA

Council of Australian Post-graduate Association Inc. (CAPA)

Ms Alana Chinn

BANGLADESH

Student Union of Bangladesh (SUB)

Mr. Ziual Haque Zia

HONG KONG

Hong Kong Students' Federation (HKSF)

Mr. Paul Less

INDIA

International Students Movement for the United Nations (ISMUN)

Mr. Bremley W.B. Lyngdoh

PHILIPPINES

LFS

Mr. Dennis Longid

EUROPE AND NORTH AMERICA

AUSTRIA

Osterreichische Hochschuler Innenschaft (OH)

Mr. Michael Unger

BELARUS

Club UNESCO de l'UNIVERSITE Transport

M. Aloah Yosimbom Diyen

BELGIUM

Vereigning van Vlaamse Studenten (VVS)

Ms Anja Kovcs

BULGARIA

Union of Bulgarian Students

Ms Svetla Tzvetkova

CANADA

Canadian Federation of Students

Ms Maura Parte

Federation Etudiante Universitaire du Quebec (FEU)

M. Nikolas Ducharme

DENMARK

Danske Studerendes Faellesraad (DSF)

Mr. Christoffer Greisen

Landssammenslutningen af Moderate Studenter (LMS)

Mr. Daniel Ostenfeld

ESTONIA

Federation of Estonian Student Unions

Mr. Lauri Koop

FINLAND

National Union of Finnish Students (SYL)

Mr. Linna Pekka

The Union of Finnish Polytechnic Students (SAMOK)

Ms Ira Salminen

FRANCE

UNEID/Union Nationale des Etudiants de France

Mlle Tifen Duchame
M. Remi Boudu
Mlle Carine Seiler
Mlle Vanessa Mujica
M. Mickael Dahan

FAGE/Federation des Associations Generales Etudiantes

M. Frederic Cuignet
M. Emmanuel Robinson

GREECE

ESEE/National Union of Students - Technological Institutes of Greece

Ms Nika Balomenou

GERMANY

Deutsches Studentenwerk (DSW)

Mr. Dieter Schaferbarthold

Freier Zusammenschluss von Student Innenschaften (FZS)

Ms Ulrike Gonzales

LATVIA

National Student Union (LSA)

Mr. Daniels Pavluts

LITHUANIA

National Student Union (LSS)

Mr. Regimantas Buozius

LUXEMBOURG

Union Nationale des Etudiant(e)s du Luxembourg

M. Frederic Krier

NORWAY

Norsk Studentunion (NSU)

Ms Anne H. Rygg

POLAND

Zrzesenie Studentow Polskich (ZSP)

Ms Agnieszka Bolimowska

UNITED KINGDOM OF GREAT BRITAIN AND NORTHERN IRELAND

National Union of Students (NUS)

Mr. Jim Gardner

UNITED STATES OF AMERICA

National Association of Graduate-Professional Students (NAGPS)

Mr. Brodie Dollinger

YUGOSLAVIA

(Federal Republic of)
Student Parliament of Belgrad

Mr. Zoran Nikolic

OTHER DELEGATES

FRANCE

Association Etudiants Solidaires Dauphine

M. Tobo Djengue

LATIN AMERICA AND THE CARIBBEAN

OCLAE: Organizacion Continental Latinoamericanna y Caribena de Estudiantes
Sr. Yosvani Diaz Romero, Cuba
Sr. Rony Corbo Gonzalez, Uruguay
Sr.Alejandro Urizar Cabrera, Guatemala
Sr. Vladimir Vinicius Camargos, Brazil
Sra. Kenia Hechavarria Marinez, Cuba,
Sr. Raul Sanchez, Argentina
Sr. Gustavo Daverio, Argentina
Sr. Robert Polanco, Brazil
Sr. Alberto Castellano Gurierrex, Mexico
Sr. Marcos Diaz Galarza, Puerto Rico

BRAZIL
Union Nacional de Estudiantes de Brasil (UNE Brasil)
Sr. Ricardo Capeelli

HAITI
Association des Etudiants de la Faculte des Sciences(AEFDS)
M. Carl Sherson Clermont

MEXICO
Federacion de Estudiantes Universitarios de Morelos (FEUM)
Sr. Miquel Angel Cuevas

NICARAGUA
Union de Estudiantes de Nicaragua (UNEN)
Sr. Elias Velazguez Florez

PERU
Federacion de Estudiantes de Peru (FEP)
Sr. Yomar Melendez Rosas

GUATEMALA
Associacion de Estudiantes Universitarios
Sr. David Estuardo Guzman Herodia
Sr./Sra. Quimy De Leon

TRINIDAD AND TOBAGO
Guild of Undergraduates
Mr. Allister Glean

INTERNATIONAL

MOTEUR/Coordination des Associations d'Etudiants Handicapes
Mr. Emmanuel Moreau, France
Mr. M.R. Tobo Djengue, Cameroon

Post-Graduate International Network (Pi-NET)
Mr. Peter Kerey, Hungary
Mr. Ronald Popma, The Netherlands

The Royal Academy of Science International Trust (RASIT)
H.R.H. Dr. Princess Nasreen El-Hashemite
Ms Donna Majab
Ms Helen Mojab
Ms Suja Abou-Khamseen
Mr. Kathim Al Sahir

Alliance for a Responsible and United World
Mr. Daniel Pop, Romania
Ms Grainne Kelly, Ireland
Ms Hobate Hatta, Togo
Ms Kerry Ann Cochrane, Canada
Ms Mariana Ferraz Duarte, Brazil
Ms Tijana Zivanovic, Yugoslavia
Mr. Rigobert Yanda, Kenya
Mr. Christophe Raoul Ewodo, Cameroon
Ms Parisudha Sudhamongkala, Thailand
Mr. Altaf Wani, India

NON UNIVERSITY HIGHER EDUCATION SECTOR

SECTEUR NON UNIVERSITAIRE DE L'ENSEIGNEMENT SUPERIEUR

SECTOR NO UNIVERSITARIO DE ENSENANZA SUPERIOR

Arab Federation for Technical Education (AFTE)
Prof. Dr. Mohammad Al-Azzawi

Association of American Community Colleges (AACC)

Dr. Anthony Zeiss
Mrs Jacquelyn Belcher
Mr. David R. Pierce

Association of Canadian Community Colleges (AACC)

Mr. Gerald Brown
Mr. Leslie O'Reilly

European Centre for the Development of Vocational Training (CEDEFOP)

Mr. Michael Adams

Committee of Technikon Principals of South Africa (CTP)

Prof. B.A. Khoapa
Prof. I.J. Mosala
Prof. Johan Pretorius

European Training Foundation (ETF)
Mr. Thomas Schroder

SEAMO VOCTECH (Southeast Asian Ministers of Education Organisation-Regional Centre for Vocational and Technical Education)

Mr. Haji Abdul Ghani Haji Omar
Mrs Judy Morente

Miami-Dade Community College
Dr. Michael J. Lenaghan

PARLIAMENTS

PARLEMENTS

PARLAMENTOS

AFRICA

NIGER

Assemblee Nationale

M. Adoutane Moutal

ARAB STATES

EGYPT

The Egyptian People' Assembly

Dr. Fathi El Baradi

LEBANON

Parlement Libanais

Mrs Bahia Hariri

ASIA AND PACIFIC

REPUBLIC OF THE PHILIPPINES

Senate

Mr. Edgardo J. Angara

EUROPE AND NORTH AMERICA

AUSTRIA

The Austrian Parliament

Mr. Josef Hochtl

ESTONIA

The Estonian Parliament

Mrs Talvi Marja

FRANCE

Assemblee Nationale

M. Jean Glavany

POLAND

The Sejm of Poland

Mr. A. Luczac

SLOVENIA

The Slovenian Parliament

Ms Helena Hren Vencelj

SPAIN

Senado

Sr. Josep Varela Serra

TAJIKISTAN

The National Parliament Maglisi Oli

Mr. H. Mamadshoh

LATIN AMERICA AND THE CARIBBEAN

RGENTINA

Camara de Diputados de la Nacion

Sra. Liliana Lissi
Dr. Eduardo Mondino

COSTA RICA

Asamblea Legislativa

Sr. Sergio Salazar Rivera

MEXICO

Senado de la Republica mexicana

Sr. Francisco Xavier Salazar Saenz

REPUBLIC OF SURINAME

The National Assembly

Mr. Ashokkoemar Ramballi

VENEZUELA

Senado

Sra. Aline Lampe Joubert
Congreso Nacional
Prof. Pablo Gonzalez Padilla

**TRADE UNIONS
SYNDICATS SINDICATOS**

EUROPE AND NORTH AMERICA

BELGIUM

Confederation Europeenne des Syndicats Independants

Dr. Walter Trapp

Confederation Syndicale Europeenne

M. Alain Mouchou

FRANCE

Federation Nationale des Syndicats Autonomes de l'Enseignement Superieur et de la Recherche (IAUPL)

M. Paul Colonge

GERMANY

DGB Confederation Internationale des Syndicats Libres

Dr. Gerd Kohler

RUSSIAN FEDERATION

General Confederation of Trade Unions

Mr. Albert Potapov

CHAMBERS OF COMMERCE/ FIRMS

CHAMBRES DE COMMERCE/ ENTERPRISES

CAMARAS DE COMERCIO/ EMPRESAS

AFRICA

SUDAN

Sudanese Business and Employer's Federation

Mr. Bakri Omer

EUROPE AND NORTH AMERICA

BELGIUM

FINA Eeducation Centre

Mme Catherine Brohee

FRANCE

Jeune Chambre Economique

Mme Chantal Rozier
M. Dominique Angels
Prof. Jacques Reynier

Groupe HEC

M. Jean-Loup Ardoin
M. Bernard Ramanantsoa

Baker & McKenzie

Dr. Wallace Baker

Assemblee des Chambres francaises de Commerce et d'Industrie

Mme Marie-Grancoise Treffel

European Bahai' Business Forum

M. George Starcher
M. Eric Zahrai

Chambre de Commerce Franco-Allemande

Mme Margarete Riegler-Poyer

HUNGARY

International Chamber of Commerce Hungarian National Committee

Dr. Karoly Ivanyi

MONACO

Jeune Chambre Internationale

M. Yannick Moati
M. Edmond Pastor

SPAIN

AFPUI Junior Empresa

Sra. Paloma Martin Nieto Merino

LATIN AMERICA AND THE CARIBBEAN

BRAZIL

Confederacao nacional do Comércio

Dr. Arnaldo Niskier

COLOMBIA

Asociacion Nacional de Industriales de Colombia (ANDI)

Dr. Luis Carlos Villegas Echeverri

URUGUAY

UDE-Chamber of Commerce de Montevideo

Lic. Luisa Peirano Basso

DONORS

BAILLEURS DE FONDS

PROVEEDORES DE FONDOS

EUROPE AND NORTH AMERICA

CANADA

Univrsite de Nebraska

M. Jil Emal

ESPAGNE

Junta de Andalucia

Dr. Luis Millan Vazquez de Miguel

FRANCE

Fondation CETELEM

M. Paul Defourny
Mme Marie-Dominique Christien
Mlle Celine Godet
M. Pierre Benedetto
M. Paul Camous
M. S. Chirache
Mme C. Baret
Mme E. Nahas

Fondation Charles Leopold Mayer

M. Pierre Calame

GERMANY

DAAD-German Academic Exchange Service

Mr. Ulrich Grothus

Gesellschaft Fur Technische Zusammenarbeit (GTZ)

Dr. Wolfgang Kueper

ISRAEL

Weizmann Institute of Science-PERACH

Mr. Amos Carmeili

ITALY

Conferenza Episcopale Italiana

Ms Stefania Gandolfi

Instituto per la Cooperazione Universitaria

Mr. Pier Giovani Palla

NORWAY

Norwegian Agency for Development Cooperation (NORAD)

Mrs Kristin Sverdrup

Ms Ingrid Braastad

THE NETHERLANDS

Netherlands Organization for International Co-operation in Higher Education (NUFFIC)

Dr. Rosita van Meel

UNITED KINGDOM OF GREAT BRITAIN AND NORTHERN IRELAND

The British Council

Mrs Rebecca Walton

UNTED STATES OF AMERICA

The Rockefeller Foundation

Dr. David J. Maurrasse

The Kellogg Foundation

Dr. Betty Overton-Adkings

LATIN AMERICA AND THE CARIBBEAN

ARGENTINA

Instituto de Aguas Subterraneas para Latinoamerica (INASLA)

Dr. Jochen de Bundschuh

PUBLISHERS

MAISONS D'EDITION

EDITORIALES

EUROPE AND NORTH AMERICA

FRANCE

Presses Universitaires de France

M. Gaston Mialaret

Agence Education et Formation

M. Olivier Dhers

GROUP III

INVITED GROUPS AND GUESTS

ADVISORY GROUP ON HIGHER EDUCATION

Professor Ab Lughod Ibrahim
Vice-President (1993-1995)
Birzeit University
Palestinian Authority

Professor Jorge Brovetto
Executive Secretary
Montevideo Group of Universities
Uruguay

Dr. Donald R. Gerth
President
International Association of
University Presidents
United States of America

Professeur Georges Haddad
President honoraire de l'Universite
de Paris I, Pantheon-Sorbonee
Conseller special du Directeur
general de l'UNESCO

Professor Grant Harman
Pro. Vice Chancellor
University of New Engalnd
Australia

Prof. Gottfried Leibbrandt
Chairman, CEPES AdvisoryBoard
The Netherlands

Prof. Lydia Makhubau
Vice-Chancellor
University of Swaziland
Swaziland

Professor Narciso Matos
Secreatry- general
Association of African
Universities
Ghana

Prof. Peter Medgyes
Hungary

Professor Yasunori Nishijima
Kyoto City University of Arts Japan

Prof. Eunice Ribeiro Durham
NUPES, Universidade de
Sao Paulo
Brazil

Prof. Charas M.D. Suwanwela
Past President and Adviser
Chulalongkorn University
Thailand

Professor Justin Thorens
Honorary President
International Assocation
of Universities
Switzerland

Professor Carlos Tunnermann
Bernheim
Nicaragua

Prof. Dr. Hans J.A, van Ginkel
Rector
United Nations University
Japan

DIRECTOR-GENERAL'S GUESTS

H.R.H. Prince Talal Bin Abdul
Aziz
President
Arab Gulf Programme for United
Nations Development
Organizations (AGFUND)
Saudi Arabia

Mr Nasser Al-Kahtani
AGFUND
Saudi Arabia

Professor Mohammad Al Mannie
AGFUND
Saudi Arabia

Dr. Abdul Aziz Al Sonbul
AGFUND
Saudi Arabia

Dr Hisham Al Sharif
AGFUND
Saudi Arabia

Mr. J. Balbir
Former Head of UNESCO
Teacher Training Section
FRANCE

Professor Kenneth Barker
Chief Executive and Vice-Chancellor
De Montfort University
United Kingdom.

Dr. L.R. Batra
Director
Big Boulder Field Station
United States of America

Mr. A. Chiappano
Former Head of UNESCO
Teacher Training Section
France

Professor Alfonso Borrero Cabal
Universidad Javeriana
Colombia

Dr. Lula Collier
Associate Vice President for
Academic Affairs
Jackson State University
United States of America

Professor John L. Davies
Pro Vice-Chancellor
Anglia Polytechnic University
United Kingdom

Dr. Thierry De Samie
Maitre de Conferences
Universite de Montpellier III
Djibouti

Monsieur Jacques Delors
President
Cellule speciale sur l'education
pour le vingt et unieme siecle
France

Professor Ricardo Diez-
Hochleitner
President
The Club of Rome
Spain

Professor Dr. Donald Ekong
Consultant in Higher Education
Management
c/o The Ford Foundation Office
for South Africa
South Africa

Dr. Nisreen El-Hashemite
The Royal Academy of Science
International Trust
United Kingdom

Dr Maria Aparecida Fernandes de Melo
Brazil

Dr Vitoria Maria Mendoca de Barros
Brazil

Dr. Gerry Hancock
AGFUND
Saudi Arabia

Dr. Gusztav Hencsey
General Manager
Computer and Automation Institute
Hungary

Dr. Attiya Inayatullah
President
International Planned Parenthood Federation
Pakistan

Ms Rita Lakin
Former UNESCO Programme Specialist
France

Prof. Istvan Lang
Advisor
Hungarian Academy of Sciences
Hungary

Dr Arnold Mitchem
President
Council for Opportunity in Education
United States of America

Mr Soungalo Ouedraogo
Directeur de l'enseignement superieur et de la formation professionnelle
Union economique et monetaire ouest africaine
Burkina Faso

Mr Jean-Claude Pauvert
Former Head of UNESCO Teacher Training Section and Former Director of UNESCO Bucharest Office
France

M. Eduardo Portella
President de la Conference generale de l'UNESCO
France

M. Michael Potashnik
AGFUND
Saudi Arabia

M. Michel Romieu
President Directeur General
Elf Aquitaine Gaz
France

M. Mihaly Rozsa
Secretary-general
National Commission for UNESCO
Hungary

Ms Seina Safa
AGFUND
Saudi Arabia

Dr. Celine Saint-Pierre
Presidente
Conseil Superieur de l'Education
Canada

Dr. Fayrouz Sarkis
AGFUND
Saudi Arabia

Prof. Michael Scott
Pro Vice Chancellor
De Montfort University
United Kingdom

Professor Zuhair Sebai
AGFUND
Saudi Arabia

Professor Malcolm Skilbeck
Former Deputy Director for Education, OECD
France

Professor Mihaly Simai
Hungarian Academy of Science
Hungary

Dr. Michael J. Stopford
Senior Assistant to the President for International Affairs
American University
United States of America

Professor Tabare Vasquez
Universidad de la Republica
Uruguay

Ms Hebe Vessuri
Instituto Venezolano de Inverstigaciones Cientificas
Venezuela

Abogado Jose Wainer Grampiner
Secretario tecnico del rector
Universidad de la Republica
Uruguay

Comenius Award Winners

Ms Cecilia Braslavsky, Argentina

Mr Ladislav Cerych, Czech Republic

Mr Burton Clark, United States of America

Mr Naguib Abu Haydar, Lebanon

Institut pedagogique national, Mali

Ms Lydia Makhubu, Swaziland

Mr Shaheen Attiqur Rahman, Pakistan

Mr Rene Remond, France

Mr Ulrich Teichler, Germany

Mr Pravase Wasi, Thailand

Mr Derek Bok, United States of America

Mr Jorge Brovetto, Uruguay

College of Science, Faculty of Science, South Africa

Mr Francisco Gonzalez Montes, Spain

Group "una empresa docentre". Colombia

Ms Palmira Juceviciene, Lithuania

Mr Quincy Lettsonne, British Virgin Islands

Mr Ferdos Hajian Pashakolace, Islamic Republic of Iran

COMMISSION RESOURCE PERSONS

AFRICA

KENYA

Prof. Florida Karani
Deputy Vice-Chancellor
University of Nairobi

SOUTH AFRICA

Dr. Jairam Reddy
Professor

ARAB STATES

IRAQ
Dr. Abdul-Ilah Al-Kahashab
President
Bagdad University

LEBANON
Dr. Abdul H.H. Hallab
Special Adviser
American University of Beirut

LIBYAN ARAB JAMAHIRIYA
Prof. Mohamed Faray Doughaim

SUDAN
Dr. Andallah Ahmad Abdallah

ASIA AND PACIFIC

INDIA
Dr. Ganesh Datt Sharma
Secretary-General
University Grants Commission

JAPAN
Prof. Cary A. Duval
Faculty of International Studies
Center for Global Education
Bunkyo University

THAILAND
Prof. Tong In Wongsothorn
Director
SEAMEO

EUROPE

FRANCE
Prof. Jean-Claude Garric
FISE

Prof. Basarab Nicolescu
Physicien theoricien CNRS
Universite Paris 6
President du CIRET

ISRAEL
Prof. Ammon Rubinstein

ITALY
Prof. Valerio Grementieri
President EDEN

NORWAY
Prof. Arild Tjeldvoll
Universite d'Osla

The NETHERLANDS
Dr. Jos Walenkamp
NUFFIC

SPAIN
Prof.Francisco Rubio
Titular de la catedra Red ISA

Sr. Lorenzo Olarte Cullen
Vice-presidente y Consejero de
Turismo y Transporte del
Gobierno de Canarias

LATIN AMERICA AND THE CARIBBEAN

ARGENTINA
Ing. Luis Julian Lima
Presidente
Universidad Nacional de la Plata
AUGM

BRAZIL
Dra. Renee Zicman
Directeur de la Coop
Universidade Pontificia Catolica
de Sao Paulo

CHILI
Dr. Ubaldo Zuniga Quintanilla
Rector
Universidad de Santiago

COLOMBIA
Dr. Luis Enrique Orozco Silva
Vice-Rector
Universidad de los andes

MEXICO

Dr. Victor Arredondo
Rector
Universidad de Vera Cruz

VENEZUELA

Dra. Carmen Garcia Guadilla
Titular de Catedra
Universidad de los Andes

THEMATIC DEBATES' PANELISTS

The Requirements of the World of Work

Chair:

M. Michael Henriques
International Labour Office (ILO)
Switzerland

Keynote Speaker:

Dr Ulrich Teichler
University of Kassel
Germany

Rapporteur:

Mr Bikas Sanyal
International Institute of
Educational Planning (IIPE)
France

Panelists:

Mr Hedi Djilani
President
General Council of the
International Council of Employers (IOE)
Tunisia

Ms Sike Nelle Sombe
President
AIESEC International
Cameroon

Dr. Gerd Kohler
Hauptvorstand
Gewerkschaft Erziehung and
Wissenschaft
Germany

Advisory Steering Committee:

Dr Donald Gerth
President
California State University
USA

Prof. Yasumori Nishijima
Former Chairman
Japanese National Commission
for UNESCO

Higher Education and Sustainable Human Development

Chair:

Prof. Hans van Ginkel
Rector, The United Nations
University (UNU)
Japan

Keynote Speakers:

Mr Gustavo Lopez
Director
UNESCO Transdisciplinary Project on
Education for a Sustainable Future

Dr Peter W. Heller
Executive Director
Canopus Foundation
Germany

Prof. Haubouot Asseypo
Rector
University of Cocody
Ivory Coast

Prof. Dr Rietje van Dam Mieras
Rector
Open Universiteit
The Netherlands

Resource Persons:

Prof. David L. Johnston
McGill Centre for Medicine,
Ethics and Law
Canada

Dr Kirit Parikh
Senior Economic Adviser to the Administrator
UNDP
USA

Dr. Ruben C. Umaly
Secretary-General
Association of Universities of Asia and the Pacific (AUAP)
Thailand

Mr Patrick Mpedzisi
UNITWIN Student
University of Zimbabwe
Zimbabwe

Mrs Roos Wemmenhove
International Students for Environmental Action (ISEA)
The Netherlands

Prof. Mihajlo D. Mesarovic
UNESCO Scientific Advisor on Global Change USA

Dr Frank W. Bosshardt
World Business Council for Sustainable Development (WBCSD)
Switzerland

Prof. Bolek Mazurkiewicz
Poland

Ms Paulette Bynoe
University of Guyana
Guyana

Dr Hans Peter Winkelmann
CRE-Copernicus
Germany

Dr Budd L Hall
Ontario Institute for Studies in Education
Canada

Dr Hilligie van't Land
International Association of Universities (IAU)
France

Advisory/Steering Committee:

Prof. Jorge Brovetto
President of UDUAL and the Montevideo Group of Universit es
Uruguay

Contributing to National and Regional Development

Chairs:

Prof. Josep Bricall
Centro de Estudios de Planificacion (CEP)
Spain

Prof. Eric Froment
Conference des Presidents d'Universities
France

Keynote Speaker:

Prof. John Goddard
University of Newcastle-upon-Tyne
United Kingdom

Moderator:

Dr Alfons Stinus
Momentum Network
Spain

Rapporteur:

Dr Madeleine Green
American Council on Education (ACE)
Association of Commonwelath Universities (ACU)
United Kingdom

Panelists:

Prof. Brahim Baccari
Universite de droit, d'economie et de gestion de Tunis
Tunisie

Prof. Susan Clark
Nova Soctia Council on Higher Education
Canada

Prof. Jacques Marcovitch
Reitor
Universidade de Sao Paulo
Brazil

Dr Francisco Gatto
UN Economic Commission for
Latin America and the Caribbean
Argentina

Prof. Dorothy D. Njeuma
University of Buea
Republic of Cameroon

Working Group Facilitarors:

Dr Mario Albornoz
Universidad de Burenos Aires
Argentina

Dr Andris Barblan
Association of European
Universities (CRE)
Switzerland

Dr Isabelle de Keyser
Natura Network
Belgium

Dr Carlo Di Benedetta
Community of Mediterranean
Universities (CUM)
UItaly

Dr Kenneth Edwards
Association of European
Universities (CRE)
Switzerland

Mr Felix Garcia Lusin
Conference of Spanish Recotrs
(CRUE)
Spain

Dr M. Kamal
Assocation of Arab Universities
(AARU)
Jordan

Dr Sebastiao Elias Kuri
Universidad Federal do Sao Carlos
Brazil

Mr Frederik Oberthur
International Association of
Agricultural Students (IAAS)
Belgium

Ms Mary O' Mahony
Association of European
Universities (CRE)
Switzerland

Prof. Rodolfo Pinto da Luz
Universidad Federal de Santa
Catarina
Brazil

Prof. Moumouni Rambre Ouiminga
Conseil Africain et Malgache pour
I'Enseignement Superieur
(CAMES)
Burkina Faso

Prof. Carlos Sola i Ferrando
Universitat Autonoma de
Barcelona
Spain

Dr Rubean Umaly
Association of Universities of Asia
and the Pacitific (AUAP) Thailand

Mr Pierre Van Der Donckt
Inter-American Organization for
Higher Education (IOHE) Canada

Dr Shirely Walters
University of the Western Cape
Republic of South Africa

Advisory/Steering Committee:

Prof. Ibrahim Abu Lughod
Birzeit University
Palestine

Higher Education Staff Development: A Continuing Mission

Chair:

Dr Cream Wright
Director
Education Commonwealth
Secretariat
United Kingdom

Rapporteur:

Mrs Alison Girdwood
Chief Programme Officer
Commonwealth Secretariat
United Kingdom

Panelists:

Mr John Fielden
Director
Commonwealth Higher Education
Management Service (CHEMS)
United Kingdom

Dr (Ms) Jasbir S singh
Consultant
Association of Commonwealth
Universities (ACU)
Malaysia

Dr Brigitte Berendt
Freie Universitat Berlin
Germany

Prof. Dr A.K. Aboul-Hassan
Treasurer
Arab Network on Staff
Development (ANSD)
Egypt

Dr Elizabeth Poskitt
President
International Federation of
Unitersity Women (IFUW)
Switzerland

Dr Yolanda Rojas
Director
Doctoral Program on Education
University of Casta Rica
Costa Rica

Prof. Narciso Matos
Secretary-General
Association of African Universities
(AAU)
Ghana

Higher Education for a New Society: A Student Vision

Chair:

Baroness Tessa Blackstone
Minister of State for Education
and Employment in the House of Lords
United Kingdom

Panel 1: Social Issues and Higher Education

Panelists :

Ms. Florence Nsumbu
Mouvement International des
Etudiants Catholiques (MIEC)
Republique Democratique de Congo

Mr. Agus Salim
International Forestry Students
Association (IFSA) Indonesia

Mr. Peter Sondergaard
National Unions of Students
in Europe (ESIB)
Denmark

Ms. Raguia ElHusseiny
Union of Progressive Youth
Egypt

Mr. Thiago Monaco
International Federation of
Medical Students Association (IFMSA)
Brazil

Professor Mihaly Simai'
Hungarian Academy of Sciences
Hungary

Dr. Willaim Lindley
Food and Agricultural
Organisation (FAO)

Panel 2: Regional Perspectives

Panelists:

Mr. Alper Akyur
Association des Etats Generaux
des Etudiants de i'Europe (AEGEE)
Turkey

Mr. Yosvani Diaz Romero
Organizacion Continental
Latinoamericana y Caribena de
Estudiantes (OCLAE)
Cuba

Mr. Keshav Raj Pandey
Asian Students Association (ASA)
Nepal

Mr. Abdallah Al Najjar
General Union of Arab Students
(GUAS)
Palestine

Mr. Felix Abeeku Yawson
International Association of
Agricultural Students (IAAS) Ghana

Dr. Tang
Chief
Technical and Vocational
Education
UNESCO

Dr. Alan Wagner
Organisation for Economic
Cooperation and Development (OECD)

Entrepreneurs Panel

Chair:

Mr. Yannick Moati
Junior Chamber International (JCT)
Monaco

Panelists:

Dr. Roberto D ' Allesandro
Legal Counsel
Malta

Ms. J. Claire K. Niala
International Federation of Business
and Professional Women (IFBPW)
Kenya

Mr. Michel Romieu
President Director General
ELF Aquitaine Gaz
France

Mr. Eric Zahrai
European Baha' i Business Forum
France

Mr. Wallace R, Baker
Baker & McKenzie
USA

Mr Luis Carlos Villegas Echeverri
Asociacion Nacional de
Industrales (ANDI)
Colombia

Ms.Cynthia Wolsdorff
Junior Association for
Development in Europe (JADE)
Germany

Ms. Alison Sutherland
International Pharmaceutical
Students Federation (ISF)
South Africa

Rapporteurs:

Ms. Agnieszka Stobiecka
European Law Students
Association (ELSA)
Poland

Ms. Christel Scholten
Association Internationale des
Etudiants en Science Economique
et Commerce (AIESEC)
Canada

Mr. Walter Prysthon
Mouvement International des
Etudiants Catholiques (MIEC)
Brazil

Mr. Benson Obua Ogwal
All African Students Association (AASU)
Uganda

Mr. Julio Casas Calderon
Jeunesse Etudiante Catholique Internationale (JECI)
Peru

From Traditional to Virtual: The New Information Technologies

Chair :

Prof. Michel Guillou
Recteur
Agence universitaire de la francophonie (AUPELF)
France

Keynote Speaker:

Prof. Bachir Diagne
Universite Cheikh Anta Diop de Dakar
Senegal

Rapporteur:

Prof. Tarcisio Della Senta
Director
Institute of Advanced Studies
The United Nations University (UNU/IAS)
Japan

Panelists:

Prof. Lourdes Feria
Universidad de Colima
Mexico

M. Bernard Loing
Vice-President
International Council for Open and Distance Education (ICDE)
France

Prof. Dyane Adam
Principal
University College Glendon
York University
Canada

Prof. Tamas Lajos
Technical University of Budapest
Hungary

Prof.. Michel Moreau
Recteur d'Academie
Directeur general
Centre National d'Enseignement a Distance (CNED)
France

Mr Piet Henderikx
European Association of Distance Teaching Universities (EADTU)
The Netherlands

Mrs Molly Corbett Broad
President
University of North Carolina
USA

M. Henrik Toft Jensen
Universite de Roskilde
Danemark

Prof. Tarek Shawki
University of Illinois at Urbana Champaign
USA

Prof. Maurice Tchuente
Recteur
Universite de Dschang
Cameroun

Dr Gottfried Leibbrandt
Chairman of the European Center for Higher Education (CEPES)
WCHE Advisory Group
The Netherlands

Resource Persons:

Prof. Dr. Horst Mohle
UNESCO Institute for Education (UIE)
Germany

M. Didier Oilo
Agence universitaire de la francophonie (AUPELF)
France

Mr Kiyoshi Nakabayashi
NTT Information & Communication Systems Laboratories
Japan

Mr Kasumasa Noda
NTT Advanced Technology Corp.
Japan

Prof. Maria Luisa Martin
The Monterrey Institute of Technology
Mexico

Dr Magdallen N. Juma
Kenyatta University
Kenya

Prof. Jum Murai
University of Keio
Japan

Mr Shirabe Orino
University of Tokyo
Japan

Mr Ng Chong
Research Associate
UNU/Institute of Advanced Studies
Japan

Mr. T. Tschang
Research Associate
UNC/Institute of Advanced Studies
Japan

Dr Sylvia Charp
University of Pennsylvania
USA

Dr. John Foster
Governing Board of the International Conference on Technology and Education (ICTE)
United Kingdom

Prof. Vladimir Tikhomirov
Rector, Moscow State University of Economics, Statistics and Informatics
Russia

Advisory/Steering Committee:

Dr Gottfried Leibbrandt
The Netherlands

Higher Education and Research: Challenges and Opportunities

Chair:

Prof. Daniel Akyeampong
International Council for Science (ICSU)
Ghana

Rapporteur:

Prof. Albert Fischli
Executive Director Hoffman La-Roche Ltd
Switzerland

Panelists:

Prof. Guy Ourisson
France

Prof. M.H.A. Hassan
Executive Director
The Third World Academy of Sciences (TWAS)
Italy

Prof. Oumar Sock
Directeur
Ecole Polytechnique de Dakar
Senegal

Prof. M.G.K. Menon
India

Dr Heather Eggins
Director
Society for Research into Higher Education (SRHE)
United Kingdom

Prof. Maxwell McCombs
Department of Journalism
University of Texas at Austin
USA

Resource Persons:

M. Andre Gouaze
President
Conference internationale des
Doyens de Facultes de Medecine
France

M. Herve de Tricornot
Directeur
Agence pour l'investissement dans
la recherche et le développement (AIRE)
France

M. Bernard Eding
Directeur
Societe Nationale de Raffinage
(SONARA)
Cameroun

Mrs Maureen Brennan
ICSU
France

Advisory/Steering Committee:

Mr Sarukhan Kermez
Universidad Nacional Autonoma
de Mexico (UNAM)

The Contribution of Higher Education to the Education System as a Whole

Chair:

M. Victor Adamets
International Bureau of Education (IBE)
Geneva

Keynote Speaker:

Prof. Phillip Hughes
Australia National University
Australia

Rapporteurs:

Mr Malmoudi Mahmoud
Tunisia

Mme Gaelle de Viron
Universite catholique de Louvain
la-Neuve Belgique

Panelists/Presentators:

Dr Cecilia Braslasvky
Director-General of Research
and Development
Ministry of Culture and National
Education
Argentiana

Mr Chung Yue Ping
Dean of Education
Chinese University of Hong Kong
China

Dr. D.G. Al Emadi
Dean, Faculty of Humanities
Qatar University
Qatar

Dr Eddah Gachukia
Executive Director
Forum for African Women
Educationalists (FAWE)
Kenya

Dr Ina Grieb
Vice President
University of Oldenberg
Germany

Mr. D Wagner
Director
International Literacy Institute (ILI)
University of Pennsylvania
USA

Mr. B. Wentworth
Deputy Minister
Ministry of Higher Education
Vocational Training, Science and
Technology
Namibia

Mr Armando Rocha Trindade
President
International Council for Open and
Distance Education (ICDE)
Portugal

Resource Persons:

Mr eric Bockstael
Secretary-General
International Institute for Policy, Practice and Research in the Education of Adult
Belgique

M. Samady
Former Director
Division for the Development of Education
UNESCO

Mr Jong-yang Kim
President
Hanyang University
Republic of Korea

Mme Stefania Gandolfi
Conferenza Episcopale Italiana
Italy

Advisory/Steering Committee:

Prof. Borero Cabal
Universidad Javeriana
Colombia

Prof. Narciso Matos
Secretary-General
Association of African Universities (AAU)
Ghana

Women and Higher Education: Issues and Perspectives

Chair:

Dr . Attiya Inayatullah
President, International Planned Parenthood Federation
Former Chairperson
UNESCO Executive Board Former Minister,
Population, Welfare and Women's Development
Pakistan

Keynote Speakers:

Dr. Berit Olsson
Swedish International Development Agency (SIDA)
Sweden

Prof. Christina Ulenius
President
University College of Karlstad
Sweden

Discussants:

Prof. Federico Mayor
Director General
UNESCO

Prof. Peter Katjavivi
Vice-Chancellor
University of Namibia
Namibia

Dr. Maria Irigoin
Consultant in Higher Education
University of Santiago
Chile

Mrs Linda Souter
President
International Federation of University Women (IFUW) Canada

Panelists:

Prof. Maria Inacia D'Avila Neto
Director, Institute of Psychology
Federal University of Rio de Janeiro
Brazil

Dr. Binod Khadria
School of Social Sciences
Jawaharlal Nerhu University
New Delhi
India

Dr Joy Kwesiga
Dean, Faculty of Social Sciences
Makerere University
Uganda

Mrs Mouna Mourad
Faculty of Medicine
St Joseph's University
Beirut
Lebanon

Dr Ralitsa Muharska
St Kliment Ohridski University
Sofia
Bulgaria

Special Panelists:

The Honourable Esi Sutherland-Addy
Forum for African Women
Educationalists (FAWE)
Nairobi
Kenya

Dr. Breda Pavlic
Director
Unit for the Status of Women and
Gender Equality
UNESCO

Rapporteurs:

Mrs Francoise Sauvage
International Federation of
University Women (IFUW)

Mrs Jeannine Jacquemin
Soroptimist International

Mrs Claire Jourdan
International Federation of
Women in Legal Careers

Promoting a Culture of Peace

Chair:

Dr Donald Gerth
President
California State University
USA

Moderator:

Dr. L. Eudora Pettigrew
Chair, IAUP/UN Commission on
Disarmament Education, Conflict
Resolution and Peace
USA

Keynote Address:

Dr Oscar Arias
Nobel Peace Prize Laureat
Fundacion Arias para la Paz
Costa Rica

Rapporteur:

Dr Maurice Harari
Secretary-General
International Association of
University Presidents (IAUP)
USA

Panelists:

Prof. Saleh Al-Mani
King Saud University
Saudi Arabia

Prof. George Benneh
University of Ghana
Accra

Prof. Betty A. Reardon
Teachers College
Columbia University
USA

Prof. Enver Sehovic
University of Zagreb
Croatio

Prof. Shen Dingli
Fundan University
People' Republic of China

Resource Person:

Dr Marshall W.M. Conley
Acadia University
Canada

Advisory/Steering Comittee:

Mr Tunnermann Bernheim
Nicaragua

Mobilizing the Power of Culture

Chair:

Prof. Rex Nettleford
Chancellor
University of the West Indies
Jamaica

Representing the Director General of UNESCO:

Mr Herrnan Crespo-Toral
Assistant Director General ai
for Culture

Rapporteur:

Mr Eduard Delgado
Director INTERPARTS
Spain

Panelists:

Dr Gisela Baumgratz
Council on International
Educational Exchange (CIEE)
France

Dr Hilary Callan
Executive Director
European Association for
International Education (EAIE)
The Netherlands

H.E. M.N. Tidjani-Serpos
Ambassador
Permanent Delegate of Benin
to UNESCO

Prof. E.L. Cerroni-Long
Prof. of Anthropology at Estern
Michigan University
USA

Prof. Nabil El-Haggar
Vice-President
Universite des sciences et
technologies de Lille
France

Mr. Y.R. Isar
Director
Culture and Development
Co-Ordination Office
UNESCO

Resource Persons:

Sr Antonio Gallo Armosino
Universidad Rafael Landivar
Guatemala

Dr Andrea Karpati
Associate Professor of Education
Eotvos Lorand University
Hungary

Autonomy, Social Responsibility and Academic Freedom

Chair:

Prof. Justin Thorens
Universitie de Geneve
Suisse

Rapporteur:

Mr Guy Neave
International Association
of Universities (IAU)
France

Panelists:

Prof. Brenda M. Gourley
Vice-Chancellor
University of Natal
South Africa

Mr Dennis Longid
Asian Students Association (ASA)
University of the Philippines
Philippines

Prof. A.H. Al Boraey
Cairo University
Egypt

Mrs Ximena Erazo
World University Service (WUS)
Chili

Mme Lise Bissonnette
Directrice
Grande Bibliotheque
"Le Devoir
Canada

Prof. Jacques Macovitch
Reitor
Universidade de Sao Paulo
Brazil

Mr Peter Preuss
President
Preuss Foundation
USA

Dr Olle Pekka Heinonen
Minister of Education
Finland

Prof. Wichit Srisa-an
Recotr
Suranaree University of Technology
Thailand

Advisory/Steering Committee:

Prof. Justin Thorens
Universite de Geneve
Suisse

UNITWIN

AFRICA

BENIN

Dr. Holo Aliaoune
Universite nationale du Benin,
Cotonou

BOTSWANA

Prof. Kemsley Edward
Botswana College of Agriculture,
Gaborone

BURKINA FASO

Prof. Traore S. Alfred
Universite de Ouagadougou,
Ouagadougou

CAMEROON

Dr. Enderley Joyce
Universite of Buea, Buea

CENTRAL AFRICAN REPUBLIC

M. Nestor Nali M.
Universite de Bangui, Bangui

CONGO

Prof. Marmoz Louis
Ecole normale superieure,
Universite Marien Ngouabi,
Brazzaville
Universite de Caen, France

Prof. Mbemba Gaspard
Ecole normale superieure,
Universite Marien Ngouabi,
Brazzaville

CONGO

(Democratic Republic of)
Dr. Kabyla Ilunga
Universite de Lumumbashi,
Lumumbashi

Dr. Nemo Jacques
Universite de Lumumbashi,
Lumumbashi
Universite de Paris X

COTE D'IVOIRE

Dr. Lezou Dago Gerard
Universite de Cocody, Abidjan

ETHIOPIA

Prof. Mogesie Ashenafi
Addis Ababa University
Addis Ababa

GABON

M. Biteghe Joel
Actuellement a I'IRIM, Universite
de Nice-Sophia Antipolis, France

GHANA

Prof. Andam Aba
University of Science and
Technology, Kumasi

KENYA

Prof. Bahemuka Judith
Nairobi University, Nairobi

Dr. Eddah Gachukia
Forum for African Women Educationalists (FAWE) Nairobi

Dr. Juma Magdallan
Kenyatta University

Dr. Konana Lois
Moi University, Eldoret

MADAGASCAR

Prof. Rakotoniaina Justin
Universite de Fianarantsoa, Fianarantsoa

MOZAMBIQUE

Dr. Ferreira Beatriz
Universidade Eduardo Mondlane, Maputo

Dr. Carlos Machili
Universidade Pedagogica, Maputo

Prof. Mazula Brazao
Universidade Eduardo Mondlane, Maputo

Prof. Sidi Daniel
Universidade Eduardo Mondlane, Maputo
Hopital Necker-Enfants Malades, Paris

NAMIBIA

Prof. Kamba Walter J.
University of Namibia, Windhoek

Prof. Mshigeni Keto E.
University of Namibia, Windhoek

NIGER

Prof. Lang Jacques
Universite Abou Moumouni, Niamey
Universite de Bourgogne, Dijon (France)

NIGERIA

Prof. Omolewa Michael
University of Ibadan, Logos

RWANDA

Dr. Musonera Augusti
National University of Rwanda

SENEGAL

Prof. J.M. de Ketele
Universite Chekh Anta Diop (UCAD), Dakar
Universite catholique de Louvain (Belgique)

Dr. Sega Seck Fall
Ecole normale superieure, Universite Cheikh Anta Diop (UCAD), Dakar

Dr. Salif Diop el Hadji
Universite Cheikh Anta Diop (UCAD), Dakar

SOUTH AFRICA

Prof. Abrahams Cecil
University of the Western Cape, Bellville

Prof. Ogunniyi Meshach
University of the Western Cape, Bellville

TANZANIA (United Republic of)

Prof. Ansere
Open University of Tanzania, Dar es Salam

Prof. Mmari G.R.V.
Open University of Tanzania, Dar es Salam

Dr. Msolla Peter
Sokoine University of Agriculture, Morogoro

TOGO

Dr. Quashie Maryse Adjo
Centre de formation a distance, Lome,

ZIMBABWE

M. Kakitiki Samson
University of Zimbabwe, Harare

M. Mpedzisi Patrick
University of Zimbabwe, Harare

ARAB STATES

EGYPT

Elmahary Yehia
Alexandria University, Faculty of Engineering

JORDAN

M.Abu Jaber Nizar
Faculty of Science,
Yarmouk University

Dr. Jawad Ali Ali
Yarmouk University

M. Safty Adel
United Nations University

MOROCCO

Professor Laouina Abdellah
Faculte des Lettres et sciences humaines
Universite Mohammed V

Professeur Mouradi Aziza
Faculte des Sciences, Kenitra

SUDAN

Professor El-Hang Ismail Hamid Ahmed
Omdurman Islamic University

SYRIAN ARAB REPUBLIC

Professor, Dr. Ghata Adnan
Al Baath University, Homs

Abdul Majid Sheikh Hussein
Al Baath University, Homs

TUNISIA

Mahbouli Abderraouf
Universite de Tunis 1

Zakia Bouaziz
CREDIF, Tunis

Professeur Mezghani Nebila
Faculte de droit et des sciences politiques de tunis

M. Triki Fathi
Univesite des Sciences Humanies et Sociales, Tunis

YEMEN

Dr. Al Bassam Ra'ad
Faculty of Agriculture
University of Sana'a

ASIA AND PACIFIC

AUSTRALIA

Assistant Professor Fien John
Griffith University

CHINA

Professor Dai Guan-Zhong
Northwestern Polytechnical University

Professor Nanzhao Zhao
China National Institute of Educational Research

INDIA

Professor Karad Vishwanath
Maharashtra Academy of Engineering and Educational Research's MIT

Professor Passi
Indira Gandhi National Open University

Professor Saraswati Baidyanath
Indira Gandhi National Centre for the Arts

JAPAN

Duval A.
Bubkyo University Foundation

KAZAKSTAN

Professor Omashev Namazaly
Kazakstan State University

PAKISTAN

Professor Siddiqui Shunukat Ali
Alama Iqbal Open University

THAILAND

Dr. Bhandhubanyong Paritud
Faculty of Engineering,
Chulalongkorn University

Dr. Chaya-Ngam Iam
Sukhothai Thammathirat Open
University

VIET NAM

Prof. Nguyen Cong Hien
The Hanio University
of Technology

Professor Nguyen Si Mao
Hanoi University of Technology

EUROPE AND NORTH AMERICA

BELGIUM

Secretaire General Isabelle de
Keyzer
NATURA

M. Louis Laurie
NATURA

Prof. Kund-Erik Sabroe Kund
COIMBRA
University of Aarhus, Asylvej,
DK. Risskov

BULGARIA

M. Darina Gueorguieva
INSA, Technical University of Sofia
Prof. Serge Monchaud
Technical University of Sofia

CANADA

Dr. Sheryl Bond
Queens University, Kingston

M. Irigoin
Queens University, Kingston

Fabienne Desroches
Universite de Montreal

M. Laval Doucet
Universite Laval

M. Claude Dionne
University de Montreal
New Brunswick

FRANCE

Prof. Raoul Caruba
I.R.I.M. Universite de Nice

Directeur Pascal Chaigneau
Centre d'Etudes Diplomatiques,
Paris

Prof. Pierre Chalvidan
Universite Paris XII

M. Jean-Louis Herman
Ingenieur de recherche
Universite des Sciences Sociales
de Toulouse

Prof. Hugo Houben
CRE Terre-Ecole d'Architecture
de Grenoble

M. Gregoire Koulbanais
Equipe Cousteau

M. Philippe Lebrasseur
Centre d'interets du
developpement economique

M. Michel Vincent
CRE Terre, Ecole d'Architecture
de Grenoble

M. Aminetou Mint Bah Nagi
Universite de Nice I.R.I.M.

Prof. Jean Francois Moreau
Universite Rene Descrtes,
Hopital Necker

President Rene Samuel Sirat
Ecole des Hautes Etudes du
Judaisme

M. Patrice Doat
CRE Terre, Ecole d'Architecture
de Grenoble

M. Christian Couralet
ACESTE, Toulouse

M. Laval Doucet
Universite Laval

M. Bousez Michel
Universite Paris 1, Paris

M. Jean-Francois Moreau
Universite Rene Descartes, Paris

Prof. Ali M.S. Fatemi
The American University of Paris,
Paris.

GEORGIA

Prof. Khomeriki Irakli
Tbilisi State University

GERMANY

Prof. Dr. Bernd Hamm
Centre for European Studies,
University of Trier

GREECE

Prof. Dimitri Papadopoulou
Aristotle University of
Thessaloniki

Prof. Michael Scoullos
Universite d'Athenes

M. Costas Rodriguez

HUNGARY

Prof. Nyarady Rozsa
College for Business and
Management Studies

ITALY

Franco Rizzi

The NETHERLANDS

Mme Maaike S. de Langen
Utrecht Group

M. Arco Van den Hamm
Utrecht Group

Dr. Henk J. van Rinsum
Utrecht Southern African
Network, Utrecht University

Dr. Lieteke van Vucht Tijssen
Utrecht Southern African
Network, Utrecht University

POLAND

Prof. Jalowiecki Bohdan
Universite de Varsovie

Dr. Luczak Elzbieta
Institut Pedagogique d'agriculture
et technologie, Olsztynie-Kortowo

Ing. Agronome Agniesza Nowakowska
Insitut Pedagogique d'agriculture
et technologie, Olsztynie-Kortowo
Universite de Bourgogne et ENS
d'Agronomie

Prof. Renate Siemenska
Institute of Sociology
University of Warsaw

PORTUGAL

Prof. Afgaan Naim
Institut Superieur Technique,
Lisbonne

ROMANIA

Prof. Dumitriu Corneliu
International Theatre Institute

Prof. Sofronie Ramiro
University of Agricultural and Veterinary Sciences in Bucharest

M. Martin Hauser
Universite de Bucarest, Bucarest

RUSSIAN FEDERATION

M. Vladimir Djanibekov
International Centre of Educational Systems

M. Savran Djavlanov
International Centre of Educational Systems

Prof. Evstafiev Alexandre
Moscow State University of Environmental Engineering

Prof. Valadimir Filippov
Universite de la Russie de I'Amitie des peuples,
Moscou

Mr. Serguei Gontcharenko
Moscow State Linguistic University

Prof. Mikhail Ivanov
Moscow State University

Dr. Larissa Konovalova
State Academy of Management

Prof. Valery Kvartalnov
Russian Chairs

Prof. Magometov Akourbek
North Ossetian State University

Prof. Serguei Peshkov
Centre international des Systemes d'education

Prof. Teodor shanin
UNESCO/INCORVUZ Chair
and network for the development of NGOs in countries in transition
State Academy of Management
Moscow

Prof. Tskhai Alexander
Altai State Technical University
Barnaul

Dr. Sc. Tatiana Vinogradova
Universite d'Etat d'Architecture et de Genie Civil de Nijni Novgorod
Ngasu

Prof. Vladimir Vragov Nicolayevich
Novobibirsk State University
Novosibirsk

Savran D. Djavlanov
International Centre on Educational Systems
Moscow

Prof. Valery Kvartalnov
Russian International Academy for Tourism

Guennadi Kalioujnyi
State Academy of Management,
Moscow

Michael Fedorov
State Academy of Management,
Moscow

Gontcharenko, Serguei
Moscow State Linguistic University,
Moscow

Prof. Vladimir Ivanov
Moscow State University,
Moscow

SPAIN

President Albert Manuel Esteban
Santander Group
University of Murcia

M. Enric Angullol
University Pompeu Fabra

M. Luis Beltran
Universidad de Alcala de Henares

Dr. Brezmes Maria Jose Saez
Universidad de Valladolid

Dr. Cesar Chaparro Gomez
Universidad de Extremadura

Dr. Concha Sofia Perez Diaz
Universidad de las Palmas de Gran Canaria

M. Francisco Rubio Royo
Universidad de las Palmas de Gran Canaria

M. Jenaro Costas Rodriguez
Universidad Nacional de Educacion a Distancia

Recteur Lobo Cabrera Manuel
Universidad de Las Palmas de Gran Canaria

Dr. Maicas Manuel
Universidad Autonoma de Barcelona

Mme Margarit Ribalta Monica
Universitat de Barcelona

M. Ricardo Marin Ibanez
Universidad Nacional de Educacion a Distancia

Prof. Maria Novo
Universidad Nacional de Educacion a Distancia

Dr. Professeur Rafael Portaencasa Baeza
Universitaria Politecnica de Madrid

Dr. Miguel Rojas Mix
Universidad de Extremadura, Caceres

Licenciado en Cienci Josep Xercavins I Valls
Universitat Politecnica de Catalunya

Mme Jose Maria Echeverria
Universidad de Deusto

SWEDEN

Prof. Guy Heyden
University of Goteborg

Skogh Elin
Lunds University

UNITED KINGDOM OF GREAT BRITAIN AND NORTHERN IRELAND

Dr. Helen Callaway
University of Oxford

Dr. David Turoton
University of Oxford

TURKEY

Prof. Kaynak Okyay
Bogazici University

Prof. Dr Kucuradi Loanna
Hacettepe University, Centre for Research and Application of the Philosophy of Human Rights

LATIN AMERICA AND THE CARIBBEAN

ARGENTINA

Prof. Camilloni de Wigdorovitz Alicia Rosalia
Universidad de Buenos Aires

Abogado- Economista Martin Bacigalupo Pedro Luis Maria
Universidad Catolica de Cuyo

Dr. Mirande Susana Laura
Universidad de Buenos Aires

Ingeniero Popovsky Ricardo
Universidad de Palermo

Ingeniero Schiavon Maria Isabel
Universidad Nacional de Rosario

M. Villar Julio
Universite Nacional de Quilmes

BOLIVIA

Crespo Callan J Renato
Universidad Mayor San Simon

Dr. Garrett Aillon Julio
Universidad Andina Simon Bolivar

BRAZIL

Antunes dos Santos Carlos Roberto
Universidad de Parana

Professor Craveiro Clelia Brandao
Universidad Catolica de Goias

Prof. da Silva Helio
Ecole d Architecture et d'Urbanisme de UNIMEP

Vice President da Silveira Cavalcanti Francisco Carlos
Universidade Federal do Acre

Vice President Gissoni Vera
Universidade Castelo

Professeur Maciel Tania
Universidad Rio de Janeiro

Mme Marcal Juliane
Federal University of Minas Gerais

Professor Martins Romeo Jose Roymundo
Colegio do Brasil

M. Messeder Pereira Carlos Alberto
Universite Rio de Janeiro

Dr. Pinheiro Paulo Sergio
University of Sao Paulo

M. Santos Carlos Roberto
Universidade Federal do Parana
UNAMAZ

CHILE

Coordenadora Peronard Marianne
Universidad Catolica de Valparaiso

M. Urzua Raul F.
Universidad de Chile

COLOMBIA

M. Munera Velez Dario
Universidad Pontificia Bolivariana

M. Munoz Luis Carlos
Universidad Pontificia Bolivariana

M. Restropo Restropo Gonzalo
Universidad Pontificia

Director Sanchez Angel Ricardo
Instituto para el desarrollo de la democracia Luis Carlos Galan

CUBA

Dr. Sabina Elvira Martin
Universidad de La Habana

MEXICO

Investigador Titular Didriksson Takayanagui Axel
Universidad Nacional Autonoma de Mexico

Dr. Espinoza elia Marum
Universidad de Guadalajara

Mtra Gomez Mont Araiza Carmen Lucia
Universidad Iberoamericana

PARAGUAY

Director Nagy Ferrari Ladislao
Asociacion de Universidades Grupo Montevideo (AUGM)

PERU

Prof. Chavez Vasquez Victor Manuel
Universidad Nacional de Ucayali

URUGUAY

Professor Contera Cristina
Universidad de la Republica

Professor Contera Rios Cristina
Universidad de la Republica, Facultad de Ciencias Sociales

Ingeniero Fernandez Odella Julio
Universidad Uruguay

Odella Fernandez
University ORT of Uruguay

VENEZUELA

Mme Mattar de Carrillo-Batalla
Fundacion Planeta Libre

M. Mattar Farid
Fundacion Planeta Libre

Dra Perez de Santos Rosa maria
Universidad Central de Venezuela

Antropologa y Dr. Texier de Gamez Ende
Fundacion International Planeta Libre

M. Villalobos Eddie
Fundacion Planeta Libre

IAU BOARD AND GUESTS

Dr. William H. Allaway
Director Emeritus
Education Abroad Program
University of California
United States of America

Dr. Thomas Bartett
Former Chancellor
State University of New York
United States of America

Professor Guoguang Mu
Former President
Nanki University
China

Professor. Triloki N. Kappor
Former Vice-Chancellor
Panjab University, Chandigarh
India

Professor Dr. Boleslaw Mazurkiewicz
Department Head
Technical University of Gdansk
Poland

Professor Hassan Mekouar
Universite Mohammed V
Faculte des Lettres
Morocco

Professor Martin Meyerson
President Emeritus
University of Pennsylvania
United States of America

Dr Gamal Eldin Mokhtar
President
Arab Academy for Science and Technology
Egypt

Dr. Hanna Nasir
President
Birzeit University
Palestinian Authority

Mr. Ahmadou Lamine Ndiaye
Rector
Universite Gaston Berger de Saint-Louis
Senegal

Dr. Avelino Porto
President
Universidad de Belgrano
Argentina

Professor Dr. Julio Teran Dutari
Former Rector
Pontificia Universidad Catolica del Ecuador
Ecuador

Dr. Abdul Majid Sheikh Hussein
President
Al-Baath University
Syrian Arab Republic

Dr Heinrich Stremitzer
Austria

IAUP BOARD

Professor Eugene Amonoo-Neizer
Former Vice-Chancellor
University of Science and Technology Kumasi
Ghana

Dr. Ruben Arminana
President Sonoma State University
United States of America

Dr. Warren Baker
President
California Polytechnic State University, San Luis Obispo
United States of America

Mr. Abdelhamid Bouab
Officer-in-charge, PFPSD, DPEPA/DESA
United Nations
United States of America

Professor Dr. Academician Vladimir Kurilov
President
Far Eastern State University
Russian Federation

Mr. Sc Ung Lee
President
Korea Industrial Gases, Ltd.
Republic of Korea

Professor V.R. Mehta
Vice-Chancellor
University of Delhi
India

Dr. James Roach
President
Western Connecticut State University
United States of America

Dr. Alvaro Romo
Coordinator of International Programs
University of Houston System
United States of America

Dr. David Strangway
President
Canada Foundation for Innovation
Canada

Dr. Edward Walsh
Vice-president
International Association of
University Presidents
Ireland

INTERNATIONAL COMMITTEEE ON ENGINEERING EDUCATION

Professor Dr. Saad el-Raghy
Professor
Faculty of Engineering, Cairo
University
Egypt

D.Sc. Hans Peter Jensen
Rector
Technical University of Denmark
Denmark

Academic Vice-President Gearold
Johnson
Chief Academic Officer
National Technological University
United States of America

Mr Clifford Smith
President Emeritus
General Electric Foundation
United States of America

Dr. Eric W. Thulstrup
The World Bank
United States of America

OTHER GUESTS

AJAYI Ade
National Universities Commission
Isadan University
Nigeria

ALCARAZ Rafael, Ing.
Instituto Tecnologico de Estudios
Superiores de Monterrey
Mexico

Al-EMADI Darwish Ghuloom, Dr.
Qatar University,
Qatar

ALI M. Shamsher
AGFUND

ALMANZAR Mary
Universidad Autonoma de Santo
Domingo (UASD)
Republica Dominicana

ALROY Gideon
Faculty of Medecine
Israel

ALVAREZ Mario
Doyen
Universite d'Etat d'Haiti, UEH
Haiti

AVNET MORSE Jean, Prof.
United States of America

AMOKRANE Arezki
Professeur d'Universite
Algerie

AMPARO Ramon
Universidad Autonoma de Santo
Domingo (UASD)
Republica Dominicana

ARCHIBOLD Sayori
Presidente de la Asociacion de
Estudiantes, Panama

AUBERT Jean Eric
Princiapl Administrator
Directorate for Science and
Technology
OCDE

BADIOLA Juan Jose
Rector de la Universidad de
Zaragoza
Vicepresidente del Consejo de
Universidades de Espana
Espana

BAHMANI FARD Tish
ICSU

BARDET Benoit
Presse et Communication
AUPELE-UREF

BARNES DE CASTRO Francisco
Rector, Universidad Nacional
Autonoma de Mexico
Mexico

BECERRA Miguel
Asociacion de Investigadores para
el Avance de la Ciencia y la
Tecnologia en Colombia
Universidad Pedagogica y tecnologica
Colombia

BONNARD Mathias
AUPELF-UREF

BENOIT Augustin
President
Organisation Scientifique
Industrielle pour le
Developpment de I'Inde
France

BENOIT Rosary
Secrétaire général
Organisation Scientifique
Industrielle pour le
Développement de l'Inde
France

BORIS Richard
Vice-President du Syndicat des
professeurs a CUNY,
NY (PSC-CUNY)
USA

BRANDAO LAVARENGA
Clelia, Dr.
Reitor, Universidade Catolica
de Goias
Brazil

BRITO Mariano
Recteur de I'Universite de Montevideo
Uruguay

BRUN Marion
Union Nationale des Etudiants
de France
France

BUCAILLE Marie
Presse et Communication
AUPELF-UREF

BUSSION Rosen
Deleguee commerciale
France

CARISTAN Alain
AUPELF-UREF

CARTA Francesco
SRHE
United Kingdom

CARUCCIO Regina
Lectrice a la Sorbonne
France

CASPARSSON Gustaf
EDS
Suede

CENATUS Berard
Universite d'Etat d'Haiti, UEH
Haiti

CHAYA-NGAM
Thailand

CHEDID Suzanne
Association des Libanaises Universitaires
Liban

COLOM MOLINA Leopoldo
Universidad Marano Galves
Guatemala

COTE Pierre
Quebec
Canada

CROWELL Anne
Maharishi Open University
The Netherlands

CROWELL Chris
Maharishi Open University
The Netherlands

CUSHINGBERRY George
Commissioner in Higher Education -USA

DABABNEH Michel
Association des diplomes de l'Universite de France en Jordanie
Jordanie

REDY Seri Faustin
Association Panafricaine de l'Anthropologie
Cote d'Ivoire

DE LA CRUZ TOME Africa AIPU

De la ROSA Jesus
Asesor del Rector
Universidad Autonoma de Santo Domingo
Republica Dominicana

De La ROSA Graciela
Universidad de la Republica
URUGUAY

DELAVAULT Huguette
AFFDU

DIOUF SI Alla
Institut pour la Renovation Industrielle en Afrique Noire
France

DJABALI Fatima
Ambassade de Bahreim
France

DORIN Silvia
IDB

DZVIMBO Peter
Pro-Vice Chancellor
University College of Distance Education, University of Zimbabwe- Zimbabwe

ELIAS KURI Sebastiao, Dr.
Universidade Federal do Sao Carlos -brazil

ENNAFAA Ridha
Professeur
Universite de Paris VIII
France

ELHACHEM Bassam
Professeur de sociologie
Institut Catholique de Paris
France

EVSTAFIEV A., Prof.
Vice-Rector, Moscow Academy of Chemical Engineering
Russian Federation

FADIGA Kanvally
Directeur du Centre de Recherche et de Publication, ENS
Cote d'Ivoire

FAVERJON Christophe
Federation mondiale de la Jeunesse Democratique
France

FERNANDEZ Nelly
Profesor
Universidad Mayor de San Andres
Bolivia

FJELLAANDSBO Bjorn Ove
EDS

FOLLET Brian, Prof.
Vice-Chancellor
University of Warwick
United Kingdom

FONGANG Frantz
AUPELF-UREF

FOTSO Kings
Cyberlab Institut Mobile
President
France

FRAPPE Benoit
Maharishi Open University
France

GARAY CUELI Dalmiro Fabian
Federacion Universitaria Argentian
Argentina

GARCIA PAREDES Gustavo, Dr.
Rector, Universidad de Panama
Panama

GARGIONE FILHO Baptista, Dr.
Reitor, Universidade do Vale do Paraiba
Brazil

GERARD Renee
AFFDU

GHALIB FARE'E Waheeba, Dr.
Open ARWA University
Yemen

GILLETTE Arthur Jr
Club UNESCO des etudiants
de Paris
France

GODINHO GOMES A., Prof.
ECOMOA
Burkina Faso

GONZALEZ Dagpnertp
Universidad Jose Matias Delgado
El Salvador

GONZALEZ PADILLA Pablo,
Prof.
Congreso Nacional de Venezuela
Venezuela

GONZALEZ PIREZ Magalys
Cuba

GOROSTIAGA Xavier, Dr.
Universidad de Managua
Nicaragua

GOURBIERE Jean
ICET
France

GRAFFE Jose Elias
Researcher
Venezuela

GRIEB Ina
Vice-president
University of Oldenburg
Germany

GROSSAT Bernard, Prof.
Institut demographique de
l'Universtite de Paris (IDUP)
France

HAAPANEN Eija
ELLLI
Finland

Hadj-YOUNES Nadia
AUPELF-UREF

HAGUNA Made
Rwanda

HAM Charlos
AUPELF-UREF

HAMMOUD Rafica
Egypte

HARTMAN Eike
Maharishi Open University
The Netherlands

HARTMAN Gabriel
Maharishi Universityo Management
the Netherlands

HEMPTINNE Charles
President
Vicariate for foreign students
Belgium

HERGOVICH Gerlinde
Autriche

HERNANDEZ LIMON Olga
ANUIES - Universidad de
Tamaulipas
Mexico

HENRY Myriam
Pays-Bas

HUAZI Saad
WFME
Jordan

HONG Mle
ICSU

HOUENNOU Pascal
Conseiller charge de la
Cooperation Internationale a
l'Universite de'Abobo-Adjame

HULTIN Goran
Assistant Director-General,
International Labour Office
Switzerland

IBRAHIM Awatif
Sudanese Women General Union
Sudan

JURI Hungo, Dr.
Rector de la Universidad Nacional
de Cordoba
Argentina

KALBACH Karl
Maharishi Open University
The Netherlands

KANTE Henri
Conseiller culturel
Cote d'Ivoire

KARAM CHEDID Suzanne
Association des libanaises
universitaires
Journaliste
Liban

KAZADI Augustin
Consultant
CNUCED
France

KENSICK Natasha
Publications
International Institute for
Educational Planning (IIEP)
France

KHALADJAN, Dr.
Rector, MEGU
Russion Federation

KOMENAN AKA Landry
Vice-President de l'Universite
de Bouake
Cote d' Ivoire

KURI Sebastiao Elias
CRE-COLOMBUS
France

LAB Pierre-Henri
FMJD
France

LAMPE JOUBERT Aline, Prof.
Congreso Nacional de Venezuela
Venezuela

LANDEAU Pascal
AUPELF-UREF

LAURILLARD Diana, Prof.
The Open University
United Kingdom

LECOURT Sophie
Presse et Communication
AUPELF-UREF

LECOZ Michel
AUPELF-UREF

LFEVRE Elvira
Periodista
Panamá

LEMELLE Wilbert
International Literacy Institute
Phelps Stokrd Fund
Etats-Unis

LEMOINE Dominique
Maharishi Open University
The Netherlands

LENIVEAU Anne-Marie
Ecole Instrument de Paix
France

LENIVEAU Anne-Marie
Ecole Instrument de Paix
Suisse

LEONARD Catherine
ICSU

LOIRET-CLAUDE Pierre-Jean
AUPELF-UREF

LONGWORTH Margaret
Finalnd

LUNA PORRAS Alvaro
Fundacion para el desarrollo
Cultural y Ecologico de la Amazonia
Colombia

MAAMOURI Mohamed
Deputy Director
UNESCO International
Literacy Institute
USA

MAIQUES MARCH Jose Maria
AIPU

MAKANY Philippe
Professeur
Congo

MALAMOUD Georges
AUPELF-UREF

MALITA M., Prof.
President, BSUF
Roumanie

MARINHO Helen
Federal Ministry of Education
National Coordinator of the
French language Project
Nigeria

MARTINOTTI Guido
Professeur
Italie

MEBARKI Fariza
Maharishi Open University
The Netherlands

MESSAD Djouhra, Prof.
CNRS-CRMD
Algerie

MICHEAU Francois
Jadanie

MONNET Agnes
Directeur de Centre de Formation
Continue, ENS
Cote d'Ivoire

MONTACLAIR Florent
Centre d'Etudes pur l'Education
et l'Interculturalite de Besancon
France

MONTACLAIR Florent
Centre UNESCO de Besancon
France

MOREAU Michel
Directeur General, CNED
France

MORRIS Bevan
Maharishi Open University
France

MOUHAYA Emmanuel
Institut pur la Renovation
Industrielle en Afrique Noire
Ouganda

MOUKOUKOU Arsene
Institut pour la Renovation
Industrielle en Afrique Noire
Gabon

MUKAMA Faustin Patrick
College Tutor
Tanzania

MUSONERA Agustin
Rwanda

NADER Tony
President
Maharishi Open University
France

NAVALO Zenon
Presidente de la Asociacion de
Estudiantes de Ingenieria
Panama

NGARBATHEM Andre
Institut pour la Renovation
Industrielle en Afrique Noire
Tchad

NIQUE Christina
Directeur de Centre International
des Sciences Pedagogiques
France

NELSEN Mme
France

NOUROUMBI
Etudiant
Congo

NUNEZ Norma, Dra.
Universidad Central de Venezuela
Venezuela

OBORNE Michael
Directeur General adjoint Science
et Technologie
OCDE
France

OLMOS Virgilio
Universidad Autonoma de
Chiriqui
Panama

OUEDRAOGO Soungalo, Prof.
ECOMOA
Burkina Faso

PANES Berta
Espana

PARIKH Kirit, Dr.
UNDP
United States of America

PARVU Gabriel
EDS
PASQUIER Pierre
AUPELF-UREF

PENALOSA LOPEZ-PIN Antonio
Deputy Secretary-General
International Organisation of Employers
Switzerland

PESTRANA Andres, Dr.
Rector, Universidad Simon
Bolivar
Venezuela

PEREZTAJU Vilma
Etudiant
Universite Rene Descartes Paris V
France

PERRET SERPA Luiz Felipe, Dr.
Reitor, Universidade Federal do Bahia
Brazil

PIPERNO Jaime
Universidad de la Republica
URUGUAY

PIRES Ieda Maia
Etudiant
Universite Rene Descartes Paris V
France

PITA MOURE Jose Manuel
Profesor-Investigador
Espana

PLEBANI Betta
CIEE
France

PLAISANCE Eric
Enseignant
Universite Rene Descartes Paris V
France

POP Daniel
Youth Network
Romania

PORRAS Alvaro Luna
Fundacion para el Desarollo
Ambiental y Cultural de la
Amazonia (FUNDARCA)

PORFIRIO GARCIA, Dr.
Universidad Autonoma de Santo
Domingo (UASD)
Republica Doninicana

PRAIZELIN Guillaume
AUPELF-UREF

PRIGOLLINI David
Secretario de Relaciones
Internaicionales
Facultad de Medicina de
Buenos Aires
Argentina

RABELO Leni Maria
Universidade Federal de
Uberlandia - Minas Gerais
Brazil

ROACH Denise
United States of America

SAAD Violette
Association des libanaises
universitaires
Liban

SA BARRETO Francisco Cesar, Dr.
Reitor, Universidade Federal de
Minas Gerais
Brazil

SALABURU ETXEBERRIA
Pello, Dr.
Rector
Universidad del Pais Vasco
Espagne

SALAZAR Francsco Xavier
Senador
Mexico

SALVATIERRA CRUZ Jorge
Asesor
Universidad de Costa Rica

SANTOS ORTEGA Carla
Profesora
Ecuador

SASSINE Somor
Liban

SCHANBACHER Volker
Maharishi University of
Management
The Netherlands

SCHEUNEMANN DE SOUZA
Inguelore, Dr.
Reitor
Universidade Federal de Pelotas
Brazil

SERI Dedy, Prof.
Directeur
Universite de Cocody
Cote d'Ivoire

SERVALLI Guido
Responsiabile Universita
Regione Lombardia
Italy

SHRIVASTAVA Shashi Kant
Senior Education Specialist World Bank
India

SHUBEROFF Oscar, Dr.
Rector de la Universidad de
Buenos Aires
Argentina

SIERRA Manuel
Rector
Universidad de Cartagena
Colombia

SOTO DE LA JARA Mariana
Estudiante Universidad Paris X
Chile

STANCIULESCU Gabriela, Prof.
Vice-Recteur, bsuf
Roumanie

STINUS S.
Director, Momentum
Espagne

TAMEZ GUERRA Reyes S.
Presidente
Universidad Autonoma de
Nuevo Leon
Mexico

TANO Yolande
Vice-President de l'Universite
d' Abobo-Adjame
Cote d'Ivoire

TIKHOMIROV V.P., Prof.
Moscow State University
Russian Federation

TOURE Vakaba
Directeur de l'Ecole Normale
Superieure côte d'Ivore

TUDOR Bogdan
EDS

VANDAM - MIERAS Maria
member of the Scientific Council
for Government Policy
The Netherlands

VAN LEEUWEN Ferdinand
Education International
Belgique

VARMA Girish
Maharishi Open University
The Netherlands

VEDOVA Patricia
Universite Catholique de Santiago
de Guayaquil
Equateur

VEZINA Patrice
EI
France

VIDAL Michel
Institut pour la Renovation Industrielle en Afrique Noire
France

VILLALBA Alesandro
Federacion Universitaria
Argentina
Argentiana

VILLARAZA Aurelia
AUAP
Philippines

WALTERS Shirley, Dr.
Centre of adult and Continuing Education
South Africa

PRESS

JOURNAUX PRENSA

AESCULAPE EUREDIC
Guiton E.M.

AFP
Coex T.

AFRICA N I
Mouckwanguy F.
Alain T.

AFRIQUE EDUCATION
Malet H.
Tedga P.

AG CHINE NOUVELLE
Yang J.

AG. EDUC. FORMATION
Bouchard P.
Guiraud M.
Taieb D.
Dhers O.

AGENCE JANA
Abdulatif A.S.

AGENCE MENA
Abdalla H.

AG. NATIONALE D'INF.
Metni J.

AITV
Tchienehon J.V.

AITV RFO
Kaplan R.

AKHBAR FL YOM
Weessa M.

Al HAYAT
Aref M.

Al Khalij
El Ayoubi I.

Al RAYAA
Souad W.

Al RIYADH
Abo Dehman A.

AL-SHAAB
Ramahi

AL YAMAMAH
Zein H.

ALGERIE PRESSE SERVICE
Ainouche A.
Zerarka Y.

AN-NAHAR
Barada A.
Sassine G.

A.P. MONDE ARABE
El Tayeb S.

AP-PHOTO
Euler M.

A.P. QATAR
Abou-Chadra N.

APTN
Tranvovez P.

A.P. XINHUA
Zheng X.

ARAB NEWS NETWORK
Al Khayer O.
Chamie T.
Khayat N.
Al- Masry

ARAB RADIO & TV
Ben Saidani A.
Gacem
El Laffi

ARTE
Laumonier M.A.

ASSAFIR
Kleib S.

ASH-SHAHID INT.
Ghamgui M.

ASS. PRESS TV
El Tayeb S.

ASSOCIATED PRESS
Dam-Van Y.

AZZAMAN
Zamzami

BATELESUD
M'Packo E.

BBC
Siraj M.
Ola-Davies G.

BBC-RADIO NEWS
Ion Miron D.

BBC SWAHILI
Nabakwer

BERLINER BEITUNG
Wetzel J.

CANA
Cox R.

CARACOL RADIO
Rico Laverde E.

CAURIS
Maiga A.A.

CCIC
Weber H.
Pere De Hemptine

CHINE YOUTH DAILY
Yonggun L.

CHR. HIGH. EDUC.
Bollag. B.
Giudice B.

COMBAT NATURE
Carlier J.

CZECH NEWS AGENCY
Mundil S.

DIDISCHE ZEITUNG
Mayer A.

DAMINA
Diatta Ngoboh T.

DEUTSCHE WELLE
Issoufou A.

DONGA DAILY NEWS
Sae-Won

DPA
Hoyer N.

ECHO DE L'AFRIQUE
Rostini P.

EFE
Gastar

EL CORREO ESPANOL
Iturribarria F.

EL MUNDO
Montoya R.

EL NACIONAL
Araujo E.

EL PERIODICO
Capdevila M.

EL TIEMPO
Morales C.

ELSEVIER
Van Leeuwen A.

FOHLA DE SAO PAULO
Rosseti Ferreira F.

France INFO
Hug H.

France INTER
Four J.M.

FRANKFURTER ALLGEMEINE
Hanimann J.

FRATERNFTE MATIN
Hien Solo

FREELANCE
Chedid S.
Saade Z.
Faria M.

GIORNALE DI BRESCIA
Carella A.

GLOBE AND MAIL
Nelles W.

HANKOOKILBO
Song T.G.

HUMANITE HEBDO
Cariou E.

IL FARO
Asem H.

INDIAN CURRENTS
Vallamattam J.

INT. HERALD TRIBUNE
James B.

INTER PRESS SERVICE
Oyog M.A.

INTER OM HOGSKOLAN
Kalvemark T.

IRIB
Mansoori AM.
Guillaume C.

JEUNE AFRIQUE
Zouari F.

JORNAL DA UNIVERSIDADE
Eichenberg F.

JORNAL DE NOTICIAS
Silva A.

KOWAIT NEWS AGENCY
Saade M.

KUNA
Al Ali A.

L'ETUDIANT
Galbaud D.
Oui M.

LA NACION
Iglesias G.

LA CLAETE
Ding Y.

LA VANGUARDIA
Luna J.

LA VIE CATHOLIQUE
Modeste J.N.

L'AUTRE AFFRIQUE
Robinet S.

LE PHARMACIEN D'AFRIQUE
Hiuguet E.

LE POINT-GRANDES ECOLES
Attia F.

LE QUOTIDIEN DU PEUPLE
Ma W.

LIETUVOS RYTAS
Urhonaite E.

L'OPINION
Fassi Fihri H.L.

L'UNION
Massanu Mukoko B.

MAGHREB ARABE PRESSE
El Hachimi A.

MARCHES TROP. ET MED.
Simonet M.C.

MASS MEDIA TRAINING INST.
Debalkew T.

MOHARER
Abou Jaafar N.

MONDE DE L'EDUCATION
Chupin J.

MORGUNBLADID
Olafsdottir M.

NAN
Momoh M.

NOUVELLES D'EUROPE
Liu C.

NOVILIST-CONVERGE
Mujadzic D.

NOVYIE IZVESTIYA
Zverev A.

NRC HANDELSBLAND
Kamerman S.

ORCHIDEES
Romay A.
Sene D.
Fantino C.

OSTDEUTSCHER RUNDFUNK
Zimmermann M.

PANA
Njoku F.

PARENTS D'ELEVES
Marage G.M.
Meaude Y.

PERSPECTIVES SOCIALES
Pelissier M.

PHOSPHORE
Michaud A.

PHOTO
Murez S.

POLITIS
Nahapetian N.

PROV. PUBL. ASS.
Sy L.R.

PUBL. ASS. PHILIPPINES
Dayang P.

RADIO ALFA
De Pina M.P.

RADIO CHINE INT.
Zhou C.

RADIO CROATE
Jergovic B.

RADIO ORIENT
Chmait W.
Hamoui H.

RADIO PRIVEE
Nkunzimana D.

RADIO ROUMANIE INT.
Aroi I.

RADIO TV DU BURUNDI
Bakenirema E.

REFORMA
Delgado M.

REGION VERTE
Benstaali D.

REPI
Dolegeal F.

RFI
Mettra G.
Garcia Herrera M.
Gaymard V.
Bras A.C.
Ninin C.
Fernandez M.
Quentin F.
Cook R.
Thank Thuy L.
Morna A.
Garcia A.
El Banna DAlle M.
Lavergne P.

RFO
Hillemand- Landucci
Barbier G.
Brauge F.

RICERCA
Bonaventura T.

RIMA
Zamzam I.

RMC MOYEN-ORIENT
El Kalache M.

RMC/MO
Tlili H.

SAARLANDISCHER RUNDFUNK
Rau B.

SABC
Louw L.

SABC-RADIO
Liesl L.

SANA
Zaaboub

SAUDI T.V.
Sayed H.

SCIENCE AND PUBLIC POLICY
Richardson J.

STANDPOINTS
Delage E.

STRATES.CNRS
Bernis M.

SUD FM
Mbaye T.

SUD QUOTIDIEN
Sow B.

SUDKURIER
Frisch A.

SUNDAY INDEPENDENT
Mac Gregor K.

TEMOIGNAGE CHPETIEN
Gairaud M.

THE HERALD
Karikoga M.A.
Ngwa A.

THE HINDU
Rajagopalan T.

THE MANILA BULLETIN
Caridad C.

THE STAR HEADLINES
Fowung I.

THE YEMEN OBSERVER
Aref S.

TIMES HIGH. EDUC.
Guillaume J.

TIMES HIGH. EDUC. SUPP.
Marshall J.
Jobbins D.

TTU MONDE ARABE
Yagoub S.

TV CROATE
Findak Zigic
Baredic M.
Osenicki M.

TV ESPAGNOLE
Sacaluga A.
Valdes C.
Agusti B.

TV IRAN
Moshrefi

TV3-TV DE CATALOGNE
Ferrerons J.
Bou D.

TVR
Cozighian P.
Necsa D.

UNESCO PANAMA
Nunez Montoto N.

UNI
Tuteja A.

URTE-TV EGYPTIENNE

Fohda H.

VIA LE MONDE

Viau G.
Viau C.
Robitaille J.
Beauchemin F.

VIE UNIVERSITAIRE

Catin J.M.
Merceron S.

WELT AM SONNTAG

Ruge E

WORLD NEWS LINK

Murr L.

UNESCO

Mr E. Portella
President of the General Conference

Mr. P. Pataki
President of the Executive Board

Mr. F. Mayor
Director-General

Mr. D. Janicot
Assistant Director-General for Directorate

Mr. A. Sayyad
Assistant Director-General for External Relations

Mr. C.N. Power
Assistant Director-General for Education

Mr M. Iaccarino
Assistant Director-General for Natural Sciences

Ms F. Fournier
Assistant Director-General for Social and Human Sciences

Mr. H. Crespo-Toral
Assistant Director-General a.i. for Culture

Mr. H. Iouchkiavitchious
Assistant Director-General for Communication, Information and Informatics

Mr. J. Hallak
Assistant Director-General, International Institute for Educational Planning

Mr. Y. Matsui
Assistant Director-General for Management and Administration

Mr. D. Chitoran
Special Adviser

Mr. H. Gurgulino de Souza
Special Adviser

Mr. S. Tanguiane
Special Adviser

Division of Higher Education

Mr M.A.R. Dias, Director
Ms M. Coursodon

Unit for the World Conference on Higher Education

Ms M.L. Kearney, Head of Unit
Ms M. L. Simionescu
Ms D. Maurisse-Oudot
* Ms N. Arnhold
* Ms H. Baligadoo
*Ms L. Bartyzel
*Ms J. Boigey
*Ms S. Brochu
*Mr. L. Calo
*Ms A. Chevert

*Ms A. Font Giner
*Mr Jin-Yeong Heo
*Ms E. Kadri-Cham
*Mr. T. Kilby
*Ms H. Kuttab
*Mr D. Lincoln
*Ms M. Nilsson
*Mr B. Schneider
*Ms A. Siniscalco
*Mr E. Tappy
*Mr J. Theiss
*Ms R. Uldall
*Mr G. Vada
*Mr L. Valdez

Section for Inter-university Co-operation
Mr K. Seddoh, Deputy Director
Ms. C. Pinan
Ms V. Beauchene-Ferreira
Ms. H. Tortian
Mr Yim Chang Bin
Ms E. Hoyer
Ms. M.R. Grosjean
*Mr H. Beck
*Ms T. Esparza
*Ms A. Salinas
*Ms A. Sant' Anna

Unit for Higher Education Policy
Mr. J. Sadlak, Head of Unit
Mr I. Mizuta
Mr. J. Emele

Unit for Academic Mobility
Mr. D. Beridze, Head of Unit
Ms J. Puech

Section for Educational Sciences
Ms M. Sauliere
Ms M. Pastel
Ms D. Veyre
*Ms S. Woloch

Culture of Peace Programme
Mr L. Atherley, Director
Mr. D. Adams, Director
Mr. F. Russell

Division of Philosophy and Ethics
Mr. P. Vermeren

Youth Co-ordinaion Unit
Ms M. Henriques Mueller,
Chief of Unit

Unit on the Status of Women and Gender Equality
Ms B. Pavlic, Director
Ms S. Sam-Vargas
Ms L. Ruprecht

Bureau for External Relations
Mr H. Godicke, Director
Mr. L. Vieira

Office of Public Information
Mr A. Da Costa, Deputy Director,
Regionalization Division
Ms E. salas C. Rossenbach, Chief
of Press Room
Ms J. Caro Gardiner

Interdisciplinary Agency Co-operation Project
Mr G. Lopez Ospina, Director
Ms M. Syed
Ms J. Damlamian
Ms M. Samman

Task Force on Education for the Twenty-first Century
Ms A. Draxler, Director
Mr J. Johansen

Office for Administration and Information
Ms S. Fernandez-Lauro, Chief
Documentalist
Ms F. Bloch, Senior
Administrative Assistant
Ms G. Britland
Ms F. Runge

Ms P. Zarka
Ms F. Jouot-Belhami
Ms M. Breda
Mr M. Bun
Mr M. Zamorano

World Education Report

Mr J. Smyth, Chief Editor
Ms M. gingras-Kovatcheva

Bureau for Programme Coordination

Mr H. Rissom, Director

Unit for ED Conferences and Meetings

Mr P. Herold
Ms M. Hassine

BPC/EXB

Mr Pokrovsky

BPC/ARB

Ms K. Shaheen
Ms S. Kaidi

BPC/EUR

Mr. A. Sannikov
Ms S. Mobley

Programming and Evaluation Unit

Mr. R. Tiburtini

Publications Unit

Ms W. McNevin

Division of Basic Education

Ms A. Bah Diallo, Director
Mr A. Yousif, Chief of Section for Litercy and Adult Education.
Mr A. Ouane
Ms S. Bokhari
Ms F. Migeon
Ms M. Lefebvre

Global Action Programme on Education for All

Mr. D. Berstecher, Director
Mr. J. Visser, Director, Learning without Frontiers Coordination Unit
Mr M. Gilmer, Director, Special Project : Youth
Mr M. Lakin, International Forum "Education for All"
Mr E. Khvilon
Ms M. Patru
Ms C. Parlea
Ms J Lefebvre
Ms J. Sullivan

Division for Renovation of Secondary and Vocational Education

Mr A. Parsuramen, Director
Ms K. Savolainen, Director
Mr. Q. Tang. Chief of Section for Technical and Vocational Education
Ms M. Schaeffer-Teissier
Ms J. Balichard
Ms J. Boulmer
Ms O. Monduc
Ms I. Odibo
Ms C. Thiounn
Ms N. Brasseur
Ms Guebre-Xabier
Ms M. Kayser

Division for the Reconstruction and Development of Education System

Ms L. Jallade, Director

Languages Division

Mr J. Poth, Director

International Institute for Educational Planning

Mr B. Sanyal, Special Adviser
Ms F. Du Pouget, Chief of Documentation Centre
Mr 1. Denison, Deputy Chief of Publications

Ms M. Martin
Ms S. D'Antoni
Ms S. Heyman
Ms K. Lezeaau

Natural Sciences Sector

Mr M. El Tayeb, Chief of Division for Policy Analysis and Operations
Mr P. Lasserre, Director of Division of Ecological Sciences
Mr A. Pinilla, Chief of Coordination and Evaluation Unit and Executive Assistant
Mr P. Dogse
Mr M. Hadley
Mr. T. Marjoram
Mr. F. Zhang
Ms R. Clair

Sector of Social and Human Sciences

Mr A. Kazancigil, Principal Director, Division of Social Science, Research and Policy
Mr. J. Symonides, Director of Division of Human Rights, Democracy and Peace
Mr. V. Volodine, Chief of Human Rights Unit
Ms C. von Furstenberg
Ms R. Ozeir

Sector for Culture

Mr Y. Isar, Director, Culture and Development Coordination Office and Director, International Fund for the Promotion of Culture
Ms D. Tennakoonge

Sector of Communication, Information and Informatics

Mr. P. Queau, Director of Information and Informatics Division

Mr. T. Tawfik, Director, Unit for Special Projects

Mr M. Chamakhi
Mr R. Cluzel
Ms I. Panevska

Bureau of Documentation, informatics and Telecommunications

Networks Division

Ms D. Tal

Information and Library Division

Ms D. Pelissier, Chief of Division

Bureau for Extrabudgetary Funding

Ms N. Ibrahim

Conference Division

Mr. H. Rais, Chief of Conference Division
Mr. F. Ghebre, Chief of Control and Planning Unit
Mr S. Latifi
Mr P. Amour

UNESCO Institutes/Regional Offices

International Bureau of Education

Mr V. Adamets, Chief of Unit
Mr M. Amadio
Ms G. Canahuati

UNESCO Institute for Education

Mr. P. Belanger, Director
Mr W. Mauch

UNESCO Institute for Information Technologies in Education

Mr V. Kinelev, Director

UNESCO Bangkok Office

Mr. V. Ordonez, Director
Mr Wang Yibing

UNESCO Beijing Office

Mr N. Noguchi, Director
Ms M. Hayashikawa

UNESCO Beirut Office

Mr. V. Billeh, Director

UNESCO Brasilia Office

Mr. J. Wertheim, Director
Mr J.L. Lombard

UNESCO Bucharest Office

Ms L. Wilson, Director
Mr L. Vlasceanu
Ms . Uvalic-Trumbic

UNESCO Cairo Office

Mr A. Shihab-Eldin, Director
Mr Amr Azzouz
Ms G. Gholam

UNESCO Caracas Office

Mr. L. Yarzabal, Director
Mr J. Silvio
Ms A. Vila
Ms N. Moccia

UNESCO Dakar Office

Mr P. Obanya, Director
Mr J. Shabani
Ms M. Lefebvre de Longeville
Ms K. Beeckman

UNESCO Doha Office

Mr A. Bubtana, Head of Office

UNESCO Guatemala City Office

Mr. F. Figueroa Rivas, Head of Office

UNESCO Jakarta Office

Mr. S. Hill, Director

UNESCO Kingston Office

Ms C. Harvey, Head of Office

UNESCO Maputo Office

Mr H. Charles, Head of Office

UNESCO Montevideo Office

Mr F.J. Lacayo Parajon, Director

UNESCO Pretoria Office

Mr L. Honwana, Director
Mr B. Ntim
Mr J. Nkinyangi

UNESCO Santiago de Chile Office

Ms A. Montenegro

UNESCO Washington Office

Mr. F. Method, Head of Office

UNESCO Yaounde Office

Cheikh T. Sy. Head of Office